PRAISE FOR

THE BIBLICAL FEASTS AND THE RETURN OF JESUS

"Travis Snow has written an amazing study on all the feasts of Israel emphasizing their future fulfillment at the end of this age and in the Age to Come. I am very in accord with the basic thrust of the book and agree with some of the detailed interpretation, but not all. But that is not the point. The point is that this book moves theology forward in a wonderful way, a theology that is often missed. This is an important book and highly recommended."

—**DANIEL JUSTER, TH.D.,** ADJUNCT PROFESSOR AT THE KING'S UNIVERSITY AND FOUNDER OF TIKKUN INTERNATIONAL

"Like many, I simply assumed that Jesus had already fulfilled the spring feasts and would fulfill the fall feasts when He came again. I assumed wrongly! Challenging us to reexamine familiar passages and dig into lesser-known prophetic pictures, Travis Snow shows us how a more complete fulfillment is still coming for each of God's appointed times. Read this book and see how the drama of the Second Coming and the Age to Come will be more beautiful than you have ever imagined."

—**NICK UVA,** PASTOR OF HARVEST TIME CHURCH IN GREENWICH, CT

"I do not know of any other book that articulates in such a detailed way how all the biblical feasts relate to Bible prophecy and the ministry of Jesus, while also bringing past and future together, all in one glimpse, with a bright perspective! *The Biblical Feasts and the Return of Jesus* is a very well-crafted book, full of insights that inspire hunger for more revelation from God's word. This resource is not for those looking for sensational prophetic trivia. It is for the serious student of Scripture and those avidly searching for biblical truth concerning the last days, the Second Coming, and the Messiah's kingdom."

—**VICTOR VIEIRA,** INTERNATIONAL HOUSE OF PRAYER KANSAS CITY

The BIBLICAL FEASTS *and the* RETURN OF JESUS

HOW *the* SPRING *and* FALL FEASTS *of* ISRAEL
WILL BE FULFILLED *in the* KINGDOM *of* GOD

TRAVIS M. SNOW

SHILOH
MEDIA

THE BIBLICAL FEASTS AND THE RETURN OF JESUS

Shiloh Media
Dallas, T.X.

Library of Congress Control Number:

Book designed by Mark Karis
www.karisworks.com

First Edition
Paperback ISBN: 978-1-7340229-6-4
eBook ISBN: 978-1-7340229-7-1
Hardcover ISBN: 978-1-7340229-8-8

For Siona

TABLE OF CONTENTS

Acknowledgments viii

1 Every Feast is About the Future 1
2 Passover in Historical Context 22
3 Passover & the Return of Jesus 51
4 The Feast of Weeks in Historical Context 110
5 The Feast of Weeks & the Return of Jesus 119
6 The Feast of Trumpets in Historical Context 143
7 The Feast of Trumpets & the Return of Jesus 161
8 The Day of Atonement in Historical Context 183
9 The Day of Atonement & the Return of Jesus 198
10 The Feast of Tabernacles in Historical Context 219
11 The Feast of Tabernacles & the Return of Jesus 234

Ways to Help Shiloh Media 247
Scripture Index 248

ACKNOWLEDGMENTS

IN MANY RESPECTS this book is the fruit of years of study at the feet of excellent Christian and messianic Jewish Bible teachers, without whose influence in my life I would never have been able to write on the topic of the biblical feasts and their relation to Bible prophecy. I am especially grateful to Rabbi Marty Waldman at Baruch HaShem Messianic Synagogue (Dallas, TX), Rabbi Lo Kaye-Wilson and his wife Mirelle, currently residing on the island of Cyprus, Rabbi David Schiller at Eitz Chaim Messianic Synagogue (Plano, TX), Dr. Daniel Juster of Tikkun International, Dr. Michael Rydelnik at the Moody Bible Institute (Chicago, IL), Dr. Kevin Spawn at the Regent University School of Divinity (Virginia Beach, VA), and Joel Richardson of Frontier Alliance International.

Special thanks are also due to Pastor Nick Uva at Harvest Time Church in Greenwich, CT for proofreading an early draft of the manuscript, Geoff Stone for his editorial work, and last, but certainly not least, Mark Karis for his design and formatting work on the book's cover and interior.

Additionally, I could not have completed this project without the constant support of my wife Avital and daughter Siona, as well as my parents Diane and James Kaufman and Joe and Candace Snow, and my wife's parents Richard and Donna Byrne. Your prayers and encouragement have brought me over the finish line, and for that I am forever grateful.

1

EVERY FEAST IS ABOUT THE FUTURE

SINCE THE 1970S, almost all Christian and messianic Jewish teaching on the biblical feasts has maintained that Jesus already fulfilled the spring feasts at the time of first coming and will thus only fulfill the fall feasts when he returns. The purpose of this book is to offer a different perspective on the historical, messianic, and future prophetic significance of the biblical holy days, and to explain how both the spring and fall feasts of Israel will be fulfilled after the Messiah's Second Coming.

We will start in this chapter by covering a few key principles that are necessary to understand before the feasts can be approached in the right way. Then, in later chapters, we will study how each feast foreshadows events that will take place after Jesus returns and sets up His kingdom.

THE FEASTS IN LEVITICUS 23

There are eight biblical festivals mentioned in Leviticus 23: the Sabbath, Passover (which includes the Feast of Unleavened Bread and First Fruits), the Feast of Weeks, the Feast of Trumpets, the Day of Atonement, and the Feast of Tabernacles. In this passage, God introduces the holy days of Israel in the following way:

> The LORD spoke again to Moses, saying, "Speak to the sons of Israel and say to them, 'The LORD's appointed times which you shall proclaim as holy convocations—My appointed times are these." (Lev. 23:1-2)

The Hebrew word that we often translate as "feasts" is *moedim* (pronounced: mo-E-deem). This word is derived from a root (*yaw-ad*) that means "to appoint," which is why these festivals are often called God's "appointed times." In addition, this Hebrew root not only implies an appointment, but it was also used in many contexts to describe a meeting in which God would impart divine revelation to His people.

For example, in Exodus 25:22, the root of moedim is used when God says, "there I will meet (*yaw-ad*) with you from above the mercy seat, from between the two cherubim which are upon the ark of the testimony." Similarly, the Tent of Meeting where Moses met (*yaw-ad*) the Lord and received guidance was literally called the "tent of appointed times" (*ohel moedim;* Exod. 29:42).

The way the term moedim is used in the Bible indicates that the festivals of Leviticus 23 were annual (or weekly in the case of the Sabbath) appointments that God established for the Israelites so that they could meet with Him and receive His revelation for their lives. These festivals were part of a cycle of sanctified time that anchored Israel's relationship with the Lord and allowed them to understand His work as their Creator, Provider, and Deliverer.

We often call the moedim feasts, which is fine at one level. However, most of the moedim did not originally involve proper feasting on food. For this reason, we should remember that facilitating a revelatory encounter with God was always the central purpose of the moedim, though thankfully, in some cases, this did involve actual feasting.

THE ISRAELITE CALENDAR

The Israelite calendar that included this cycle of moedim was much different than our modern 365-day solar-based Gregorian calendar. The calendar in ancient Israel was lunar, meaning each month lasted from the sighting of the first visible crescent of the new moon to the next new moon (Num. 28:11–15). This lunar cycle usually lasted 29-30 days, making the average lunar year 354 days long.

Moreover, the typical lunar year did include twelve months in biblical times. However, because the Israelite moedim were linked to the seasons and the harvest of agricultural products, the ancient Israelites, as well as most other surrounding nations, would add a thirteenth month to their calendar on a regular basis (usually seven times every nineteen years, or every two to three years). This ensured that the harvest festivals did not move around to different times of the year.

If the Israelites did not add this thirteenth intercalary month to their lunar calendar, they would have sometimes ended up with their harvest festivals in the winter when nothing was ripe, which would have been a problem. Thus, the lunar year was reconciled with the solar year by adding the extra "leap month" every two to three years, which implies that the Israelites used a combination of a lunar and solar calendar.

Watching the cycles of the moon provided the best way to track time on a monthly basis, from the new moon at the beginning of the month to the full moon in the middle of the month, which ended with the waning crescent and finally the next new moon. But the annual calendar was still in sync with the cycles of the sun through the addition of the thirteenth month when necessary. Though many prophecy teachers have made false claims to the contrary, if we were to take the three-year average the Israelite year was still 365 days long.[1]

1 Some prophecy teachers have utilized what they call a "360-day prophetic year" when interpreting certain prophecies. However, there is no biblical basis to the 360-day prophetic year, and this theory has been disproven by many scholars. For a discussion of the prophetic-year fallacy, see chapter 11 in *The 70 Weeks Jubilee.*

THE NEW YEAR WAS IN THE SPRING

Another key feature of the biblical calendar is that its new year begins in the spring, in the month of *Aviv* (which is also called *Nisan* in modern Judaism). Aviv usually overlaps with March and/or April on our modern calendars, and this time was chosen to mark the start of the Israelite year because it was when the first agricultural products in the ancient Near East were harvested. The barley harvest began in March or April and then in subsequent months other produce items were gathered from the fields. As a result, Israel's new year commenced right before the spring harvest and ended after the fall harvest was complete.

DID ISRAEL HAVE TWO NEW YEARS?

Today, it is common in some circles to hear that Israel may have had two separate new years, one in the spring, in the first month, and one in the fall, in the seventh month. To support this claim, many people point to Exodus 23:16 and 34:22 (cf. 1 Sam. 11:1), because these passages mention "the end of the year" and "the turn of the year" in the fall, at the time of the Feast of the Ingathering (i.e., the Feast of Tabernacles).

For example, Exodus 23:16 states:

> Also you shall observe the Feast of the Harvest of the first fruits of your labors from what you sow in the field; also the Feast of the Ingathering at the end of the year when you gather in the fruit of your labors from the field.

The Feast of the Ingathering referred to in Exodus 23:16 is the Feast of Tabernacles (cf. Lev. 23:34), which began on the fifteenth day of the seventh month. Because the Feast of Tabernacles is associated with the "end of the year" and "the turn of the year" in Exodus, some have argued that there was a second new year that began in the seventh month, or that the proper biblical new year began at this time.

This line of reasoning, however, is faulty for two reasons. First, Exodus 23:16 and 34:22 never mention a new year starting in the seventh month. Instead, these passages simply link the Feast of Tabernacles to the end of the year because it was in the seventh month, toward the end of the year. Even though there were still technically five months left on the calendar until the first month (i.e., the proper new year), in a general sense the Feast of Tabernacles still represented a turning from one year to the next.

Second, because the Feast of Tabernacles was the last festival on Israel's calendar, it was natural to connect this appointed time to the end of the year. After the Feast of Tabernacles, the year's festivities were complete, and the people switched their focus to the next year's harvest. Thus, Exodus 23:16 and 34:22 note how the end of the seventh month was regarded as the conclusion of the year, even though, again, the year did not officially end for another five months (i.e., after the twelfth month).

THE USE OF NONTECHNICAL LANGUAGE

To understand why Exodus 23:16 and 34:22 speak of the "end" or "turn" of the year in the seventh month, even though the year did not technically end at this time, think about how people today might say at 5 p.m. when their workday ends, "I'm so glad this day is over." We all know that in a literal sense the day does not end until 12:00 a.m., seven hours later, but this does not mean it is wrong for people to say in a relative sense that their day is over at 5 p.m. when they leave their job.

The same type of relative language is also used in Exodus 23:16 and 34:22 to describe the end of the Israelite year. The Feast of Tabernacles marked the end of the year in a general sense in the same way 5 p.m. marks the end of our modern workday. But there is nothing in these texts about a biblical new year in the seventh month.

In his commentary on Exodus, Old Testament scholar Douglas K. Stuart clarifies how Exodus 23:16 and 34:22 use non-technical language to describe the end of the year. He writes:

> [This] is simply phenomenological, informal language, much as people today speak of the day "ending" with dusk or "beginning" at dawn, even though they well know that it technically ends/begins at midnight.[2]

THE SPRING NEW YEAR IN THE ANCIENT NEAR EAST

The Bible is clear that the new year begins in the spring, right before Passover, which is why Exodus 12:2 says, "This month [referring to Aviv in the spring] shall be the beginning of months for you; it is to be the first month of the year to you." Also, the festivals in the fall are said to take place in the seventh month, which negates the idea that the new year in ancient Israel could have started at this time (Lev. 23:23).

In his book *The Cultic Calendars of the Ancient Near East*, historian Mark Cohen explains how common a spring new year was in the ancient world. He writes:

> [T]he evidence overwhelmingly indicates a "universal" spring New Year [in ancient Mesopotamia]. The concept of a beginning to the year is manifested in three ways: (1) as a starting point for counting and naming years; (2) as the start of the fiscal year (i.e., performing year-end accounting and starting the ledgers for the coming year); and (3) as the start of the religious/agricultural year's cycle. [...] Throughout almost all Mesopotamia the beginning of the year occurred in the spring.[3]

Stuart concurs with Cohen and writes:

> It is clear that in terms of formal teaching in the Pentateuch [i.e., Torah], the new year is firmly established as commencing in the spring, the month of Aviv (what we would call March-April) being

---

2 Douglas K. Stuart, *The New American Commentary: Exodus, Volume 2* (Nashville: Broadman & Holman Publishers, 2006), 272.

3 Mark E. Cohen, *The Cultic Calendars of the Ancient Near East* (Church: Capital Decisions, 1993), 14.

> the first month, and that the seventh month was the one to which the fall festival was dated.[4]

Like the Israelites, other nations in Mesopotamia observed a spring new year as well, including the Babylonians and Sumerians. These ancient cultures began their year around the time of the barley harvest in the spring, right after the spring equinox, and ended their year after the fall harvest of olives, grapes, and other fruits and vegetables, just after the fall equinox. The Israelite moedim fit this ancient pattern perfectly, and understanding when the year officially starts according to the Bible will also reveal many important lessons once we begin a deeper study of the prophetic significance of the biblical feasts in later chapters. But for now, below is a chart that outlines when the biblical feasts occur on the biblical calendar:

SPRING FEASTS

1st Month—Aviv	Passover, Unleavened Bread, First Fruits
2nd Month	
3rd Month	Feast of Weeks (Shavuot/Pentecost)
4th Month	
5th Month	
6th Month	

4 Stuart, *Exodus*, 273.

FALL FEASTS

7th Month (approaching the end of the year)	Feast of Trumpets, Day of Atonement (and Jubilee), Feast of Tabernacles
8th Month	
9th Month	
10th Month	
11th Month	
12th Month	
13th Month (Every 2-3 years)	

THE CONSENSUS VIEW ON THE FEASTS

Most people familiar with the biblical feasts understand that these appointed times in Leviticus 23 have layers of meaning connected to the life of the Messiah and future prophetic events. But unfortunately, as noted earlier, the popular view on the feasts since the 1970s has maintained that Jesus already fulfilled the spring feasts (Passover, Unleavened Bread, First Fruits, and Weeks) at the time of His first coming.

This assumption has in turn led to a second assumption, namely that only the fall feasts (Trumpets, Atonement, & Tabernacles) will be fulfilled at the time of the Messiah's Second Coming. In other words, almost all modern teaching on the prophetic significance of the feasts is built on the premise that the spring feasts relate primarily to past events whereas the fall feasts relate primarily to future events.

Below is an overview of how many people explain the fulfillment of the spring and fall feasts:

- **Passover, Unleavened Bread, and First Fruits:** Fulfilled when Jesus was crucified as the Lamb of God on Passover and raised from the dead on the day of First Fruits.

- **Weeks (Pentecost):** Fulfilled when the Holy Spirit was poured out on the early church.

- **Trumpets:** Will be fulfilled when Jesus returns at the sound of the trumpet.

- **Atonement:** Will be fulfilled when Jesus saves Israel and judges the nations.

- **Tabernacles:** Will be fulfilled when Jesus dwells on the earth in the millennial kingdom and we feast with Him at the marriage supper of the Lamb.

This common explanation of the prophetic meaning of the feasts is based on the timing of events recorded in the Gospels and the book of Acts. We know Jesus was crucified on the day of Passover (the fourteenth of Aviv) in the first century, which is why the idea that Jesus is our true Passover Lamb is so prevalent in the New Testament (1 Cor. 5:7). Moreover, Jesus was also raised from the dead on the day of First Fruits (1 Cor. 15:20), which occurred just two days after Passover, on the sixteenth of Aviv. Then, seven weeks later, the Holy Spirit was poured out on the early messianic community during the Feast of Weeks (aka. Pentecost; Acts 2).

Because the crucifixion and resurrection of Jesus, as well as the outpouring of the Holy Spirit, coincided in such a precise way with the spring feasts of Leviticus 23, it is tempting to conclude that these feasts have already been completely fulfilled and reached their prophetic end goal. Some have even gone so far as to suggest that because the spring feasts have already (in their view) been fulfilled, future end-time events such as the Rapture, the Second Coming itself, and the defeat of the Antichrist must take place in the fall, during the Feast of Trumpets or on the Day of Atonement, in the seventh month.

EVERY FEAST HAS THREE LAYERS OF MEANING

Since the purpose of this book is to explain how all the biblical feasts foreshadow events that will take place when Jesus returns and sets up His kingdom, we need to cover why this consensus view on the fulfillment of the spring and fall feasts is not accurate. Without a doubt, it has been a good thing that so many ministries and Bible teachers have helped God's people understand some of the deeper messianic layers of the moedim in Leviticus 23, because Jesus is indeed our Passover Lamb, and the way God linked the crucifixion, resurrection, and outpouring of the Holy Spirit to the spring feasts is one of the most beautiful elements in the biblical storyline of redemption.

As we will learn in this book, however, Scripture never says certain feasts have been fulfilled already whereas others still await their final fulfillment. The biblical writers never connect the spring feasts only to the Messiah's first coming and the fall feasts only to His Second Coming. Instead, the Bible teaches that every feast has three layers of meaning or fulfillment:

1. A historical meaning in ancient Israel.
2. A first-century fulfillment through the work of the Messiah.
3. A future fulfillment tied to end-time events and the Messiah's Second Coming.

These multiple layers of meaning do not minimize those aspects of the feasts that Jesus has already fulfilled, nor do they negate the connection between the feasts and His first-century ministry. However, they do indicate that if we want to truly understand the prophetic significance of the biblical feasts, we need to adopt a different perspective on the feasts than the one that has been popular for the last fifty years.

THE DAY OF ATONEMENT EXAMPLE

One example that illustrates how a biblical feast can encompass multiple layers of meaning and fulfillment can be seen if we take a closer look at the Day of Atonement. The Day of Atonement was when Israel's annual rite of purification took place in the Tabernacle or Temple (historical meaning). We also know the Messiah made atonement for our sins, a point that the book of Hebrews establishes by drawing heavily from the Day of Atonement sections of Leviticus (first-century fulfillment). However, it is also widely accepted in many prophecy circles that the Day of Atonement foreshadows what the Messiah will do in and for Israel, and by extension for all the nations of the earth, after His Second Coming (future fulfillment).

There is no sense in which the Day of Atonement was fulfilled only in the past or will be fulfilled only in the future. Instead, the Day of Atonement points to multiple historical and prophetic fulfillments, some of which have already come to pass and some of which we are still waiting for.

This is only one example, but the same can also be said about the other feasts besides the Day of Atonement. Every feast carries these multiple layers of meaning, and it is not until we grasp this basic point that we will be able to understand the full prophetic power and beauty of God's appointed times.

Ironically, many people who say Jesus already fulfilled the spring feasts, and that only the fall feasts await a future fulfillment, accept that He did fulfill certain aspects of the Day of Atonement (a fall feast) in the first century, particularly when he made atonement for our sins. They will allow that a fall festival like the Day of Atonement can have multiple fulfillments tied to the Messiah's first and Second Coming. But then, when they teach on the spring feasts, they emphasize an exclusive past-tense fulfillment and negate any future fulfillment!

It is not hard to see that this approach to the feasts, as popular as it has been for fifty years, is illogical and inconsistent. This view is weak because it attaches both a first-century and Second-Coming fulfillment to some of the feasts (in this case the Day of Atonement) but not to the others.

A better approach is to accept that every feast in Leviticus 23 points back in some way to what the Messiah has already done, while also pointing forward in some way to what He will accomplish when He returns and sets up His kingdom. This means that while we should certainly study and celebrate how Jesus already fulfilled certain aspects of the feasts (both spring and fall), we should simultaneously explore what the feasts (both spring and fall) can teach us about the days to come.

PAUL'S VIEW ON THE FEASTS IN COLOSSIANS

To the surprise of many, the Apostle Paul also taught that the biblical feasts in Leviticus 23 will only reach their final prophetic fulfillment after the Messiah returns. For example, in Colossians 2:16–17 Paul wrote:

> Therefore, no one is to act as your judge in regard to food or drink or in respect to a festival or a new moon or a Sabbath day, things which are a mere shadow of what is to come; but the substance belongs to Christ.

Most New Testament scholars accept that when Paul refers to the festivals and Sabbath days in this passage, he has the holy days of Leviticus 23 in mind. With that point established, notice how Paul also says here that these festivals are a "shadow of what is to come."

This phrase "what is to come" is used numerous times in the New Testament to refer to the end times, the Second Coming, and the kingdom of God. In addition to Colossians 2:17, derivatives of this phrase can be found in Romans 8:38, 1 Corinthians 3:22, Ephesians 1:21, Hebrews 2:5, Hebrews 6:5, Hebrews 13:14, 1 Peter 5:1, and Revelation 1:19, and in each of these passages the focus is always on the return of the Messiah. For example, in Ephesians 1:21 Paul speaks of how Jesus is above all rule and authority "not only in this age but also in *the one to come*" (emphasis added). Similarly, in Hebrews 2:5 and 6:5 we find parallel language to what Paul uses in Colossians 2:17

when the "world to come," or age to come, are the topic of discussion.

This linguistic usage confirms that when Paul says in Colossians 2:17 that the Sabbaths and festivals of Leviticus 23 are a "shadow of what is to come," he is indicating that these Sabbaths and festivals foreshadow prophetic events that will take place in the future. Moreover, Paul does not say only certain festivals have future prophetic meaning, or that some of the feasts have already been fulfilled whereas others still await their final fulfillment.

Quite the opposite, Paul paints with a broader brush and says all the moedim point to prophetic fulfillments that have not yet transpired. For Paul, the spring and fall feasts, as well as the Sabbath, have a substance in Christ that offers revelation concerning what is to come. There is no more clear or concise statement regarding the future prophetic significance of all the biblical feasts in the entire Bible. In the rest of this book, we will explore exactly what Paul meant when he said this, as well as how each of the appointed times in Leviticus 23 foreshadow the events of the future.

AN OUTLINE OF THE NEW PARADIGM

In my first two books, *The Passover King* and *The 70 Weeks Jubilee*, I made the same basic argument regarding the fulfillment of the spring and fall feasts that I will make in this book. Those books, however, were focused almost exclusively on Passover, the Jubilee, and Daniel's 70 weeks prophecy (Dan. 9:24–27), as well as other biblical and theological issues.

In this book, we will have to cover some of the main points from *The Passover King* and *The 70 Weeks Jubilee*. Nevertheless, our broader goal here is to go deeper into the other feasts besides Passover and the Jubilee, and to develop a more detailed framework and chronology that outlines how the feasts will be fulfilled after the Messiah's Second Coming.

Over the years, numerous people have said to me, "Ok, if you don't think the spring feasts have already been fulfilled, what's your basic overview of how all of the feasts will be fulfilled when Jesus returns?"

The Biblical Feasts and the Return of Jesus was written to answer this question in a thorough manner, and I also hope that it will help to move the discussion on the feasts in a new direction.

To give an overview on the front end of where we are headed, below is a summary of the prophetic fulfillments of the feasts that we will cover in later chapters:

- **Passover, Unleavened Bread, First Fruits:** The Messiah will return as a greater Moses, Divine Warrior, and Miracle Worker. He will rescue Israel from captivity, lead a second exodus through the wilderness, and defeat the forces of evil with a series of Passover plagues.

- **Weeks:** After Jesus returns, there will be a great harvest of souls and spiritual revival; the nations will be gathered to Jerusalem, the Spirit of God will be poured out on all people, and the renewal of the earth will begin.

- **Trumpets:** Israel and the nations will attend the Messiah's formal enthronement and coronation ceremony on Mount Zion. At this time, the nations will hear the great trumpet blast that announces Jesus is King of the messianic age, and He will from that point on extend His justice and rule over all the earth.

- **Atonement:** The land of Israel and its people will be cleansed of all impurities, the space for the messianic Temple will be anointed and consecrated, and the Messiah will begin His high priestly ministry on the earth.

- **Tabernacles:** The earth will experience healing and agricultural abundance like never before. Israel and the nations will feast and rejoice in God's presence, and His glory will dwell among His people forevermore.

As this outline indicates, the annual feasts of Leviticus 23 will be fulfilled in a successive and glorious fashion after Jesus returns, and every feast foreshadows how God's redemptive plan for Israel and the nations will play out in the future. Though many people may only have a vague picture in their minds of what will take place when Jesus again sets foot on this earth (e.g., He returns on the clouds, defeats the Antichrist, and then reigns from Jerusalem), studying the feasts with their deepest prophetic meaning in mind can help us piece together a much more detailed mosaic of prophetic fulfillments that will be tied to the Second Coming and the inauguration of the messianic kingdom.

This, in turn, will not only allow us to understand at the intellectual level what will happen when Jesus returns, as important as that is. But it should also inspire us to align with God's prophetic plan in a practical way and worship Jesus with renewed enthusiasm, reverence, and hope.

Personally, since I began my theological studies nearly two decades ago, I have not found anything else in Scripture that reveals the breathtaking glory of Jesus and "the hope of His calling" (Eph. 1:18) quite like the biblical feasts. These holy days unlock a magnificent vision of the King of kings and His plan of salvation for His people, which can anchor our souls in the midst of life's tumultuous storms, even as we await their final fulfillment and our future inheritance in the age to come.

THE HISTORICAL CONTEXT IS KEY

In addition to accepting that every feast in Leviticus 23 will be fulfilled when Jesus returns, another key to approaching the feasts in the right way is to study them in their original historical context. This might seem like a basic point, but it is one worth emphasizing because many teachings on feasts are not based on enough study of how the ancient Israelites would have viewed these holy days when they were first instituted thirty-five hundred years ago.

For example, many popular explanations of the feasts rely more on Jewish traditions from the rabbinic literature than an in-depth analysis of the biblical text. In some cases, these Jewish traditions shed light on the true meaning of a particular feast, but in many other cases they are more of a hindrance, or a distraction, than a help. Consequently, we should be aware of the need to return to what the Bible itself says about the feasts and avoid relying exclusively on Jewish traditions.

Beside Jewish traditions, many Christians traditions also disconnect the prophetic fulfillment of the feasts from their original historical significance. This often leads to speculative theories that lack a biblical basis, such as the view that Jesus must return and save Israel on the Day of Atonement in the future (more on this in chapter 9).

In this book, we will cover some Jewish traditions that dovetail with and confirm the biblical teaching on certain feasts. We will also engage with various Christian perspectives when necessary. However, we will still prioritize the biblical text and a historically based approach to the feasts more than Jewish or Christian traditions.

First and foremost, we will seek to answer the question: Why was this feast celebrated in Israel and what central ideas would have been associated with this feast in the minds of the ancient Israelites? Until we do the legwork necessary to answer this question, we will not be able to discern the future prophetic fulfillment of the holy festivals in Leviticus 23, quite simply because the final prophetic fulfillment of the feasts will be directly tied to their original historical meaning.

To that end, this book is laid out in such a way that will allow us to move progressively from the historical material to the prophetic material. As we look at each feast in more detail, we will cover one chapter that explains that particular feast in its original historical context. Subsequently, the next chapter will cover how the historical meaning of that feast will lead to its final prophetic fulfillment after the Second Coming.

A PREMILLENNIAL & ISRAEL-CENTRIC FRAMEWORK

Now that we have covered the importance of a kingdom-focused and historically grounded approach to the feasts, it is also worth noting that the prophetic meaning of the biblical feasts can only be understood if we adopt a premillennial and Israel-centric framework of eschatology (i.e., study of the end times).

PREMILLENNIALISM

Premillennial eschatology is characterized by the belief that Jesus will return to this earth after a period of tribulation, then set up an earthy kingdom for about a thousand years after which point the final judgment of all the living and the dead will take place, which will then lead to the inauguration of the "eternal state" in a completely new heavens and new earth. In summary, premillennial eschatology posits three major eras of redemptive history after the Fall: (1) Our current phase of history in this fallen world, (2) the millennial kingdom on this earth, and (3) the eternal state in the new heavens and new earth[5] (cf. 1 Cor 15:20–28; Rev 20:1–6).

There is no need to wade into the depths of premillennialism now, except to say that this book will cover many of the events that will take place right before and during the millennium. What we will learn is that the biblical feasts offer a very detailed, yet often overlooked, picture of what will unfold in the first year of the Messiah's millennial reign.

THE NATION OF ISRAEL

As far as the nation of Israel is concerned, although the biblical feasts relate to God's purposes for the entire world, they also more specifically pertain to how God will complete His plan of salvation for the Jewish nation. For this reason, we must approach the feasts from an Israel-centric vantage point and seek to understand how they reveal what the Messiah will do for the Jewish people after the Second Coming, within their geographical homeland and territorial boundaries in the Middle East.

5 This system of thought is called premillennial because it upholds that Jesus comes back before the millennium. Other systems of eschatology, such as post-millennialism, uphold that Jesus will return after a utopian age ushered in through the gospel, whereas amillennialists do not believe there will be a transitional millennium at all, meaning, they believe Jesus returns and immediately establishes the eternal state.

Just like in the past, the nation of Israel will be the central hub of God's activity in the future. Jerusalem will be the capital city of the Messiah's kingdom and the eschatological fulfillment of the biblical feasts will highlight the centrality of the nation of Israel within God's redemptive economy.

This of course does not imply unfair favoritism toward Israel and the Jewish people. Rather, the centrality of Israel in the unfolding plan of God is simply connected to God's covenants with the biblical patriarchs, and to the very nature of Jesus Himself.

When God entered into covenant with Abraham, Isaac, and Jacob in the book of Genesis, He bound Himself to a people and to a physical land for all eternity. Thus, the reign of Jesus from the land of Israel in the future will represent the fulfillment of God's original promise to give the Promised Land to Israel's "seed" (i.e., the Messiah; Gen. 17:8).

Jesus will forever live in solidarity with His ethnic kinsman and blood relatives, the people of Israel, in the land promised to His fore-fathers. This was true at the time of His first coming and nothing will change in this regard at the time of His Second Coming. Just as the nations were blessed when the Messiah came to Israel the first time, all the nations will be blessed in an even greater way when Jesus returns to Israel and reigns from the throne of David in the future. God's eternal plan of salvation is both Christo-centric and Israel-centric from beginning to end.

THE QUESTION OF THE LAW OF MOSES

The final principle that can help us in our study of the feasts is to remain focused on their messianic significance rather than controversies over the Law of Moses. Often when the topic of the biblical feasts comes up, people will simultaneously begin discussing the Law and its practical application. These discussions typically revolve around questions such as:

> If the feasts have so much intrinsic messianic and prophetic meaning, shouldn't all followers of Jesus be keeping them today?

> Jesus said He did not come to "abolish the Law" (Matt. 5:17), so why not do our best to keep the Mosaic Law today, at least to whatever extent possible?

These are important questions, but they are also complex, and I do plan to publish a resource on the relationship between the Law of Moses and the New Covenant in the future. That said, it would be impossible to do this topic justice in the present volume, because it is not a topic that is as simple as people on different sides of the issue often try to make it.

Consequently, for now, I will only offer one morsel to chew on as we think about the feasts and their practical observance today. In Colossians 2:16 Paul said, "No one is to act as your judge in regards to a festival...or Sabbath day."

As noted earlier, Paul makes this statement because these festivals and Sabbaths are "a shadow of what is to come, but the substance belongs to Christ." I do not believe Paul was discouraging the celebration or practical observance of the feasts here, as many Christian commentators have erroneously argued.[6] However, the fact remains that for Paul, the most important thing is that we understand how the feasts point to the work of the Messiah. Judging others or adopting a posture of moral superiority in response to how they celebrate or do not celebrate the biblical feasts is out of line with Paul's admonition here.

With this in mind, my intention in this book is not to use the topic of the feasts as a bridge to argue for one position or another on the Law of Moses. Instead, my goal is to help readers understand how the feasts reveal the "substance" of what Jesus will do when He returns so that we can be more grounded in the "blessed hope" of His future kingdom (Titus 2:13). If we keep the focus here, on the Messiah and the glories

6 Note: Colossians 2:16–17 is a disputed passage that most likely reflects a historical context in which some people (possibly outsiders and some insiders) were judging certain Colossian believers over the particulars of their Sabbath and festival observances, or lack thereof. In this context, Paul does not argue against the observance of these celebrations, as many Christian commentators have assumed. Rather, he addresses judgmental attitudes and how they can become a distraction from the proper messianic focus when celebrating the feasts.

of the messianic age, more people will be open to studying the feasts and considering the ways that practically celebrating them can help them in their walk with the Lord.

CHAPTER SUMMARY

The purpose of this chapter was to establish a foundation that will help us approach the biblical feasts in the right way. To do this, we covered a number of interpretive principles which are summarized below:

1. There are seven annual feasts mentioned in Leviticus 23: Passover, Unleavened Bread, First Fruits, Weeks, Trumpets, Atonement, and Tabernacles. In this passage, God's festivals are called moedim (i.e., appointed times), which is a Hebrew word that denotes a revelatory appointment with God.

2. The ancient Israelites used a lunar calendar of twelve months that started in the spring. The typical lunar year was 354 days long. However, Israel's lunar calendar was reconciled with the earth's rotation around the sun through the addition of a thirteenth month when necessary, which meant that over time Israel's annual cycle averaged out to 365 days (though it was shorter some years and longer in leap years).

3. The Bible never says some feasts have been completely fulfilled whereas other have not. Rather, Scripture is clear that every feast has a historical meaning and a partial fulfillment through the Messiah's first coming, even as they all still await their final fulfillment in the kingdom of God.

4. To decipher how the biblical feasts will be fulfilled when Jesus returns, we must look at them in their original historical context, without relying exclusively on Jewish and Christian traditions. A critical point to grasp is that the final fulfillment of the feasts in the kingdom of God will be intricately tied to their original historical meaning in ancient Israel.

5. The future prophetic significance of the feasts is best explained within a premillennial and Israel-centric framework of eschatology, one that upholds that Jesus will set up the millennial kingdom on this earth with the nation of Israel at its center.

6. The Apostle Paul taught that our primary focus when studying and celebrating the feasts should be the Messiah Himself, not religious disputes about the Law that stoke a judgmental attitude (Col. 2:17).

Keeping these principles in mind will put us in position to comprehend the mystery of the moedim in Leviticus 23. As we turn now to analyze the individual feasts in subsequent chapters, our first goal will be to establish a historical framework that can help us understand the feasts from the vantage point of the ancient Israelites. From there, we will branch out and study what each feast reveals about the return of Jesus and His future kingdom.

BIBLE STUDY QUESTIONS

1. How did the ancient Israelites organize their calendar, and how should we understand Exodus 23:16 and 34:22?

2. What principles did you learn that will change the way you approach the biblical feasts?

3. What New Testament passages use the same language as Colossians 2:16–17 and what does this language reveal about Paul's understanding of the feasts?

2

PASSOVER IN HISTORICAL CONTEXT

PASSOVER is probably the most well-known biblical feast in the Bible. The majority of Jews and Christians, as well as many people from other faith backgrounds, are at least somewhat familiar with the story of the exodus plagues, the Passover lambs, and the parting of the Red Sea, so much so that the Passover has achieved a certain level of iconic status within both popular and religious culture.

Yet still, and even in spite of our general familiarity with Passover, the early chapters in Exodus that contain the record of Israel's miraculous encounter with God in Egypt are not widely understood on their own terms. Due to a lack of scholarly teaching on the Old Testament, most Christians and Jews do not fully grasp the main point of Exodus 1–15, or how the events recorded in this text would have been understood by the ancient Israelites living thousands of years ago.

To remedy this problem, our first goal when studying Passover should be to interpret the early chapters in Exodus in light of their ancient Near

Eastern historical and cultural context. Before anything else we must seek to comprehend how the Israelites living in the second millennium BC (c. 1500 BC) would have viewed the works of God in Egypt. Taking this historical approach to Exodus 1–15 will not only yield a better baseline interpretation of the Passover story itself, but it will also set us up in the next chapter to grasp how Passover will be fulfilled when Jesus returns and the prophetic events that this story pointed forward to all along.

EXODUS 1–15 IS A NEW CREATION WARFARE TEXT

If we place the Passover story within its original historical context, it becomes more and more clear that the themes of warfare and new creation dominate Exodus 1–15. These chapters present God as a mighty Divine Warrior who goes to battle against His enemies, redeems His people, and then establishes the nation of Israel as the firstfruits of His renewed cosmos. In Exodus, God steps onto the battlefield, defeats His foes, and then takes His elect through the waters of regeneration so they can enjoy a new life in His presence. Everything in the Passover story proclaims the victory of the Lord over the forces of darkness and His plan of redemption for the entire world.

To be sure, Passover is not often approached with the themes of warfare and new creation in mind. However, it will become clear in this chapter and the next that the rich layers of historical, messianic, and future prophetic meaning embedded within this iconic tale of miracles and divine intervention cannot be fully uncovered until these particular themes are appreciated.

Thus, we will begin our study of Passover by setting the Passover story against its ancient Near Eastern, historical backdrop. Then, we will progress into a more detailed study of the Passover story itself, before moving on in the next chapter to consider how Passover will be fulfilled after the Messiah's Second Coming.

THE ISRAELITES IN EGYPT

The story of Passover traces its roots to the book of Genesis, which recounts how the Israelites ended up in Egypt during the time of Joseph. After he was betrayed by his brothers, Joseph was sold into Egyptian slavery around the year 1683 BC (Gen. 37).[1] Furthermore, Genesis tells us that Joseph started out as a servant in the Egyptian court, but due to God's favor he eventually became the vizier of Egypt, second only to Pharaoh himself.

Around twenty years later (1662 BC), Joseph was reunited with his father Jacob and eleven brothers in Egypt, who had fled the land of Canaan due to a severe famine (Gen. 42–50). Notably, numerous Egyptian documents and archaeological findings confirm that during this time period it was common for Semitic peoples from the Middle East to travel to Egypt for food and sustenance, as they sought relief from "climactic problems," drought, and famine.[2]

For example, the Egyptian Prophecy of Neferti (c. 2000 BC) says, "Enemies have arisen in the east, Asiatics [i.e., Semites] have come down to Egypt."[3] This same text also pejoratively calls these Asiatic Semites "feeders," indicating that they spread "throughout the land" in search of food.

In his famous historical study, Old Testament scholar James Hoffmeier summarizes how the events referred to in Genesis make sense in light of written and archaeological evidence. He writes:

> Thus, for a period roughly from 1800 to 1540 B.C., Egypt was an attractive place for the Semitic-speaking people of western Asia to migrate [...] This span of time coincides with the traditional "Patriarchal Period" and therefore fits the period and circumstances described in Genesis when Abraham, Isaac (almost), and Jacob went to Egypt in search of food, water, and green pastures.[4]

1 Most of the dates in this chapter are based on the Egyptian New Chronology of Egyptologist David Rohls, which he outlines in his book *Exodus: Myth or History* (St. Louis Park: Thinking Man Media, 2015), 80.

2 James K. Hoffmeier, *Israel in Egypt: The Evidence for the Authenticity of the Exodus Tradition* (Oxford: Oxford University Press, 1997), 68.

3 "The Prophecy of Neferti," in Hoffmeier, *Israel in Egypt*, 58.

4 Hoffmeier, *Israel in Egypt*, 68.

THE EGYPTIAN PERIOD

In the beginning of this period in Egypt, the Israelites lived freely as shepherds in the land of Goshen (Gen. 47). Goshen was likely in the eastern portion of the Nile Delta, an extremely fertile region just south of the Mediterranean Sea.

Over time, however, "a new king arose over Egypt, who did not know Joseph" (Exod. 1:8). This new Pharaoh forced the Israelites into slavery and used the abundance of free Israelite labor to enrich his kingdom and build some of the great Egyptian cities of his empire, including "Pithom and Raamses" (Exod. 1:11).

Exodus 1:13–14 describes the scene:

> The Egyptians compelled the sons of Israel to labor rigorously; and they made their lives bitter with hard labor in mortar and bricks and at all kinds of labor in the field, all their labors which they rigorously imposed on them.

There are different views on how long Israel was in Egypt prior to the exodus, as well as different views on the precise date of the exodus itself. In all likelihood, Israel was probably in Egypt for around 215 years total, with the period of slavery lasting around 100 years.[5] Also, their

5 In Genesis 15:13, God told Abraham that his descendants would live in a foreign land for four hundred years. Some have interpreted this to mean that Israel was in Egypt for four hundred years. However, another possibility is that the four hundred years in Genesis 15:13 included the entire period of patriarchal wandering, beginning in the time of Abraham. If true, this would mean that the Israelites were only in Egypt for roughly two hundred years after Jacob entered that land. This interpretation was adopted by the Jewish historian Josephus (*Antiquities,* XV:2) and seems to be confirmed in the Septuagint (LXX) and Samaritan Pentateuch (SP) versions of Exodus 12:40. Also, in Galatians 3:16–17 Paul links the four hundred years of Genesis 15:13 to the entire period between the promise to Abraham and the giving of the Law, not specifically to Israel's Egyptian period after Jacob.

departure from Egypt can probably be dated to circa 1450 BC, during the reign of either Pharaoh Thutmose III or Pharaoh Dudimose.[6]

THE SUPERPOWER OF THE ANCIENT WORLD

In any case, for our purposes, the most important point to note is that the exodus took place at the height of Egyptian power and influence (c. 1450 BC). By this time, Egypt had already been a unified empire for at least fifteen hundred years. The Great Pyramids of Giza and the adjacent Egyptian Sphinx, known to many as the most recognizable wonders of the ancient world, had already been standing for one thousand years by the time of Moses, having been built around the year 2550 BC.

Nurtured by the Nile River, which produces some of the most fertile soil in the world, and protected by desert on three sides and the Mediterranean Sea to the north, Egypt was in many ways buffered from conquest with a robust natural defense. This allowed the Egyptians to prosper and develop one of the most advanced civilizations in the ancient world.

In terms of religion, Egyptian life was regulated by a complex religious piety centered around the worship of hundreds of gods and goddesses. But at the heart of the Egyptian culture and religion was the Pharaoh himself.

The Pharaoh was viewed not simply as a representative of the gods, but as a divine intermediary, responsible for maintaining the order of the unseen gods on the earth. As the head statesman and the chief religious leader of Egypt, the Pharaoh waged wars, provided food for the people, participated in religious ceremonies, and initiated building projects that enabled Egypt's major cities to become the largest and most magnificent in the ancient Near East.

6 Many scholars have chosen a later date for the exodus, circa 1250 BC. However, this later date does not fit with numerous chronological statements in the Bible, including 1 Kings 6:1 and Judges 11:26. For example, 1 Kings 6:1 says Solomon began to build the Temple 480 years after the exodus, and we know he started this work circa 966 BC. Choosing a later date for the exodus (1250 BC) does not allow for enough time between the exodus and the building of Solomon's Temple whereas the circa 1450 BC exodus date fits this chronological scenario perfectly.

For example, the original capital city of Egypt, Memphis, reached a population of at least thirty thousand by the 2000s BC, and the later capital, Thebes, had at least eighty thousand inhabitants by the 1300s BC, making it the largest city of its time. In addition, Thebes (modern Luxor, Egypt) was widely known as a city of unsurpassed splendor and beaty. Imposing and meticulously sculpted and painted monuments brought the landscape of Thebes to life, and sites such as the Valley of the Kings and Queens and the Luxor Temple still draw tourists to Thebes today.

All this to say, when we encounter Egypt in the book of Exodus, we are encountering the most dominant military, economic, and cultural superpower of the day. Very few nations would dare mess with Egypt, and those who did were often met with devastating defeat and humiliation on the battlefield.

THE LIFE OF MOSES

While Egypt enjoyed unsurpassed military, economic, and cultural dominance in the ancient Near East, the young child Moses entered the world around the year 1530 BC. Exodus 2 tells us how Moses was born to Hebrew parents in Egypt yet placed in a basket and floated down the Nile River as a baby to protect him from the murderous reach of the Pharaoh, who sought to annihilate all the male Hebrew children in his kingdom (Exod. 2:1–4).

In God's providence, Moses was taken out of the Nile by Pharaoh's daughter and raised as her adopted son (Exod. 2:5–10). The Jewish historian Josephus further adds that during his twenties and thirties Moses became one of the most successful generals in the Egyptian army.[7]

When he was forty years old, however, Moses murdered an Egyptian whom he saw beating a Hebrew slave. As a result, he was forced to flee into the wilderness for another forty years and became completely cut off from the life of prominence and luxury he had known before (Exod. 2:11–15).

The famous story of the burning bush, which opens Exodus 3, takes

7 Josephus, *Antiquities of the Jews,* II.

place when Moses is already eighty years old. In this passage, God finds Moses pasturing a flock of sheep "on the west side of the wilderness," at the foot of the "mountain of God," which would eventually become known as Mount Sinai (Exod. 3:1).

THE PLAGUES AGAINST EGYPT

When God encountered Moses in the wilderness, He commanded him to go back to Egypt to set the Israelites free from slavery, because He was moved to compassion in light of Israel's intense suffering. As we read in Exodus 3, God says:

> I have surely seen the affliction of My people, who are in Egypt, and have given heed to their cry because of their taskmasters, for I am aware of their sufferings. So I have come down to deliver them from the power of the Egyptians, and to bring them up from that land to a good and spacious land, to a land flowing with milk and honey. (vv. 7–8)

> Therefore, come now, and I will send you to Pharaoh so that you may bring My people, the sons of Israel, out of Egypt. (v. 10)

Because God also foresaw that Pharaoh would not willingly let the Israelites leave, He promised to break Pharaoh's will through a cycle of plagues, signs, and wonders:

> So I will stretch out My hand and strike Egypt with all My miracles which I shall do in the midst of it; and after that he will let you go. (Exod. 3:20)

> But I will harden Pharaoh's heart that I may multiply My signs and My wonders in the land of Egypt. When Pharaoh will not listen to you, then I will lay My hand on Egypt and bring out My hosts, My people the sons of Israel from the land of Egypt by great judgments. The Egyptians shall know that I am the Lord, when I stretch out

My hand on Egypt and bring out the sons of Israel from their midst. (Exod. 7:3–5)

The plague narrative that ensues then recounts how God, through Moses and Aaron, brought down ten plague judgments against Pharaoh and the Egyptians. In order, these plagues included:

- Turning the entire Egyptian water supply, including the Nile River, streams, pools, and reservoirs of water, into blood (Exod. 7:19).
- Frogs throughout all of Egypt, in the houses, bedrooms, beds, ovens, and kneading bowls (Exod. 8:1–6).
- Gnats as abundant as the dust of the earth (Exod. 8:16–19).
- Swarms of flies that "laid waste" the land (Exod. 8:20–24).
- Pestilence and disease that killed most of the Egyptian livestock (Exod. 9:1–7).
- Putrid boils and sores on "man and beast" (Exod. 9:8–10).
- Thunder, hail, and fire "flashing continually" from the sky, which destroyed most of the trees and crops in Egypt (Exod. 9:18–26).
- A host of locusts that consumed whatever was left after the hail (Exod. 10:1–15).
- "Thick darkness in all the land of Egypt for three days" (Exod. 10:21–23).

- And finally, with the tenth plague, the Angel of the Lord killed all the firstborn in Egypt, "from the firstborn of Pharaoh who sat on his throne, to the firstborn of the captive who was in the dungeon, and all the firstborn of cattle as well" (Exod. 11:1–7; 12:29–32).

A NATURAL EXPLANATION OF THE PLAGUES?

Given the extraordinary character of the Exodus plague narrative, many scholars have attempted to explain the ten plagues in naturalistic terms, rather than accept that they were caused by God's supernatural intervention. One of the most popular naturalistic explanations of the plagues suggests that they were caused by an unusually high inundation of the Nile, which occurred every year in July and August when the water levels of the Nile would rise. By September, the Nile would then overflow its banks and water would spread into the surrounding areas, irrigating the farmland and depositing mineral-rich silt that nurtured the Egyptian crops.

Scholars who adopt a naturalistic interpretation of the plagues argue that the blood of the first plague was nothing more than red soil and reddish microorganisms that happened to be in the Nile River in higher quantities that year. These conditions allegedly killed the fish, displaced the frogs (second plague), and created a breeding ground for mosquitos, gnats, flies, and other insects (third and fourth plagues). In this scheme, the plague of pestilence that killed the livestock (fifth plague), as well as the boils (sixth plague), were caused by harmful bacteria that was left in Egypt after the frogs died, which was then allegedly carried by the insects into the rest of the land. The intense weather and locusts of the seventh and eighth plagues could be explained as natural phenomena as well, and likewise, the ninth plague of darkness is sometimes attributed to an intense sandstorm (*hamsin*) that blotted out the light of the sun.[8]

8 This interpretation is found in the famous work: *Old Testament Survey: The Message, Form, and Background of the Old Testament,* eds. William Sanford Lasor, David Allen Hubbard, & Frederic William Bush (Grand Rapids: Wm. B. Eerdmans, 1996), 69–70. Though I do not agree with this view, it is summarized in the following way: "An important study shows that the nine plagues fit precisely the natural phenomena of Egypt. In this study all the plagues (except the hail) form a sequence of severe natural events which exhibit a cause-and-effect relationship in the very order of their happening. The plagues begin with an abnormally high inundation of the Nile."

THE SUPERNATURAL NATURE OF THE PLAGUES

There can be no doubt that God used the elements of nature to judge Pharaoh and the Egyptians. However, there are a number of problems with the view that the plagues were merely the result of a cause-and-effect sequence of naturally occurring phenomena tied to the inundation of the Nile.

First, the plagues are called "miracles" (3:20) and "signs and wonders" (7:3) that were performed by God's "hand" and "the finger of God" (8:19). This language suggests that the plagues were much more than the aftereffects of a flood caused by the overflow of the Nile River.

Second, at different points in the Exodus narrative, Egyptian magicians perform the same miracles as Moses and Aaron with "their secret arts" (7:11; 7:22; 8:7; 8:18). This implies that in four cases the religious leaders in Egypt were able to access the demonic realm to mimic the work of God, which again reveals the supernatural character of the plagues.

Third, the first plague of blood did not only affect the Nile River. Exodus 7:19–21 says this plague affected other rivers, streams, pools, reservoirs of water, and even the water in vessels of wood and stone. As we read in Exodus 7:21, "the blood was through all the land of Egypt."

If the Nile River being filled with red sediment and red microorganisms caused the plague of "blood," it would have affected only the Nile itself, but it did not. We know that other sources of water in Egypt were affected as well.

Also, Exodus uses the word "blood" to depict how the waters of Egypt were transformed. It does not describe a natural change in pigmentation, nor is there any indication in the biblical text that the blood of the first plague should be interpreted in a metaphorical sense. The most straightforward reading of Exodus 7 is that the first plague involved literal blood throughout the entire Egyptian water supply. This was a miracle, something that produced awe and fear in the people who witnessed it. It was not a natural occurrence the Egyptians were already familiar with due to normal seasonal changes in their country.

Fourth, Moses was able to control how long the plague of frogs lasted (8:8–15). This would not have been the case if the frogs appeared only because of the inundation of the Nile.

Fifth, there is no causal link between the inundation of the Nile River and the seventh, ninth, and tenth plagues (extreme weather, darkness, and slaying of Egyptian firstborn). The overflow of the Nile could not have caused fire and hail to burst forth from the heavens. Nor could it have caused the land to go dark for three days and the death of only the firstborn in Egypt. Thus, we have to ask: if the plagues really exhibit such a clear "cause-and-effect relationship in the very order of their happening,"[9] which was set off by the inundation of the Nile, as many scholars claim, then why do three of the final plagues that bring the plague narrative to its climactic conclusion have no connection at all to the inundation of the Nile? When the inconsistencies in the naturalistic explanation of the plagues are framed in this way, it becomes clear that a much better reading of the biblical text maintains that all ten Exodus plagues were independent miracles carried out by the hand of God.

Sixth, and finally, the Israelites were protected from the plagues. This is stated in the account of the fourth, seventh, ninth, and tenth plagues (8:22; 9:26; 10:23; 11:7). However, it is obvious that the Israelites did not suffer from any of the other plagues either.

This distinction between what the Israelites experienced in comparison to the Egyptians indicates that the plagues were selective supernatural judgments, not natural phenomena. Of course, it still requires faith to believe that God performed these miracles in Egypt thirty-five hundred years ago. Either way, there is nothing in the book of Exodus that suggests that the Israelites or the Egyptians viewed the plagues in a naturalistic way. Everyone knew they were having an encounter with the living God, who was miraculously manipulating the forces of nature to display His power.

9 Lasor & Hubbard, *Old Testament Survey*, 69–70.

IMAGINE THE PLAGUES

Due to our familiarity with the book of Exodus, it is easy for us to move quickly through the plague narrative without letting the magnitude of what God did to Egypt at this time sink in. But just pause for a second and think about what happened prior to the exodus.

Imagine waking up in the morning and seeing blood coming out of your faucet as you turn on the water to brush your teeth, and then blood coming out of the shower as you attempt to get ready for the day. Then imagine thousands of filthy frogs coming out of your cabinets and closets and into your house through the windows, overrunning your entire home. Then imagine a million mosquitos and flies swarming around your head as you try to leave your house to go to work or run some errands.

Imagine painful boils popping up all over the body of your favorite dog or cat and all over your own body as well. Then imagine turning on the news and hearing that there would be no meat available at the grocery stores for the next six months because a plague of pestilence had destroyed every cow in the land. Then you get in your car and find yourself stuck in a hailstorm that turns your vehicle into shrapnel and Swiss cheese, as lightning from heaven strikes power lines and trees all around you, setting buildings on fire, destroying crops, and ruining the economic infrastructure of your city for years. Then somehow you make it home and find your firstborn son or daughter lying dead on the floor of their room.

I have personally experienced a tornado that destroyed hundreds of houses and businesses in my neighborhood, a hurricane, and many severe thunderstorms. I have also dealt with my fair share of sickness and orthopedic injuries in almost forty years of life. But none of us have every experienced anything close to the Exodus plagues. This was a sustained outpouring of judgement and wrath that God inflicted on the most powerful nation in the world, which affected every stratum of Egyptian society in unfathomable ways for probably close to six months or longer. When God said He would stretch out His hand against Pharaoh and the Egyptians, He meant it.

THE REASON FOR THE PLAGUES

We know the plagues were supernatural judgments that God used to break Pharaoh's will. However, many questions remain regarding the exact significance of the plagues, such as why these specific plagues were chosen by God in the first place. After all, God could have delivered Israel in any way He wanted, or in a matter of minutes, so why did He subject Egypt to a sequence of plague judgements that lasted many months?

To answer this question, we must first understand that the plague narrative in Exodus revolves around the idea that prior to Israel's first Passover God went to war against the Egyptians and the demonic forces that controlled their nation (i.e., their gods). The plagues were part of a sustained military bombardment campaign that systematically destabilized the Egyptian kingdom, delegitimized the Egyptian gods, and exalted Israel's God alone as the supreme Lord of heaven and earth in a way that could not have been achieved were it not for the protracted nature of the plague sequence. Put simply, the plague narrative in Exodus 7–15 is a warfare text that recounts the Lord's victory on the battlefield, and this is a vital point to grasp if we want to both properly interpret the Passover story within its original historical context and understand many deeper lessons about how Passover will be fulfilled by Jesus at the time of His Second Coming.

THE PLAGUES AND THE GODS OF EGYPT

One of the major clues that the early chapters in Exodus revolve around this theme of spiritual warfare can be found in Exodus 12:12. In this verse, God said that on the night of Passover He would "fatally strike all the firstborn" of Egypt and "execute judgments against all the gods of Egypt" (cf. Num. 33:4).

This statement indicates that the plagues had something to do with the Lord's confrontation with the supernatural powers of darkness (i.e., the gods) that controlled Egypt, and many scholars have noted that there is a link between the plagues and certain Egyptian deities. For example, the Egyptians had multiple gods associated with the Nile River, including

Hapi (or Apis), the bull god of the Nile, Isis, the goddess of the Nile, and Khnum, the ram-god guardian of the Nile. In addition, the Egyptian goddess of birth, Heqet, had the head of a frog, because frogs were associated with fertility, and one of the most prominent Egyptian goddesses (Hathor) was often depicted with the ears of a cow. There were also other gods associated with disease (Sekhmet), insects (Uatchit), the sky (Nut, Hathor), crops (Osiris), weather and desert storms (Set), the sun (Amon-Re), and childbirth and life (Min, Heqet, Isis).

Though some scholars remain unconvinced that the plagues were directed against various Egyptian gods, there does seem to be a connection here because the plagues relate to major areas of life and nature that were controlled by different Egyptians deities. Especially with the ninth plague of darkness, it is hard to imagine that the Israelites and Egyptians would not have viewed this as a direct attack against the primary Egyptian deity, the sun god, Amon-Re, and it is probably a safe bet that the Egyptians would have viewed the other plagues as attacks against many of their other gods as well.

Thus, with His ten plagues, the Lord judged the gods of Egypt and their divine representative on the earth, Pharaoh. The Lord showcased His sovereignty (and their impotence) over every realm that was previously thought to be under their control. The plagues were spiritual warfare directed against the Egyptian pantheon, and throughout the plague narrative God quite literally tramples on His enemies.

THE LORD AS THE DIVINE WARRIOR

Another clue that the plague narrative in Exodus depicts a military battle between the Lord and the supernatural powers of darkness can be seen when we consider the extent to which God is portrayed as a divine warrior in this text. To briefly elaborate, the plagues in Exodus 7–12 were not only used by God because they targeted individual Egyptian deities. Rather, at a more fundamental level, these specific plagues were used by God because various popular mythologies known to the ancient Israelites, Canaanites, Mesopotamians, and Egyptians depicted the gods engaging in warfare, and it was understood that in many cases a divine warrior would use the forces of nature as their primary weapon in battle.

As noted by Old Testament scholar Charlie Trimm, "One of the key characteristics of the divine warrior was his employment of natural elements against his enemies," and this use of nature weapons was especially common "among those gods identified as storm gods."[10] According to Trimm, "lighting and thunder were quintessential tools of a storm god," and many stories written by ancient Near Eastern peoples depict their gods using these natural elements on the battlefield. Moreover, because the peoples of the ancient world were much more dependent on and afraid of nature than we are today, storm gods were often regarded as the supreme and most important deities who controlled and ruled all the others (e.g., Zeus in the Greek pantheon with his lightning bolts).

Consequently, when God used the plagues as His weapon of choice in Exodus, this made clear, in a way that would have made sense to an ancient Near Eastern audience, that He is the ultimate Divine Warrior and chief Storm God of the universe.

THE STORM GOD IN THE ANCIENT NEAR EAST

To understand how Exodus draws on this divine warrior motif that was already well-known in the ancient Near East, we need to compare the biblical account to some other popular stories that were in circulation at the time of the exodus.

Outside of the Bible, a great example of a storm god in battle is found in the Babylonian creation epic Enuma Elish. In this story, the Babylonian chief god, Marduk, "employed thunder bolts in his battle against [the chaos dragon] Tiamat."[11] Furthermore, Marduk often holds a thunderbolt in artistic renditions, and in the Enuma Elish we read of how Marduk controlled the forces of nature—in particular lightning,

10 Charlie Trimm, *"YHWH Fights for Them!" The Divine Warrior in the Exodus Narrative* (Piscataway: Gorgias Press: 2014), 47.

11 Trimm, *"YHWH Fights for Them!"* 39.

fire, wind, and water—to defeat Tiamat.

Here is a passage from Enuma Elish that describes Marduk as a storm god who goes to battle against Tiamat:

> [Marduk] fashioned a bow, designated it as his weapon, feathered an arrow, set it in the string. He lifted up a mace and carried it in his right hand, slung the bow and quiver at his side, put lighting in front of him, his body was filled with an ever-blazing flame. He made a net to encircle Tiamat within it, marshalled the four winds so that no part of her could escape: South Wind, North Wind, East Wind, West Wind, the gift of his father Anu, he kept close to the net at his side. He created the (evil wind), the tempest, the whirlwind, the Four Winds, the Seven Winds, the tornado, seven of them. They advanced behind him to make turmoil inside Tiamat. The lord [Marduk] raised the flood-weapon, his great weapon, and mounted the frightful, unfaceable storm-chariot.[12]

Like the Babylonians, the Canaanites also believed that their chief god, Baal, went to war against Death with clouds, rain, wind, and thunderbolts. Trimm also writes that the "Egyptian god Seth was associated with the use of thunder and rainstorms in war,"[13] and the Assyrian king Sargon declared that the Assyrian weather god, Adad, "let loose his fierce tempest against [Sargon's enemies] and, with bursting cloud and thunderbolt (lit. stones of heaven), totally annihilated them.'"[14]

THE SUPREME STORM GOD AND DIVINE WARRIOR

It is not a coincidence that in Exodus, the God of the Israelites displays complete control over nature and uses many of the same weapons of war that were commonly employed by the storm gods of the surrounding

12 "The Epic of Creation," section IV, in *Myths from Mesopotamia: Creation, the Flood, Gilgamesh, and Others*, trans. Stephanie Dalley (Oxford: Oxford University Press, 1989), 251.

13 Trimm, *"YHWH Fights for Them!"* 48–49.

14 Trimm, *"YHWH Fights for Them!"* 48.

nations in various mythological accounts and mythic retellings of history. In Exodus, the Lord speaks the cultural-religious language of the day and presents Himself in a way that would have been winsome, compelling, and magnificent in the eyes of an ancient Near Eastern audience already familiar with different storm gods.

Especially with the seventh plague of thunder, hail, and fire from heaven (Exod. 9:18–26), the storm-god theme is demonstrably present in the Exodus account. Likewise, because the other plagues showcase God's complete control over nature as well, they are also part of this composite picture that depicts Him as the chief Storm God.

Unlike the gods in the mythic accounts of the surrounding nations, however, in Exodus the Lord enters the field of tangible history. He does in real time and real space what many other peoples could only dream of through myth and storytelling, and this clarified, for both the Israelites and the surrounding nations, that the Lord is the true and living God who is above all others. Furthermore, the use of common ancient Near Eastern divine warrior and storm god motifs in Exodus confirms that warfare is one of the central themes of the Passover story.

OTHER DIVINE WARRIOR ELEMENTS

In addition to the plagues themselves, there are many other elements in Exodus 7–15 that highlight the warfare theme in this text. First, many of the terms associated with the plagues carry military and warfare connotations. For example, God says multiple times He will "smite" (*nagaf*) Pharaoh and the Egyptians (Exod. 8:2; 12:23; 12:27). This Hebrew term nagaf is used multiple times elsewhere in the Bible to depict a military battle (e.g., Judg. 20:39; 1 Sam. 4:10; 2 Sam. 18:7; Zech. 14:12; 14:18).

Likewise, the Hebrew term *nakah* is also frequently used in connection with the plagues (Exod. 3:20; 9:15; 12:13; 12:29). This word is often translated "to strike," and it is used hundreds of times to depict warfare in the Bible (e.g., Josh. 12:7; 13:12; 1 Sam. 7:11; 14:48; 2 Chron. 25:13).

Another term, *naga*, is used to describe the plagues themselves in Exodus 11:1. According to Trimm, this word "denotes touching, but also often means 'to strike' (2 Sam. 14:10; Isa 53:4) or reflects military defeat (Josh 8:15)." It can refer to disease (Lev. 13–14; Deut. 24:8) or a military assault. Trimm notes that another translation, "like 'blows' or 'assaults,' might be preferable for these terms to show their common martial [i.e., military] connotation."[15]

Below is a brief comparison list that illustrates how the Hebrew terms nagaf (smite), nakah (strike), and naga (assault) from Exodus carry warfare connotations within the Passover narrative and elsewhere in the Bible:

- "But if you refuse to let them go, behold, I will smite [nagaf] your whole territory with frogs." (Exod. 8:3)

- "So I will stretch out My hand and strike [naka] Egypt with all My miracles which I shall do in the midst of it." (Exod. 3:20)

- "Then the men of Israel turned in the battle, and Benjamin began to strike [naka] and kill about thirty men of Israel, for they said, 'Surely they are defeated [nagaf] before us, as in the first battle.'" (Judg. 20:39)

- "Now the LORD said to Moses, 'One more plague [naga] I will bring upon Pharaoh and on Egypt.'" (Exod. 11:1)

- "Joshua and all Israel pretended to be beaten [naga] before them, and fled by the way of the wilderness." (Josh. 8:15)

THE HAND OF GOD IN BATTLE

Finally, the anthropomorphic language in Exodus, which is language that depicts God with human characteristics, also conveys a military

15 Trimm, *"YHWH Fights for Them!"* 45.

battle. The three most common anthropomorphisms in Exodus describe the Lord acting with His "hand" (*yad*), His "arm" (*zeroah*), and His "right arm" (*yameen*).

- "So I will stretch out my hand [yad] and strike Egypt with all My miracles which I shall do in the midst of it." (Exod. 3:20)

- "I will redeem you with an outstretched arm [zeroah] and with great judgments." (Exod. 6:6)

- Your right arm [yameen] O LORD, is majestic in power, Your right arm [yameen] O LORD, shatters the enemy." (Exod. 15:6)

Trimm points out that these anthropomorphisms (hand, arm, and right arm) are used in Exodus because a warrior's hand "held their weapons," and their strong arm was a symbol of their power.[16] These terms confirm that the plagues were meant to be understood as a weapon of war, and numerous ancient Near Eastern documents also associate a divine warrior's hand with their weapons and other actions on the battlefield.

The Babylonians for example wrote that their chief god, Marduk, "lifted up a mace and carried it in his right hand, slung the bow and quiver at his side."[17] Similarly, the Assyrian king "Sennacherib inscribed 'the might of my conquering hand' upon a monument describing military conquests." Also, numerous ancient Near Eastern images depict the gods "holding weapons in their hands."[18]

The same general idea of strength and power in battle is conveyed through the emphasis on the arm as well. The Egyptian Pharaoh

16 Trimm, *"YHWH Fights for Them!"* 15.

17 "The Epic of Creation," in *Myths from Mesopotamia,* trans. Stephanie Dalley, 251.

18 Trimm, *"YHWH Fights for Them!"* 15–17. Trimm adds that in the "Old Testament, the hand often represented armies (Num. 20:20; Judg. 6:1–2; 1 Sam. 12:9)."

Thutmose III "described himself as 'the good god who captures with his powerful arm, smiting southerners and beheading northerners,'" and the Assyrian king "Sargon II boasted that he had captured an enemy king with his 'strong arm.'"[19]

When understood as a whole, both the plagues and the specific terminology in Exodus 7–15 imply that this is a warfare text through and through. In many ways, the plague narrative is analogous to other ancient Near Eastern myths and histories that detail the exploits of a storm god or divine warrior in battle. The gods often carried their weapons in their hands, stretched out their arms in battle, and used the forces of nature to defeat their enemies. In Exodus, the Lord also displays His strong arm, only not in the realm of fantasy, but instead, with real fire, real lightning, and real hail within the tangible sphere of history. The plagues were part of a shock-and-awe military bombardment campaign that exalted the Lord alone and sealed His victory on the battlefield.

THE FIRST PASSOVER

The climax of the warfare narrative in Exodus takes place with the tenth plague, on Passover, and also about a month or two later at the Red Sea. Before the tenth plague, God commanded each Israelite household to slay a young lamb, put some of its blood on their doorposts, and then eat the lamb, roasted by fire, that same night. According to Exodus 12:8, the Passover lamb was to be eaten with unleavened bread and bitter herbs.

On the calendar, the slaying of the Passover lambs in Egypt took place in the late afternoon or early evening on the fourteenth of the first biblical month, known as Aviv (or Nisan in modern Judaism), which is in the spring, usually in March or April by modern reckoning. After these Passover lambs were slain, God sent "the destroyer" throughout the land of Egypt (Exod. 12:23), and "it came about at midnight that

19 Trimm, *"YHWH Fights for Them!"* 17–18. Trimm notes that in the "Old Testament, the arm symbolized primarily strength (1 Sam. 2:31; Job 22:8; Pss. 71:18; 79:11), although it could refer more concretely to military forces (Dan. 11:15, 22, 31)."

the Lord struck all the firstborn in the land of Egypt, from the firstborn of Pharaoh who sat on his throne to the firstborn of the captives who was in the dungeon, and all the firstborn of cattle" (Exod. 12:29).

Whereas the first nine plagues represented a more generalized military assault against Egypt, the tenth plague was more akin to what we might consider in modern terms a precision military strike. It was a laser-guided missile right to the heart of Pharaoh. As man, child, and beast lay dead on the battlefield, there was no longer any question as to whose god was supreme, and in this way the Lord prevailed completely over "the gods of Egypt" (Exod. 12:12).

THE FEAST OF UNLEAVENED BREAD

Shocked, broken, and demoralized after the tenth plague, Pharaoh kicked Moses, Aaron, and the Israelites out of Egypt, which then led to their subsequent journey to the Red Sea. At this time, on the day after Passover, a separate appointed time called the Feast of Unleavened Bread was also instituted for the Israelites. As God said in Leviticus 23:6, "On the fifteenth day of that month, the Lord's festival of unleavened bread begins; for seven days you must eat bread made without yeast."

During the days of Unleavened Bread, Israel was commanded to remove everything containing yeast from their houses and then eat only unleavened bread for the next seven days, from the fifteenth to the twenty-first of Aviv. The Feast of Unleavened Bread commemorated how God delivered Israel with such haste through the tenth plague that they had to leave Egypt eating only unleavened loaves because their bread did not have enough time to rise and become naturally fermented (Exod. 12:39).

THE FINAL DEATH BLOW AT THE RED SEA

We all know the rest of the story well. Pharaoh chased the Israelites to the edge of the Red Sea, which led to one of most iconic events in biblical history. Moses lifted up his staff against the sea and the waters parted, as we read in Exodus 14:

> And the Lord swept the sea back by a strong east wind all night and turned the sea into dry land, so the waters were divided. The sons of Israel went through the midst of the sea on dry land, and the waters were like a wall to them on their right hand and on their left. (Exod. 14:21–22)

Pharaoh and his chariots pursued, but by the time they entered the sea the Israelites had already crossed safely to the other side. Then, early in the morning, "Moses stretched out his hand over the sea, and the sea returned to its normal state, and at daybreak," Pharaoh's entire army was drowned beneath the waters (Exod. 14:27–31). Additionally, the warfare theme in Exodus is confirmed when God says in Exodus 14:14, "The Lord will fight for you," and again when the Egyptians say in Exodus 14:25: "The Lord is fighting for them against Egypt."

THE SONG OF THE SEA IN EXODUS 15

After the Israelites crossed the Red Sea, they sang the Song of the Sea, which is recorded in Exodus 15:1–18. Not surprisingly, this hymn of praise also has many of the same warfare elements that appeared earlier in the Exodus plague narrative. A selection reads as follows:

> Then Moses and the sons of Israel sang this song to the Lord, and said: "I will sing to the Lord, for He is highly exalted; the horse and its rider He has hurled into the sea. [. . .] The Lord is a warrior, the Lord is His name. Pharaoh's chariots and his army He has cast into the sea; and the choicest of his officers are drowned in the Red Sea." (Exod. 15:1–4)

> Your right hand, O Lord, is majestic in power, Your right hand, O Lord, shatters the enemy. And in the greatness of Your excellence You overthrow those who rise up against You. (Exod. 15:6–7)

In these verses, we see that the Lord is again presented as a great Divine Warrior and Storm God. He manipulates the "wind" and the "sea" (Exod. 14:21) to His advantage and is explicitly called a "warrior" in Exodus 15:3, which translates literally as "a man of war."

When the events at the Red Sea are viewed alongside the warfare elements that appear earlier in Exodus (i.e., the plagues, the military terminology, and the anthropomorphic warrior language), it is easier to see how they bring this story of the Lord's great victory on the battlefield to its climax. After all, prior to Israel's flight from Egypt, their God did win some individual battles against the Pharaoh. But at the Red Sea, He won the war, and His warrior status was dramatically confirmed through one final flourish of miraculous intervention.

Trimm also explains that the Lord's victory at the Red Sea marked the point when His reign as the King of the Israelite nation officially began. He writes:

> The kings of the ancient Near East frequently portrayed themselves as powerful warriors to legitimate their status as kings. New kings often went on military campaigns in their first year to demonstrate to their people that the gods had chosen them to be the king. [...]. In the two most extensive divine warrior myths in the ancient Near East, Enuma Elish and the Baal Cycle, Marduk and Baal respectively were proclaimed as kings after the defeat of their enemies as divine warriors. [...] The god's role as king includes his duty to defend his people and bring order to the world, which necessitated taking on the role of a warrior.[20]

In the Exodus account, the Lord fulfilled the basic criteria that any ancient Middle Easterner would need to see met before exalting one god as supreme above all others. He went on a military campaign against Pharaoh, used the forces of nature as His weapon of war, defeated the enemies of His people with a magnificent display of sovereignty and power, and thereby legitimized His right to the throne of the Israelite nation.

---

20 Trimm, *"YHWH Fights for Them!"* 38.

Furthermore, that God's actions in Exodus 1–14 were undertaken with the ultimate goal of establishing His throne in Israel is explicitly emphasized in Exodus 15. At the end of the Song of the Sea, the Israelites formally accept God as their King when they proclaim, "the LORD shall reign forever and ever!" (Exod. 15:18). Put simply, Israel acknowledged the Lord's kingship immediately after the Red Sea crossing because they witnessed His complete victory on the battlefield, which then lead to their formal covenant with Him as their Sovereign at Mount Sinai (Exod. 19).

THE RED SEA AND THE NEW CREATION

In addition to the themes of warfare, military victory, and kingship, there is also a prevalent new-creation theme in Exodus 1–15. These chapters highlight how through the exodus, God was working to restore His originally good world, despite the tragic Fall of man and the consequent corruption of the natural world outlined earlier in Genesis. In effect, the redemption of Israel in Exodus is portrayed as having cosmic significance and an intricate connection to God's broader plan to bring all nations into a restored Edenic paradise.

We see this new-creation theme most clearly in Exodus 14, which records the Red Sea crossing. However, in order to understand how Exodus makes an important point regarding God's desire to build a new creation, we need to look first at how the language used in this passage parallels the language in Genesis 1–9.

THE NEW CREATION IN GENESIS

In Genesis 1, the creation account begins with "formless and void and darkness over the surface of the deep [...] the surface of the waters" (Gen 1:2). Then God speaks "light" over the darkness and gathers the waters together into one place until the "dry land" appears (Gen. 1:9). From there, little by little, God's good creation emerges.

Likewise, in the time of Noah, when God judged the world, He brought "a flood of water upon the earth" (Gen. 6:17). The reason

God chose a flood as the instrument of His judgment in Genesis 6 was because this brought His world back to the original pre-creation and chaotic state of Genesis 1:2. By the time of Noah, mankind had corrupted the earth and destabilized God's creation through their immorality, effectually reversing the good work God did in Genesis 1. As a result, in Genesis 6–8, God sends the Flood and allows creation to revert to a state of watery chaos and darkness. With this move, God was basically saying to mankind in Genesis 6–8, "If you do not want to live in My good world, according to My laws, then I will give you back the 'formless and void' of Genesis 1."

Then, with Noah and his family, God starts His work of creation again. This is why in Genesis 8 the new creation emerges out of water, just as it does in Genesis 1.

Moreover, just like in Genesis 1:1, where we were told that the "spirit (ruach) of God hovered over the waters, in Genesis 8:1 we see that God "caused a wind (ruach) to pass over the earth, and the waters subsided," until the dry land eventually emerged and "the water was dried up from the earth" (Gen. 8:13). Subsequently, when the Flood account reaches its climax, the order of creation is confirmed when God again establishes the regular cycle of seasons in Genesis 8:21–22, just as He had in Genesis 1:14, and blesses Noah and his family, tells them to "be fruitful and multiply, and fill the earth," and gives them dietary stipulations (Gen. 8:20–9:7), just as He had done with Adam and Eve in Genesis 1:28–31.

THE NEW CREATION IN EXODUS 14

There is a consensus among scholars that Genesis 6–9 parallels Genesis 1 in that both accounts describe a new and blessed creation with dry land emerging out of the waters of chaos and disorder through the work of the Spirit (ruach). What is less well understood, however, is that Exodus 14–15 parallels these accounts in Genesis and qualifies as a new-creation text as well.

For example, Exodus 14 says that Israel reached the edge of the Red

Sea at "night" when it was dark. Furthermore, when Israel crossed the sea, "the Lord swept the sea back by a strong east wind [ruach] all night and turned the sea into dry land." Already, the emphasis on darkness, as well as the reference to the "wind" (ruach) and the "dry land" in Exodus 14, highlights that this passage is meant to be interpreted in light of the creation texts in Genesis 1–9.

Another key parallel between God's creative work in Genesis and Exodus can be found in Exodus 14:27. This verse says that Israel reached the other side of the Red Sea "at daybreak," or literally, in the "morning." The image of Israel passing from darkness at night to light in the morning dovetails with the account in Genesis 1:1–2 where we see that the world was in a state of "darkness" until God said, "Let there be light!" which then led to the "evening" and "morning" on the first day of creation (Gen. 1:5).

In many ways, Exodus 10–14 draws on the creation accounts in Genesis 1–9. In Exodus, God carries His people through the chaos of the plagues and the water and darkness of the Red Sea. He creates order and dry land with His Spirit/wind (ruach) and then brings Israel into the glory of His presence, signified by the morning light. And finally, just as God delivered His commandments to Adam, Eve, and Noah as they stood on the threshold of His new creation, He does the same with Israel at Mount Sinai.

The broader point of these parallels in Genesis and Exodus is that through His deliverance of Israel, God brought the world one step closer to the original creation ideal foreshadowed in Genesis 1–2. The exodus, as it turns out, was a stepping stone back to the garden of Eden. This is why the same themes of darkness, water, spirit/wind, dry land, and light from Genesis appear again in Exodus 14, particularly during the account of the Red Sea crossing.

This moment in biblical history established a pivotal signpost that demonstrates how God intends to move His entire creation out of chaos and back into a state of divine order and blessing, and in a very real sense, the entire book of Exodus qualifies as a new-creation text. When God redeemed Israel, He expressed His intent to redeem the entire world, and the salvation of the Jewish nation in Exodus was only the very first fruits of the renewal and redemption that will someday be experienced by the entire cosmos. The Passover story highlights that Israel's God is the King of the new creation.

PASSOVER IN HISTORICAL CONTEXT

The original Passover story revolves around many important themes, and among these the theme of redemption is perhaps the most well known. Just as important, however, when we look at the early chapters of Exodus in their ancient historical context, we see that other central themes emerge as well, including the themes of warfare, victory, and new creation.

Grasping these additional themes, and being able to situate Exodus 1–15 as a warfare text that recounts the victory of the Lord on the battlefield and His work of establishing a new creation, is essential for the task of interpretation, especially if we want understand the book of Exodus as the ancient Israelites would have. At the same time, coming to grips with the multilayered theological themes of Exodus 1–15 is important for reasons besides historical contextualization as well.

In the next chapter, we will study how the warfare, victory, and new-creation elements in Exodus also reveal many deeper lessons about the end times and the Second Coming of Jesus. After all, the first thing Jesus will do when He returns is redeem Israel and go to war against the powers of darkness, which should be our first hint that the Passover story might have quite a lot to teach us about the future.

CHAPTER SUMMARY

Below are some basic points from this chapter that are worth reviewing and keeping in mind as we continue to study the prophetic implications of Passover.

1. It appears that the Exodus plagues targeted various Egyptian deities. However, the plagues also need to be interpreted more holistically, as part of an overall picture that depicts Israel's God as the supreme Storm God of creation who is above all other principalities and powers (including Baal, Marduk, Pharaoh, the Egyptian pantheon, etc.). In the religious literature of the ancient world, storm gods often used the forces of nature as their weapon of war, and thus, the plague narrative fits in this ancient Near Eastern context as a warfare text that presents the Lord as a powerful Divine Warrior who controls the created order (Exod. 12:12).

2. Along with God's use of nature weapons in Exodus, other elements in the Passover story also underscore the warfare theme in this text. For example, the plagues are frequently described using military terminology, and the anthropomorphic language that depicts God acting with His "hand," "arm," and "right arm" carried warfare connotations in its original historical context as well (Exod. 3:20; 6:6; 15:6).

3. The miracle at the Red Sea represented God's final military strike against the Egyptians, but it also clarified that He is King of the new creation. Throughout the Bible, God's new creation always emerges out of the waters of chaos. As a result, Israel emerging out of the waters of the Red Sea at the break of dawn symbolically communicated that the exodus was a key moment in this larger story of how God is working to bring His originally good but fallen creation back to the Edenic paradise first spoken of in Genesis (Exod. 14:14; Gen. 1:2; Gen. 8:13; Exod. 14:21–31).

4. Overall, these warfare and new-creation elements in the Exodus story have important implications related to the messianic and end-times significance of Passover. Passover is the holy day that celebrates and looks forward to redemption, new beginnings, and the ultimate victory of God and His people on the battlefield.

BIBLE STUDY QUESTIONS

1. What is the most important thing you learned about the history of Egypt or the book of Exodus that you did not know before?

2. What key lessons about the Exodus plague sequence are often overlooked?

3. How would God's use of nature weapons against the Egyptians have been understood by an ancient Near Eastern audience?

4. In what ways does Exodus 7–15 parallel Genesis 1–9, and what do these parallels imply?

3

PASSOVER & THE RETURN OF JESUS

MANY CHRISTIANS AND MESSIANIC JEWS are familiar with the elements of the Passover story Jesus fulfilled already. And without a doubt, the correspondence between the first-century ministry of Jesus and Passover is both profound and beautiful.

JESUS IS THE PASSOVER LAMB

For example, in Exodus, God commanded every Jewish household to select their Passover lambs on the tenth day of the first month (Exod. 12:3). Four days later, these lambs were to be sacrificed on the fourteenth of the same month, sometime before sunset (Exod. 12:6).

These commandments concerning the Passover lambs foreshadowed what would happen in the final days before Jesus' crucifixion. We know from the Gospels that Jesus probably entered Jerusalem on the tenth of Aviv, on the very day the Passover lambs were selected for each Jewish family in Jerusalem. Moreover, just as the Passover lambs had to be tested and declared spotless before they could be sacrificed, Jesus Himself was also tested in Jerusalem and declared to be innocent and blameless by the Roman governor Pontius Pilate, when he said, "I find no fault in Him" (Luke 23:4).[1]

Then, at the exact time when the Jewish priestly class in Jerusalem sacrificed their Passover lambs in the Temple, Jesus was crucified on the cross. God sovereignly orchestrated that our true Passover lamb, the Messiah, would die on Passover, at the most significant time of the day, when the final Passover sacrifices were offered in the holy city.

This brought about the deepest messianic fulfillment of God's statement in Exodus 12:13. In this verse God said, "The blood shall be a sign for you on the houses where you live; and when I see the blood I will pass over you, and no plague will befall you to destroy you when I strike the land of Egypt."

Based on this statement, we can be confident that if we trust in the sacrifice of the Messiah and take refuge under His blood by faith, God's judgment will pass over us, just as it passed over the Israelite houses in Egypt. In the words of the Apostle Paul, "Christ our Passover also has been sacrificed" (1 Cor. 5:7). He is the ultimate Passover Lamb whose blood washes us clean from sin and protects us from the wrath of God.

JESUS IS THE UNLEAVENED BREAD

Like Passover, the seven-day Feast of Unleavened Bread that begins the day after Passover also has a fulfillment tied to the ministry of Jesus. To grasp this fulfillment, we need to remember that the unleavened bread was the food that sustained Israel when they were leaving Egypt. It was the physical provision that carried God's people out of the land of slavery and darkness and into His holy presence.

In the same way, the Messiah Himself is the true Unleavened Bread from heaven that delivers us from spiritual bondage and allows us to

1 Summary of Sam Nader, *Messiah in the Feasts of Israel* (Charlotte: Word of Messiah Ministries, 2010), 37.

have a relationship with God. He is the spiritual sustenance that God has provided for us on our journey from slavery to freedom. Just as the Israelites had to consume the unleavened bread on their way out of Egypt, we have to consume the Messiah by faith, both spiritually and through Holy Communion, to be delivered from the darkness of this world. Even as Jesus said in John 6:51: "I am the living bread that came down from heaven. Whoever eats this bread will live forever. This bread is my flesh, which I will give for the life of the world" (NIV).

REMAINING UNLEAVENED IN THE MESSIAH

Besides the way the Feast of Unleavened Bread reminds us that Jesus is our spiritual sustenance, it should also remind us to continually clean out the sin of this world from our lives. This connection between the Feast of Unleavened Bread and the need for ongoing repentance in our relationship with God is rooted in the symbolic meaning of leaven in the first-century Jewish world.

During the time of Jesus, many Jewish teachers believed that leaven symbolizes sin (Matt. 16:11–12). This meant that the physical removal of leaven from every Jewish household prior to Passover and the Feast of Unleavened Bread also reminded the people to purge the sin from their lives at this time as well.

In 1 Corinthians 5:6–8, Paul drew this same spiritual application from the Feast of Unleavened Bread and admonished the Church with these words:

> Your boasting is not good. Do you not know that a little leaven leavens the whole lump of dough? Clean out the old leaven so that you may be a new lump, just as you are in fact unleavened. For Christ our Passover also has been sacrificed. Therefore, let us celebrate the feast, not with old leaven, nor with the leaven of malice and wickedness, but with the unleavened bread of sincerity and truth.

As Paul indicates, those of us who trust the Messiah are "in fact unleavened," meaning, we are sinless in the eyes of God. For this reason, we should celebrate the Feast of Unleavened Bread by cleaning out the "old leaven" of sin from our lives, looking with eyes of faith to Jesus, who has made us spotless and blameless before the Lord. Paul's basic point here is that the Feast of Unleavened Bread should encourage us to live up in a practical sense to the level of holiness that we have already attained in a spiritual sense.

THE FEAST OF FIRST FRUITS

Last but not least, there is a third biblical feast in the first month that Jesus also partially fulfilled in the first century; namely, the Feast of First Fruits. As we saw in chapter 1, the biblical feasts are linked to the turning of the seasons and are closely associated with the harvest of various crops. According to Leviticus 23:9–14, the barley harvest in the spring began with the "first fruits" offering, which was made on the second day of Unleavened Bread (i.e., the sixteenth of Aviv).

In the first century, when the time came to cut the first sheaf of barley in Israel, members of the Sanhedrin would tie bundles of barley together while it was still standing in the field. This special barley for the first-fruits offering was grown on a small plot of land in the Kidron Valley, just east of the Jerusalem Temple.

After the first-fruits barley had been demarcated by the Sanhedrin, a group of Temple representatives and worshippers from the surrounding villages would assemble in the field at sunset on the first day of the Feast of Unleavened Bread (i.e., the fifteenth of Aviv). Once the sun set it was officially the next day (i.e., the sixteenth of Aviv),[2] at which point ten omers of grain, about forty pounds worth, would be cut down and transported to the Temple.

2 Leviticus 23:11 says the first-fruits offering was to be made "on the day after the Sabbath." The Pharisees believed the Sabbath mentioned here was the first day of the Feast of Unleavened Bread (the fifteenth of Aviv), not the weekly Sabbath, which meant that First Fruits was celebrated on the sixteenth day of the first month (the sixteenth of Aviv), two days after Passover.

At the Temple, most likely on the morning after the barley was harvested (which would still be the sixteenth), the priests would thresh the grain out of the husk, lightly roast it in a perforated pan, and grind it into flour. Then, only one omer of grain, about four pounds worth, would be mixed with oil and frankincense and waved before the Lord at the northeast corner of the altar. After the wave offering, a handful of the flour was sprinkled on the fire of the altar and offered with the other required sacrifices (Lev. 23:11–13). Subsequently, the priests would bake the rest of the omer into bread and eat it (Lev. 23:11–13), and from that point forward grain from the spring harvest could be sold in the markets.

From a historical vantage point, Israel offered the first fruits of barley at the Temple because they wanted to thank God for His provision and consecrate the entire harvest to follow to Him. As Bible teacher Richard Booker points out, the "first fruits represented the whole harvest," and by giving God the first fruits, the Israelites declared that "all of the harvest rightfully belonged to Him."[3]

Though the barley harvest began right after Passover, it would continue throughout the following month (March/April). Then, wheat, figs, grapes, olives, dates, and pomegranates would also be harvested at various times in the spring, summer, and fall.

With this entire harvest cycle in mind, we can see more clearly how the first-fruits offering two days after Passover linked Israel's holy festivals not only to their experience in Egypt, but also to the land God had given them. The Feast of First Fruits was the initial taste of the agricultural abundance that was to come later in the year.

JESUS IS THE FIRST FRUITS

Besides its agricultural and religious significance in ancient Israel, like Passover and Unleavened Bread, the appointed time of First Fruits also

3 Richard Booker, *Celebrating Jesus in the Biblical Feasts: Discovering Their Significance to You as a Christian* (Shippensburg: Destiny Image, 2006), 81.

had a messianic fulfillment in the first century. The Apostle Paul spoke of how Jesus fulfilled the Feast of First Fruits in this way:

> But now Christ has been raised from the dead, the first fruits of those who are asleep. For as in Adam all die, so also in Christ all will be made alive. But each in his own order: Christ the first fruits, after that those who are Christ's at His coming. (1 Cor. 15:20–23)

Here Paul explains that Christ was the "first fruits" of the resurrection. Just like the first fruits of barley in Israel implied the entire harvest in the rest of the year, the resurrection of Christ as the first fruits from the dead guarantees that all who trust in Him will be resurrected at the time of "His coming" (v. 23).

Furthermore, what is even more amazing about this parallel is that Jesus Himself was raised from the dead on the sixteenth of Aviv, on the exact day when the Feast of First Fruits was celebrated in Jerusalem. We know Jesus was crucified before sundown on Passover, the fourteenth of Aviv, which in the year of His death fell on a Friday. Then He was buried and raised from the dead early Sunday morning, on the third day (Matt. 16:21).

This timeline indicates that Jesus emerged from the grave right when the first-fruits offering was being made in the Temple, on the sixteenth day of the first biblical month. Then, as the Jewish inhabitants of Jerusalem brought their new grain to the marketplace, Jesus, the ultimate source of new life for the people of God, appeared to His disciples and preached the fullness of the gospel to them for the very first time (Matt. 28; Luke 21; Jn. 20).

THE GOSPEL IN THE SPRING FEASTS

It is truly fascinating and encouraging to see how God sovereignly aligned the crucifixion, burial, and resurrection of the Messiah with Passover, the first day of Unleavened Bread, and the Feast of First Fruits. By orchestrating redemption history in this way, God made an emphatic statement about the work of the Messiah and the core of the gospel message itself: Jesus is the only one who can set God's people free from spiritual bondage and bring us into the glories of the age to come. He is the true Passover Lamb, the true Unleavened Bread from heaven, and the First Fruits forerunner of the future resurrection.

PASSOVER HAS NOT YET BEEN FULFILLED

The relationship between the first three spring feasts and the ministry of Jesus is so striking and profound that it is not hard to see why many prophecy teachers have concluded that Jesus already completely fulfilled Passover, Unleavened Bread, and First Fruits at the time of His first coming. As noted in chapter 1, this connection between the ministry of Jesus and the spring feasts has also led many Bible teachers to argue that the return of Jesus will only coincide with the fall feasts. In other words, the consensus view on the prophetic meaning of the feasts maintains that since Jesus already fulfilled the spring feasts, the fall feasts must be next up on God's prophetic calendar, which more or less (according to these teachers) guarantees that Jesus will return right around the Feast of Trumpets and then fulfill the Day of Atonement and the Feast of Tabernacles shortly thereafter.

In later chapters, we will cover how the fall feasts will be fulfilled after the Messiah's Second Coming. For now, however, it is only necessary to understand that Passover was not completely fulfilled through the first-century ministry of Jesus. The fact that Jesus brought certain elements of the Passover story to prophetic fulfillment in the first century, such as the Passover lamb element, does not mean that every element of this feast has now been fulfilled, or that Passover no longer has any future prophetic significance. In fact, this chapter will demonstrate that Jesus connected His Second Coming more to Passover than to any other biblical feast, because it is the original Passover story that reveals many of the precise events that will take place immediately following His return to this earth.

Though this idea will no doubt be new to many, Israel's original exodus from Egypt paints one of the clearest pictures in all of Scripture of what will take place right after the Second Coming of the Messiah. When Jesus comes back, He will fulfill Passover before any of the other biblical feasts, and then the subsequent feasts, including Weeks, Trumpets, Atonement, and Tabernacles, will be fulfilled in a sequential fashion during the initial phases of His millennial reign.

In order to unpack how Passover is related to the Second Coming, we will now begin our study of the numerous prophecies in the Old and New Testaments that attach an end-times and future prophetic significance to the original Passover story. We will also look at a number of Jewish and Christian traditions that shed more light on the final eschatological fulfillment of Passover.

JESUS AND THE FULFILLMENT OF PASSOVER

While most Christians and messianic Jews believe Jesus already fulfilled the Passover, Jesus said something very different about this holy appointed time on the night before He was crucified. At the Last Supper, Jesus sat with His disciples and began their Passover meal with these words:

> I have earnestly desired to eat this Passover with you before I suffer. For I say to you, I shall never again eat it until it is fulfilled in the kingdom of God. (Luke 22:15–16)

Right there, Jesus said Passover will only be "fulfilled in the kingdom of God." The Greek word for "fulfilled" in this verse is *plerao*, which means to fill up or make full, and in first-century Judaism the phrase "in the kingdom of God" designated the time when the messianic kingdom will be fully established on the earth.

Jesus' use of this language in Luke 22:15–16 indicates that Passover will not be filled up with its deepest level of prophetic meaning until after He returns. Jesus did not say, "Passover will be fulfilled tomorrow when I'm crucified." He said, it will be "fulfilled in the kingdom of God," at some point in the distant future.

FULFILLED IN THE CHURCH?

Over the centuries, Christian commentators have experienced confusion when reading Jesus' words in Luke 22:15–16, especially when thinking about this idea that Passover will be "fulfilled in the kingdom of God." As a result, some of the early church fathers and Protestant reformers argued that "the kingdom of God" in Luke 22 is the Church and that Passover is fulfilled each week when Christians take the bread and wine of Holy Communion together.

The problem with locating the fulfillment of Luke 22:15–16 in the Church, and prior to the Second Coming, however, is twofold. First, this view ignores that the kingdom of God will not be fully established until Jesus returns. In other words, strictly speaking, the Church is not the kingdom of God. The kingdom of God is the kingdom Jesus will set up on the earth after His Second Coming and numerous New Testament texts make this clear (cf. 2 Tim. 4:1–8; Heb. 12:28).

Second, the idea that Holy Communion fulfills the prophetic words of Jesus in Luke 22:16 makes no sense in light of what does and does not happen during Communion. In Luke 22, Jesus said that when Passover is fulfilled He will eat the meal with us, whereas at Holy Communion it is only us, not Him, who do the eating. There is no meal offered to Jesus during Holy Communion, so this rite could not qualify as the meal He referred to in Luke 22.

No doubt Communion is rooted in the Jewish Passover meal. However, in Luke 22 Jesus still spoke of another Passover meal that He will eat with His disciples in the kingdom of God, which will mirror the Passover meal He enjoyed with His disciples the night before He was crucified.

PASSOVER IS ABOUT THE FUTURE

A much better approach to Luke 22:15–16 is to accept what Jesus said at face value. Certain aspects of the Passover story have already been fulfilled to be sure, and this is something we should all celebrate. But there are still many other aspects of Passover that point forward to future prophetic events as well. Some of these Passover-connected events will transpire during the end times, and some of them will take place soon after Jesus returns. But in either case, it is precisely because Passover will not be fulfilled until after the Second Coming that we should not neglect Passover when constructing a paradigm that outlines the prophetic fulfillment of the feasts.

As a matter of fact, I would even go so far as to say that until a person understands the intrinsic relationship between Passover and the return of Jesus, they will not be able to envision an accurate biblical picture of what will take place at the time of the Messiah's Second Coming. Perhaps more than anything else, the Passover story reveals the epic and glorious events that will unfold right before the messianic kingdom is established, and Jesus knew this, which is why He said what He did in Luke 22:15–16.

PASSOVER AND THE VICTORY OF GOD

To understand why Jesus said Passover will not be fulfilled until after His Second Coming, we need to go back to what we learned in the last chapter about the historical meaning of Passover. It was before, during, and after the first Passover that God went to war against the forces of evil as a great divine warrior and set His people free from oppression. It was in Egypt that God displayed His miraculous signs and wonders for the world to see, and it was in Egypt that God rightly exalted Himself above all other false gods and established His right to the throne of Israel through His military victories over Pharaoh.

Also, the Red Sea crossing itself was closely tied to God's work of building a new creation, with the nation of Israel at its center. Israel traveled through the water, stood on dry land, met with God at Mount Sinai, and then received His holy law in a way that evoked the sequence of events in Genesis and the experience of Adam and Eve in the garden of Eden, thereby signaling that the deliverance of the Jewish nation carried cosmic significance and was connected to God's new-creation plan for the entire world.

When these warfare, kingdom, and new-creation themes within the original Passover story are understood, it is easier to grasp why Jesus said Passover will not be completely fulfilled until after He returns. From the beginning, Passover pointed forward to much more than just the Messiah's work as the Lamb of God. As important as that work was, Passover also prefigures how the Messiah will step onto the stage of history as a great Divine Warrior in the future, defeat the powers of evil, redeem His people from political oppression, and then lead them into a new world where He is both Lawgiver and King, just as the Lord did in the book of Exodus.

While the death and resurrection of Jesus have allowed believers to experience certain aspects of Passover in a spiritual sense now (i.e., victory, freedom, redemption, and new life in God's kingdom), it will only be after Jesus returns that the entire earth will experience the fullness of what Passover always prophetically foreshadowed in the first place; namely, God's total triumph over the forces of darkness and a renewed creation where the Messiah is King.

Unfortunately, most Christians and messianic Jews do not know how Passover will be fulfilled when Jesus returns because they do not understand the warfare and new-creation themes in Exodus 1–15, nor how these themes are related to Jesus' statement in Luke 22:15–16. This blind spot again illustrates why it is so important to establish the historical meaning of each feast before trying to ascertain its prophetic meaning.

In its original historical setting, Passover was inseparable from the victory of the Lord (YHVH) over His enemies and the establishment of His new creation, and it is these aspects of Passover that infuse the Exodus story with eschatological overtones and link this feast to the events that will take place at the time of the Messiah's Second Coming. In a certain way, everything from the book of Exodus will repeat again in the future. Jesus partially fulfilled Passover by first becoming our Passover Lamb, Unleavened Bread, and First-Fruits Offering, but He will completely fulfill Passover as the magnificent Divine Warrior when He returns.

And the cool thing is, Jesus knew this. He knew about the future prophetic fulfillment of Passover, and this was what He was looking forward to on the night before He was crucified (Luke 22:15–16). Even as Jesus grieved that He would have to suffer as the Lamb, He found hope in the idea that He would soon return as the conquering Passover King.

THE PROPHETIC FRAMEWORK OF JESUS

Besides His deep understanding of the Exodus story, and in particular the warfare, kingdom, and new-creation elements in this story, another reason Jesus connected Passover to His Second Coming was because of His comprehensive grasp of the writings of the Hebrew prophets. Many of Jesus' forefathers, including Moses, Isaiah, Jeremiah, and Ezekiel, described the end times and the Second Coming using symbols, themes, and language from the book of Exodus. In other words, the Hebrew prophets were already talking about a future second exodus and a future fulfillment of the Passover story centuries before Jesus lived. Thus, in Luke 22:15–16, Jesus simply articulated an idea He learned from the Jewish Scriptures, with which many of His disciples would have been familiar.

THE SECOND EXODUS ROADMAP

In the rest of this chapter, we will survey the key passages in the Old Testament that speak of the second exodus and the final fulfillment of Passover. These texts will explain Jesus' statement in Luke 22:15–16 and further reveal how the events that unfold after the Second Coming will in many ways follow the contours of the original Passover story. At the end of this chapter, we will also cover some other Jewish and Christian traditions that highlight the relationship between Passover and eschatology before finally considering what the future fulfillment of Passover may imply about the timing of the Messiah's return to this earth.

THE TIME OF JACOB'S TROUBLE

As we all know, prior to the first Passover, the nation of Israel was not living in the Promised Land. They were in Egypt and held captive by an oppressive foreign power.

Though this idea will be new to many and difficult for others to accept, the Bible is clear that prior to the return of Jesus the nation of Israel will experience one final period of exile and captivity. During this time, large portions of the nation will flee their land and others will be forced into imprisonment and slavery.

This end-times period of tribulation and exile for the Jewish nation is often called the Time of Jacob's Trouble based on Jeremiah 30:5–7:

> I have heard a sound of terror, of dread, and there is no peace. Ask now, and see if a male can give birth. Why do I see every man with his hands on his loins, as a woman in childbirth? And why have all faces turned pale? Alas! For that day is great, there is none like it; and it is the time of Jacob's trouble, but he will be saved from it. (Jer. 30:5–7, NIV)

We know Jeremiah 30 is about Israel's final period of tribulation and exile during the end times, because the context says that after Israel experiences this time they will be saved by the Lord, dwell in peace and security, never be afraid again, and live under the reign of their Davidic King (vv. 8–11). In addition, many of the other Hebrew prophets spoke about the Time of Jacob's Trouble using similar, but in some cases even more detailed, language.

For example, the prophet Daniel said the Time of Jacob's Trouble will result in the "shattering" of "the power of the holy people" (i.e., Israel; Dan. 12:7). Daniel also linked this time to the midpoint of the Seventieth Week (Dan. 9:27), or to the halfway point of what some call the seven-year tribulation.

From this midpoint of the Seventieth Week, Daniel says the Time of Jacob's Trouble will last 1,290 days, or, three and a half years (Dan. 12:10). It will begin when the Antichrist breaks a covenant of peace with Israel, desecrates the end-times Temple in Jerusalem, and invades the entire land with a massive military force (Dan. 8:9–14; 9:27; 12:5–13). Then, for three and a half years Israel will live in exile and under slave conditions until the Messiah saves them, as prophesied in Jeremiah 30:8–11.[4]

THE FINAL INVASION OF JERUSALEM IN ZECHARIAH 14

Whereas Jeremiah 30 speaks in general terms about the Time of Jacob's Trouble and Daniel 8–12 gives an overview of the Seventieth Week timeline and other key events, Zechariah outlines in more specific terms the military attack against Israel and Jerusalem that will lead to the Jewish nation's final three-and-a-half-year period of exile. In this verse we read:

> I will gather all the nations to Jerusalem to fight against it; the city will be captured, the houses ransacked, and the women raped. Half of the city will go into exile, but the rest of the people will not be taken from the city. (Zech. 14:2, NIV)

Though the next verses in Zechariah 14 (vv. 3–5) describe the Lord fighting for Jerusalem, this does not mean God's deliverance will come immediately after the attack, which will be carried out by the armies of the Antichrist. Instead, Zechariah 14:2–5 compresses three and a half years into the space of a few verses.

According to Zechariah, "half of the city" of Jerusalem, and presumably many other Israelis living in other cities as well, will "go into exile" during the end times. Moreover, due to the similarities between Zechariah 14:2 and the other prophecies that describe the actions of the Antichrist (i.e., Dan. 8:9–14; 9:27; 12:5–13), we can be confident that the invasion Zechariah refers to will happen at the midpoint of Daniel's Seventieth Week, right after the Antichrist appears in the Temple as "the abomination of desolation" (cf., Matt. 24:15–21; Luke 21:20–24; 2 Thess. 2:4).

THE FINAL INVASION OF JERUSALEM IN LUKE 21

In Luke 21:20–24, Jesus also spoke of the same invasion of Jerusalem as Zechariah did in Zechariah 14. In this passage the Messiah said:

---

4 For a more detailed study of Daniel's seventy weeks, I refer readers to my book *The 70 Weeks Jubilee: Israel, the Messiah, and the End of the Age in Daniel 9:24–27.*

> When you see Jerusalem being surrounded by armies, you will know that its desolation is near. Then let those who are in Judea flee to the mountains, let those in the city get out, and let those in the country not enter the city. For this is the time of punishment in fulfillment of all that has been written. How dreadful it will be in those days for pregnant women and nursing mothers! There will be great distress in the land and wrath against this people. They will fall by the sword and will be taken as prisoners to all the nations. Jerusalem will be trampled on by the Gentiles until the times of the Gentiles are fulfilled. (Luke 21:20–24)

Like Zechariah, Jesus does not imply in this passage that Israel will escape the wrath of God in the last days. Rather, He says Jerusalem will experience "desolation" and be "trampled on by the Gentiles" until the time of His Second Coming (cf., Luke 21:25–28). Jesus also said those who live in Jerusalem will have to "flee to the mountains," a reality that implies a time of exile.[5]

Thus, when viewed as a whole, the picture of Israel's experience during the last-days tribulation is remarkably consistent throughout the writings of the prophets. All the prophets predicted that Israel will endure one final period of exile and captivity before they are saved by the Messiah at the end of the Seventieth Week.

ISRAEL'S FINAL PERIOD OF COVENANT DISCIPLINE

The reason the Time of Jacob's Trouble will be necessary has to do with God's eternal covenant with the Jewish nation. According to Scripture,

5 Many Christian scholars have argued that Luke 21 was fulfilled in the first century when Jerusalem was invaded and destroyed by the Romans. There are numerous problems with this view, however, including the fact that Jesus said in verse 22 that this invasion would bring to fulfillment "all that has been written." This statement carries end-time connotations because it will only be during the end times, and shortly after, that all prophecies in Scripture will be fulfilled. For a deeper analysis of Jesus' teaching in Luke 21, see chapter 16, "The 70th Week in the Gospels and Revelation" in *The 70 Weeks Jubilee.*

this covenant always included both covenant blessings as a reward for obedience and covenant discipline as a recompense for unfaithfulness. Furthermore, in Deuteronomy 4:25–30, when Moses articulated what Israel would experience in the last days if they turned away from the Lord, he specifically highlighted exile. In this passage, God told Israel:

> When you become the father of children and children's children and have remained long in the land, and act corruptly, and make an idol in the form of anything, and do that which is evil in the sight of the LORD your God so as to provoke Him to anger, I call heaven and earth to witness against you today, that you will surely perish quickly from the land where you are going over the Jordan to possess it. You shall not live long on it, but will be utterly destroyed. The LORD will scatter you among the peoples, and you will be left few in number among the nations where the LORD drives you. There you will serve gods, the work of man's hands, wood and stone, which neither see nor hear nor eat nor smell. But from there you will seek the LORD your God, and you will find Him if you search for Him with all your heart and all your soul. When you are in distress and all these things have come upon you, in the latter days you will return to the LORD your God and listen to His voice. (Deut. 4:25–30)

As Moses indicates in these verses, God warned Israel that if they did not obey His word, they would "perish quickly from the land" and be scattered among the nations in "the latter days." Today, modern Israel is a nation that for the most part has chosen to rebel against God and His laws. As a result, there should be no doubt that the covenant judgments mentioned in Deuteronomy 4, including exile, will be experienced by the Jewish nation in the days ahead. Though the Jewish people are indeed God's Chosen People, with great privileges come great responsibility. To be true to His own word and to do what is right for Israel in the long term, God will have no other choice but to severely discipline the nation during the end times, so they will be purged of their iniquity and come to a place where they are willing to "return to the LORD" and "listen to His voice" (Deut. 4:30).

THE FINAL EXILE INTO NORTH AFRICA AND THE MIDDLE EAST

In terms of location, Scripture is clear that the Jewish exiles will reside in North Africa and the Middle East during the Seventieth week. Various biblical texts point specifically to Egypt as well.

For example, Isaiah 11:11 mentions that when the Messiah returns, Jewish exiles will be found in "Assyria, Egypt, Pathros [southern Egypt], Cush [Sudan], Elam [Iran], Shinar [Iraq], Hamath [Syria]" and on "the islands of the sea [the Mediterranean, likely including Cyprus]." Another key passage in Deuteronomy 28:68 says that if Israel did not obey the Lord, He would bring them back to Egypt, where they would once again experience slavery and poverty:

> And the LORD will bring you back to Egypt in ships, by the way about which I said to you, "You will never see it again!" And there you will offer yourselves for sale to your enemies as male and female slaves, but there will be no buyer."

Along with Isaiah 11:11 and Deuteronomy 28:68, Isaiah 27:12–13 also elaborates on where Israel will experience exile in the last days. This prophecy mentions Israelis who will be "perishing in the land of Assyria" and "scattered in the land of Egypt" prior to the Second Coming.

Therefore, when we look at these passages as a composite whole, they predict that many Israelis will be living in exile and under slave conditions in Egypt and the surrounding North African and Middle Eastern nations prior to the return of Jesus. In addition, although these circumstances will be extremely difficult, it will be Israel's final exile into North Africa and the Middle East that will set the stage for the ultimate fulfillment of Passover when Jesus returns.

For just as Pharaoh used Israelite slave labor to fuel the growth of his empire and his war machine, the Antichrist will do the same. And even more importantly, just as Pharaoh was miraculously defeated when the Lord went to war on behalf of His people in the book of Exodus, so too the Antichrist, the end-times Pharaoh, will be defeated when the Messiah steps onto the battlefield to fight for His people at the dawn of the messianic age.[6]

WHERE WILL JESUS RETURN?

The end-times fulfillment of Passover will start when Jesus returns on the clouds of heaven. However, to determine exactly how this final fulfillment of Passover will play out, we need to understand what the Scriptures say about where the Messiah will return, that is to say, where He will first land after He descends to the earth.

Most popular teaching on the Second Coming is built on the idea that Jesus will descend from heaven and immediately land on the Mount of Olives in Jerusalem. This view is based on this passage in Zechariah:

> Then the LORD will go out and fight against those nations, as he fights on a day of battle. On that day His feet will stand on the Mount of Olives, east of Jerusalem. (Zech. 14:3–4, NIV)

In light of Zechariah's words here, there should be no doubt that Jesus will indeed "stand on the Mount of Olives" at some point after He returns. However, the idea that Zechariah 14:4 implies that Jesus will descend from heaven directly to the Mount of Olives, or somewhere else in Jerusalem, lacks biblical support for two primary reasons.

One, Zechariah 14:4 does not say anything about the Messiah descending from heaven directly to the Mount of Olives. It only says He will stand there prior to the time He defeats the nations allied with the Antichrist.

---

6 I do not mean to suggest with this comparison that the Antichrist will be an Egyptian. However, Scripture is clear that the Antichrist will come from the Middle East, and that his kingdom will be made up of nations in the Middle East and North Africa. For discussion of where the Antichrist will come from, see chapters 6, 7, and 14–17 in *The Passover King.*

Second, there are many other prophecies that say Jesus will return first to Egypt and then lead a second exodus out of Egypt and the surrounding Middle Eastern nations before He arrives in Israel. Consequently, to place Jesus on the Mount of Olives immediately after His Second Coming, before these other second-exodus prophecies have been fulfilled, is to overlook key events that must transpire before His final battle with the Antichrist can take place in Jerusalem.

The next part of this chapter will focus on the various second-exodus prophecies in the writings of the Hebrew prophets, starting with those that outline the Messiah's journey into Egypt immediately after He returns. As we conduct this study, it should become clear that the Messiah's return to Egypt is the natural corollary to Israel's final exile during the Seventieth Week. After all, before Jesus can make the trip up to Jerusalem, as the greater Moses He will first have to rescue a surviving Jewish remnant from exile and slavery, just as the first Moses did thirty-five hundred years ago.

THE CLOUD RIDER RETURNS TO EGYPT (ISAIAH 19)

Several prophecies highlight the Messiah's return to Egypt. One of the most important is found in Isaiah 19:1, which reads:

> Behold, the LORD is riding on a swift cloud and is about to come to Egypt; The idols of Egypt will tremble at His presence, and the heart of the Egyptians will melt within them.

That the Lord rides on a cloud in Isaiah 19:1 is the first major hint that this text is about the Second Coming, quite simply because the Messiah is often depicted as returning on the clouds in Scripture (cf. Dan. 7; Matt. 24:30; Rev. 1:7). As prophecy teacher Joel Richardson notes, "the most well-known image for Jesus' return in the New Testament is His coming back in the clouds," and this image was developed by the New Testament writers precisely because they understood the messianic implications of the Old Testament passages that speak of the Lord riding on a storm cloud, including Isaiah 19:1.[7]

Another key component of Isaiah 19:1 that indicates this prophecy is about the Second Coming is the language that portrays the idols of Egypt trembling at God's "presence." The Hebrew word for "presence" here is *panim*, which literally means "face." When used with reference to God, the "face" of the Lord often describes God's manifest presence in a physical form, such as when Jacob wrestled with God in Genesis 32:30 and said he had seen "the face [panim] of God."

The appearance of the term "face" or "presence" in Isaiah 19:1 confirms that this text describes God descending to the earth, riding on a cloud, in a physical form. In light of New Testament revelation, we can be sure that this Cloud Rider in Isaiah 19:1 is none other than Jesus Himself, the glory of God in the flesh.

Yet contrary to popular belief, Isaiah 19:1 teaches that the Messiah will ride "on a swift cloud" and go first to Egypt, not Jerusalem. Though this piece of the prophetic puzzle is often overlooked, once we understand that Jesus will rescue the scattered Jewish remnant from North Africa and the Middle East immediately after His Second Coming (Isa. 11:11; 27:12–13; Deut. 28:68), His return to Egypt in Isaiah 19:1 makes perfect sense. Before He marches up to Jerusalem, the Messiah will ride on the clouds into the land of Egypt, set His people free from slavery, and gather the Jewish survivors who were exiled during the Seventieth Week.

JESUS IS THE EXODUS STORM GOD

A final important point made in Isaiah 19:1 is that the Savior who rides on the clouds into Egypt is the same Storm God who originally appeared in the book of Exodus. As we saw in chapter 2, Exodus presents the Lord as the supreme Storm God who wages war against His enemies with the elements of nature. In addition, Exodus specifically links the

7 Joel Richardson, *Sinai to Zion: The Untold Story of the Triumphant Return of Jesus* (Leawood: Winepress Media, 2020), 216.

glorious appearance of the Lord to a "pillar of cloud" (Exod. 13:21) and a "thick cloud" resting upon Mount Sinai (Exod. 19:16; 24:16).

Isaiah 19:1 purposefully develops this storm-god motif from Exodus and weaves it into a prophetic rendition of the Second Coming. This theological move in turn signals that the events that transpire when Jesus returns will mirror those recorded in the book of Exodus. To put this another way, the repetition of the Exodus storm-god theme in Isaiah 19:1 foreshadows that Jesus will appear first and foremost as a "man of war" (Exod. 15:3), one who will perform miracles, use the forces of nature as His weapon on the battlefield, confront the enemies of Israel, and make all the gods of darkness tremble at His presence.

THE GATHERING OF ISRAEL IN ISAIAH 27

Another text that builds on Isaiah 19:1 and outlines the gathering of the exiled Jewish remnant after the Seventieth Week is Isaiah 27:12. This verse states:

> In that day the Lord will start His threshing from the flowing stream of the Euphrates to the brook of Egypt, and you will be gathered up one by one, O sons of Israel.

Notice that in Isaiah 27:12 the Lord gathers the "sons of Israel" from the Euphrates River, which would include the regions of Turkey and Syria, to the brook of Egypt. When this text is read alongside Isaiah 19:1, it becomes harder to know if Jesus will descend first to Egypt, or if He will descend first to somewhere else near the Euphrates River and then travel to Egypt shortly thereafter. In other words, whereas Isaiah 19:1 mentions only Egypt, in Isaiah 27:12 there is a progression from the Euphrates River to the land of Egypt.

Of course, Isaiah 27:12 could only be giving us an overview of the general region where Jesus will be soon after His return, in which case He could still go to Egypt first. Or, it could be giving us a more detailed geographical itinerary, starting in Syria or Turkey.

All this to say, because there are different locations specified in these two passages, Isaiah 19:1 may or may not indicate that Jesus will return on the clouds directly to Egypt. He may do so, but He could also land somewhere else near the Euphrates first, so we should not be dogmatic on this point. Either way, both Isaiah 19:1 and Isaiah 27:12 do make clear that the Messiah will be in Egypt shortly after His return to this earth, and there is no biblical text that suggests His immediate return to the city of Jerusalem.

BELIEVERS WILL BE WITH JESUS

As a brief aside, we should also note here that according to the New Testament, Christians, messianic Jews, and Old Testament saints will be with Jesus when He returns on the clouds to Egypt and the Middle East. This is important to grasp because it highlights how everything we will cover in the rest of this chapter about the fulfillment of Passover has just as much to do with our destiny in the Messiah as it does with Israel's destiny.

The New Testament teaches that when Jesus is revealed from heaven, the saints will be resurrected and raptured before He descends to the earth. Additionally, Matthew 24:30 links the gathering of believers (i.e., the Rapture) to the time when Jesus is seen coming on the clouds (cf. 1 Thess. 4:15–17).

We will not dive deep into the debates on Rapture timing in this chapter. But no matter which view on the Rapture one subscribes to, every Rapture scenario accepts that believers will return to the earth with Jesus as He descends from heaven. This means that when Jesus goes down into Egypt and rescues the exiled Jewish remnant in the Middle East, as Isaiah 19 and Isaiah 27 say He will, resurrected and glorified believers will be with Him.

Moreover, as I outlined in my first book, *The Passover King*, the book of Revelation depicts the body of Christ as the core of the Messiah's end-times military force, which He will strategically use to rescue Israel and defeat the powers of darkness when He returns. For example,

Revelation 17:14 says that when Jesus goes to war against the armies of the Antichrist, "the called and chosen and faithful" (i.e., believers) will be with Him.

From this text we can deduce that Christians and messianic Jews from across the ages will have front row seats to witness the real-time fulfillment of every second exodus prophecy in the Bible. Even though the Old Testament prophecies that describe the second exodus do not directly mention the saints being with Jesus during this time, later New Testament revelation fills in the picture and includes believers as part of the story. Once Jesus is back on the earth, wherever He goes, we will go as well.

JESUS COMES OUT OF EGYPT AND WAGES WAR (NUMBERS 24)

The third prophecy that links the return of Jesus to Egypt is Numbers 24:5–9. This text reads:

> How fair are your tents O Jacob, your dwellings, O Israel! Like valleys that stretch out, like gardens beside the river, like aloes planted by the LORD, like cedars beside the waters. Water will flow from his buckets, and his seed will be by many waters, and his king shall be higher than Gog (SP; LXX),[8] and his kingdom shall be exalted.
>
> God brings Him out of Egypt, He is for Him like the horns of the wild ox. He will devour the nations who are His adversaries, and will crush their bones in pieces, and shatter them with His arrows. He couches, He lies down as a lion, and as a lion, who dares rouse Him? Blessed is everyone who blesses you, and cursed is everyone who curses you (author's translation).

8 Nearly all modern English versions translate the name of Israel's adversary in Numbers 24:7 as "Agag." However, the earliest manuscripts of the Torah, including the Samaritan Pentateuch (SP) and the Greek Septuagint (LXX), say Gog not Agag. For a detailed discussion of Gog in Numbers 24:7 that interacts with the most recent scholarship, see chapter 6 in, *The Passover King.*

Numbers 24 is one of the most overlooked and misinterpreted Second Coming prophecies in the entire Bible, and for those who are interested I cover this text in a detailed way in my book *The Passover King*. Though we will not analyze this prophecy in depth now, the main idea to take away here is that Numbers 24:7 uses two direct titles for the Messiah.

First, it calls Him the "seed" of Israel. This "seed" language in Numbers 24:7 parallels what we also find in Genesis 3:15, where the Messiah is identified as the human "seed" of Eve who will crush the Serpent.

Second, Numbers 24:7 calls the Messiah the "king" of Israel who will have an exalted "kingdom." This terminology evokes the earlier prophecy in Genesis 49:10, which describes the future messianic king from Judah as one who will possess the "scepter" and the "ruler's staff" on behalf of the Lord.

Once the messianic nature of this prophecy is established through clear messianic references, Numbers 24:8 then says, "God brings Him out of Egypt," meaning, He will bring the Messiah (with the people of Israel) out of Egypt. Subsequently, the rest of the prophecy describes how the Messiah will wage war like a "wild ox," "devour the nations who are His adversaries," "crush their bones in pieces," and "shatter them with His arrows." Then, the concluding portion of the text also describes the Messiah as a ravenous "lion" who will destroy his prey.

The powerful symbolism and imagery in Numbers 24:7–9 was inspired by the divine warrior motif in Exodus. However, this text draws on this historical motif in a creative way and uses it as a backdrop to contextualize the Messiah's initial war campaign, which He will initiate in the early days after His Second Coming.

Put another way, Numbers 24, just like Isaiah 19, presents the Messiah as the Divine Warrior from the book of Exodus in a visible and incarnate form. These texts are two sides of the same coin, and when read alongside one another, they explain with glorious language how the Messiah will ride on a storm cloud back to the earth, travel into Egypt and the Middle Eastern nations, and then lead a second exodus out of those nations as He wages war against the powers of darkness on behalf of His people.

Isaiah 19:1	Numbers 24:8
"Behold, the Lord is riding on a swift cloud and is about to come to Egypt; The idols of Egypt will tremble at His presence, and the heart of the Egyptians will melt within them."	"God brings Him [the Seed and King of Israel] out of Egypt, He is for Him like the horns of the wild ox. He will devour the nations who are His adversaries, and will crush their bones in pieces, and shatter them with His arrows."

COMMON CHRISTIAN INTERPRETATIONS OF NUMBERS 24

We should also note here that Christian commentators typically ignore that Numbers 24 is messianic and opt for a strictly historical reading of this chapter. They say this passage only describes Israel coming out of Egypt at the time of the original exodus.

A handful of other commentators do accept that Numbers 24 is messianic. However, they only connect the "out of Egypt" language in Numbers 24:8 to the first coming of the Messiah, because Jesus did live in and come out of Egypt as a child (Matt. 2).

Though they remain popular, both of these approaches to Numbers 24 are unacceptable. The messianic terminology proves that the Messiah is in view in this passage, and the warfare language cancels out the idea that the first coming of Jesus is the topic of discussion. After all, Jesus didn't start any wars when He was a kid![9]

Bottom line, a consistent method of interpretation that takes the words of Scripture in their historical context requires a still-future exodus when the Messiah returns, and Numbers 24:8 is the first text in the Bible that speaks directly of this second exodus. This prophecy

9 It is also important to note that Matthew 2:15 does not cite Numbers 24:8 when it refers to Jesus coming out of Egypt as a child. Instead, this passage only cites Hosea 11:1, which implies that Numbers 24:8 is still to be fulfilled in the future. Moreover, the reason the Gospel of Matthew depicts Jesus reliving portions of the Exodus story when He is a boy, is because this was Matthew's way of indicating that Jesus is the greater Moses who (1) has already inaugurated a spiritual exodus for God's people, and (2) will one day also bring every second exodus prophecy (including Numbers 24:8-9) to fulfillment when He returns.

literally says that right before the Messiah sets up His kingdom He will "come out of Egypt" and wage war against the nations.

THE PARTING OF THE RED SEA IN ISAIAH 10

After Jesus comes "out of Egypt" (Num. 24:8), Scripture is clear that He will part the Red Sea a second time and perform other miracles over various bodies of water. For example, Isaiah 10:26–27 speaks of how God will judge Israel's enemies in the last days and lift up the sea with a staff in His hand. This passage says:

> The LORD of hosts will arouse a scourge against him [i.e., Antichrist & his armies] like the slaughter of Midian at the rock of Oreb; and His staff will be over the sea and He will lift it up the way He did in Egypt. So it will be in that day, that his burden will be removed from your shoulders and his yoke from your neck, and the yoke will be broken because of fatness. (Isa. 10:16–17)

In the same way that God was personified and depicted as riding on the clouds and manifesting His presence in Isaiah 19, He is also personified in Isaiah 10 as one who will hold a "staff" in His hand and part the Red Sea yet again. Because we know from many other texts that the Messiah will come out of Egypt when He returns, and because we know the Messiah is God in human form, there should be no doubt that Isaiah 10:16–17 is a description of what Jesus will do after He comes "out of Egypt," sometime shortly after His Second Coming.

Additionally, Isaiah notes here that when the Messiah parts the sea, this will effectively remove the yoke of the Antichrist from Israel's neck. This language could imply that just like the armies of Pharaoh in Exodus 14, some of the armies of the Antichrist will be drowned and destroyed in the Red Sea after Jesus returns, perhaps because they will be foolish enough to chase after Israel as the Messiah is bringing them out of Egypt. Regardless, there is a clear connection drawn in Isaiah 10:16–17 between the future parting of the Red Sea and Israel's deliverance from their eschatological enemeis.

THE MESSIANIC MIRACLES IN ISAIAH 11

Besides Isaiah 10:16–17, Isaiah 11:15–16 also speaks of how the Messiah will perform miracles over the seas and rivers of the earth when He returns. In this passage Isaiah said:

> And the Lord will utterly destroy the tongue of the Sea of Egypt; And He will wave His hand over the River with His scorching wind; And He will strike it into seven streams and make men walk over dry-shod. And there will be a highway from Assyria for the remnant of His people who will be left, just as there was for Israel in the day that they came up out of the land of Egypt. (Isa. 11:15–16)

The "tongue of the Sea of Egypt" is the Red Sea and "the River" is the Euphrates River. Thus, the prophetic picture in Isaiah 11:15–16 complements that which was presented one chapter earlier, in Isaiah 10:16–17. More specifically, Isaiah 11:15–16 notes that when the Messiah returns, He will "wave His hand" over these bodies of water and either destroy them, dry them up, or disperse them into smaller streams, so the scattered Jewish remnant can experience safe passage back to the Promised Land. Also, whereas Isaiah 10:16–17 emphasized how the miracle over "the sea" will bring judgment upon the armies of the Antichrist, Isaiah 11:15–16 emphasizes how the drying up of the Red Sea and the Euphrates River will make a pathway for Israel through treacherous terrain during the second exodus.

THE PARTING OF THE SEA IN ZECHARIAH 10

Like his forefathers, the prophet Zechariah also spoke of how the Messiah will exert complete control over the oceans, rivers, and streams after His Second Coming. For example, in Zechariah 10 the Lord proclaimed to Israel:

> I will bring them back from the land of Egypt and gather them from Assyria; and I will bring them into the land of Gilead and Lebanon

> until no room can be found for them. And they will pass through the sea of distress and He will strike the waves in the sea, so that all the depths of the Nile will dry up; and the pride of Assyria will be brought down and the scepter of Egypt will depart. (Zech. 10:10–11)

Here, Zechariah appears to describe the same Red Sea miracle as described in Isaiah 11:15–16. In this context, God again mentions how He will bring Israel back from Egypt and Assyria, but also how Israel will pass through "the sea of distress," at which point He will "strike the waves in the sea." When this miracle takes place, Zechariah notes that the Nile River will also dry up and the government (i.e., "the scepter") of Egypt will fall.

THE SECOND EXODUS BEGINS

Taken as a whole, these prophecies that chronicle how the Messiah will part the Red Sea, dry up the Nile River, and disperse the Euphrates River into seven streams when He returns are an important part of the second exodus story. When we piece these texts together, we can better understand that the common view that Jesus will return immediately to Jerusalem fails to incorporate key aspects of God's prophetic plan.

Throughout the writings of the Hebrew prophets, the Messiah is often presented as a greater Moses, Divine Warrior, and Storm God in the flesh who will return on the clouds of heaven, travel into the land of Egypt, rescue "the remnant of His people" with His own "hand" (Isa. 11:11), and at the same time perform supernatural miracles over the Red Sea and the Euphrates River, in order to both give Israel safe passage back to the Promised Land and bring judgment against the nations that will hold them in slavery during the end times. Then, as we will soon discover, the Messiah will march on a warpath through Saudi Arabia, Jordan, and the other Middle Eastern nations, before He ultimately confronts the Antichrist in Jerusalem.

As a brief review of what we have covered so far, prophecy teacher Joel Richardson offers a helpful summary of this second exodus out of Egypt. He writes:

Thus, the concept of the Lord splitting the Red Sea yet again, specifically in the context of the final redemption of Israel, is actually a theme that pops up multiple times throughout the prophets. All things considered, the view that Jesus will return to Egypt and retrace the entirety of the Exodus route enjoys some very significant scriptural support. Of the various positions, this view, although almost never considered by students of Scripture, seems to be the most biblical view. Jesus, as the greater Moses, and the glory of God in the flesh, will execute the greater Exodus march from Egypt, through the Red Sea, to Mount Sinai, and proceed all the way to Jerusalem.[10]

THE NEW CREATION AND THE RED SEA MIRACLE

As miraculous as these second exodus events will be at the grassroots level, we should also understand that they have a deeper theological significance that is rooted in the symbolic meaning of the original Red Sea miracle. In the last chapter, we learned that the parting of the Red Sea in Exodus 14 foreshadowed the emergence of God's new creation, because in Scripture God's renewed cosmos always emerges out of water, by the power of His spirit or wind (ruach; cf. Gen. 1:2).

When this theological symbolism is understood, it is easier to comprehend why Jesus will part the Red Sea and create dry land out of the Euphrates River when He returns. He will do so because this will signal that He is the true King of the new creation, who has finally arrived on the scene of history to fully restore God's originally good but fallen world.

Just as the parting of the Red Sea foreshadowed the emergence of the new creation in the book of Exodus, it will also signify the next phase of God's new-creation work when Jesus returns. Shortly after the Second Coming, God will again baptize His people in the sea, and we will emerge out of the waters of chaos standing on dry ground, in the light of His holy presence, ready to enter the millennial kingdom.

---

10 Richardson, *Sinai to Zion*, 269.

THE DESERT WARRIOR PROPHECIES

In addition to the prophecies that speak of the return of Jesus to Egypt and the parting of the Red Sea, there are other texts that outline the military battles He will fight during the second exodus. I call these texts the Desert Warrior Prophecies, because they each refer to how Jesus will march with His people from Egypt, through the Sinai and Arabian deserts, waging war against the powers of darkness as He methodically moves up towards Israel and prepares for His final battle with the Antichrist in Jerusalem.

THE DIVINE WARRIOR IN HABAKKUK 3

One of the most important Desert Warrior Prophecies is found in Habakkuk:

> God comes from Teman, and the Holy One from Mount Paran. His splendor covers the heavens, and the earth is full of His praise. His radiance is like the sunlight, He has rays flashing from His hand, and there is the hiding of His power. Before Him goes pestilence, and plague comes after Him. He stood and surveyed the earth; He looked and startled the nations, yes the perpetual mountains were shattered, the ancient hills collapsed. His ways are everlasting. I saw the tents of Cushan under distress, the tent curtains of Midian were trembling. Did the LORD rage against the rivers, or was your anger against the rivers, or was your wrath against the sea, that You rode on Your horses, on Your chariots of salvation? Your bow was made bare, the rods of chastisement were sworn. You cleaved the earth with rivers, the mountains saw you and quaked; the downpour of waters swept by, the deep uttered its voice, it lifted high its hands.
>
> Sun and moon stood in their places, they went away at the light of your arrows, at the radiance of Your gleaming spear. In indignation You marched through the earth; In anger You trampled the nations. You went forth for the salvation of Your people. For the salvation of Your anointed. You struck the head of the house of evil, to lay him

> open from thigh to neck. You pierced with his own spears the head of his throngs, they stormed in to scatter us; Their exultation was like those who devour the oppressed in secret. You trampled on the sea with your horses, on the surge of many waters. (Hab. 3:3–15)

The reason Habakkuk 3 is so significant, is because this passage is an expanded prophetic commentary on the Second Coming prophecy in Numbers 24, which we looked at earlier. Though Habakkuk 3 uses the generic title for God, like in Numbers 24, in this text God is presented in a personified way marching "through the earth" and waging war. Additionally, like He does in Isaiah 19, God emerges from the sky in this passage, with His "splendor covering the heavens."

All things considered, it is these warrior elements and the way God appears from the sky in Habakkuk 3 that confirm that the glorious return of the Messiah is in view here, because these are two of the most common motifs associated with the Second Coming in Scripture (i.e., warfare and appearing from the sky). In the words of Old Testament scholar Palmer Robertson, Habakkuk 3 describes "the great final epiphany of the glory of God, when the Son of Man shall come in the clouds [...] Then every eye shall see Him, and the vision of Habakkuk shall receive its finalized fulfillment."[11]

THE SECOND EXODUS ROUTE IN HABAKKUK 3

Notably, Habakkuk 3 does not depict the Messiah returning immediately to Jerusalem. Instead, this prophecy adds to the second exodus story of Isaiah 19, Numbers 24, Isaiah 10–11, and Isaiah 27, and delineates the war march of the Messiah after He comes "out of Egypt" (Num. 24:8). Verse 3 also specifically highlights how Jesus will travel through Teman and Mount Paran (i.e., Saudi Arabia and Jordan) on His way to Jerusalem.

Verse 7 adds that right after the Second Coming "the tents of Cushan" will be "under distress" and "Midian" will be "trembling."

11 Quoted in Richardson, *Sinai to Zion*, 216.

Cushan and Midian could include both Saudi Arabia and Jordan, and thus, we see here how the Messiah will emerge from Egypt, travel through the Red Sea, and then march from the south due north into the land of Israel.

In his book *Sinai to Zion*, Joel Richardson articulates one of the best prophetic commentaries on Habakkuk 3. He explains how this text fills in more geographic details related to the second exodus and writes:

> As Jesus strides forth, pouring out the plagues of God, the rebellious Gentiles are likened to collapsing mountains. Specifically, we are told that Cushan and Midian are in a state of panic. Both tribal names were associated with the region of Arabia and were close to Mount Sinai on the eastern side of the Red Sea. Thus, as Jesus proceeds forward out of Arabia, northward toward Jerusalem, the peoples from those regions are trembling in terror.[12]

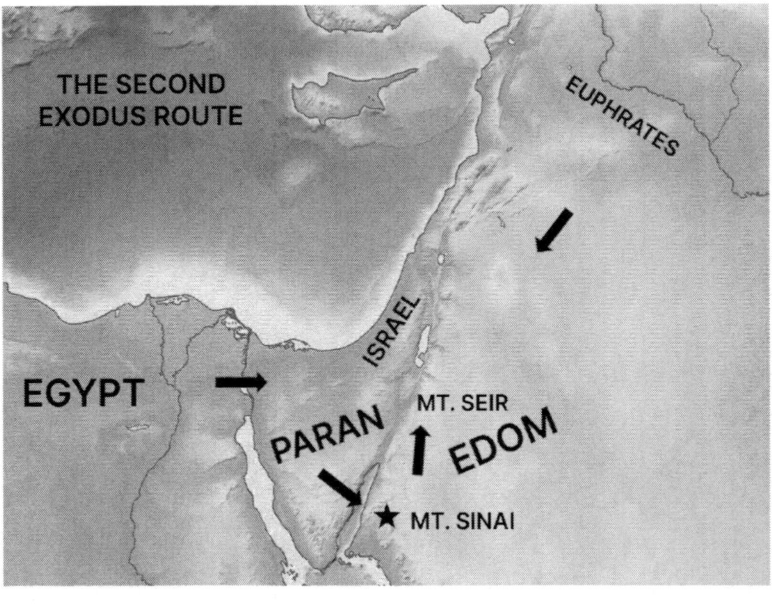

12 Richardson, *Sinai to Zion*, 222.

THE GLORIOUS DIVINE WARRIOR IN HABAKKUK 3

There is so much rich imagery in Habakkuk 3 that it can be difficult to take it all in. But in general terms, Habakkuk 3 gives us one of the most profound glimpses into the glorious Second Coming of the Messiah in all of Scripture, and it does so using the same storm-god and divine-warrior themes from the book of Exodus.

This is a vision of Jesus returning in glory, decked out in battle array with His weapons of war, riding through the clouds on his chariots of salvation, shining like the sun in its brilliance, shattering His enemies with the light of His arrows and His gleaming spear, calling down plagues and pestilence against his enemies, dispersing rivers and seas in His anger and wrath, shaking mountains and causing earthquakes, saving Israel from exile in the Middle Eastern and North African nations, and preparing to confront the Antichrist at the final battle in Jerusalem. Put simply, this is a vision of the second exodus led by the great Divine Warrior Himself, Jesus the Messiah, the Storm God YHVH in the flesh.

THE DESERT WARRIOR IN ISAIAH 63

Isaiah 63:1–6 and Zechariah 9:13–17 are also important prophecies that elaborate on the second exodus. Isaiah 63 describes the Lord as a divine warrior coming from Edom (i.e., Saudi Arabia and Jordan), "majestic in His apparel [...] marching in the greatness of His strength" (v. 1). With a rhetorical flourish, Isaiah expresses his amazement when he sees the divine Son of Man marauding through the desert and pouring out His wrath on Israel's enemies. Then, he is answered by God Himself who describes the events and purpose of the second exodus. Isaiah writes:

> Who is this who comes from Edom, with garments of glowing colors from Bozrah, this One who is majestic in His apparel, marching in the greatness of His strength? "It is I who speak in righteousness, mighty to save." Why is Your apparel red, and Your garments like the one who treads in the wine press? "I have trodden the wine trough alone, and from the peoples there was no man with Me. I also trod them

in My anger and trampled them in My wrath; and their lifeblood is sprinkled on My garments, And I stained all My raiment. For the day of vengeance was in My heart, And My year of redemption has come." (Isa. 63:1–4)

The message of Isaiah 63:1–6 harmonizes with the message of Habakkuk 3. Both texts depict the Messiah "marching" from the south, coming "from Edom," and waging war against the Gentile nations as He makes His way up to Jerusalem.

THE DESERT WARRIOR IN ZECHARIAH 9

Similarly, Zechariah 9:13–17 also mentions the Messiah's war march into Israel from the south. This text says the Messiah will "appear over" Israel, send "His arrow" forth like "lightning" against their enemies, and "march in the storm winds of the south" (v. 14).

Notice particularly how Zechariah 9:14 develops the storm-god theme from Exodus and describes the Messiah as one who will be immersed in a "storm wind" or "whirlwind" as He fights against the powers of darkness and travels through the southern desert. To imagine the scene, just recall the most terrifying yet spectacular thunderstorm you have ever been in. Then place Jesus on the earth in the midst of that storm, parading through the desert in a tornado as lightning flashes all around Him, flaming arrows fly away from Him in every direction, and a torrential downpour of rain, hail, and other plagues devastate legions of armies lined up against Him on the battlefield.

That is the picture here. Many of the Hebrew prophets received a glorious revelation of the Messiah's war march up to Jerusalem through the deserts of Egypt, Saudi Arabia, and Jordan, and this is truly one of the most awe-inspiring aspects of His Second Coming detailed in Scripture.

THE DEFEAT OF THE ANTICHRIST IN EZEKIEL 38

After He strides through the desert with Israel and the host of glorified believers who will accompany Him on His journey (Rev. 17:4), Jesus will reach Jerusalem and confront the Antichrist. One of the most important but widely misinterpreted prophecies in the Bible that reveals the Messiah's confrontation with the Antichrist can be found in Ezekiel 38:18–23.

This passage is usually misinterpreted by pastors, prophecy teachers, and Bible commentators because they believe the Lord's primary antagonist in this passage, a figure named Gog, is a political leader who will be defeated prior to the return of Jesus. In other words, most prophecy teachers within evangelicalism subscribe to the view that Gog is a second-tier, end-times dictator who is distinct from the Antichrist.

Both Scripture and Jewish tradition, however, confirm that Gog is the military-political leader who will invade Israel during the Seventieth Week, send Israel into exile, and not be defeated until he is dealt with by the Messiah.[13] Gog is the name given to the man who is later identified in the New Testament as "the Beast" (Rev. 13), the "man of lawlessness" (2 Thess. 2:3), and the Antichrist (1 John 2:18).

Below are some comments from Christian and Jewish scholars who have also recognized that Gog is the Antichrist:

- Old Testament PhD, Michael Heiser, in his book *The Unseen Realm*: "Gog would have been perceived as either a figure empowered by supernatural evil or an evil quasi-divine figure from the supernatural world bent on the destruction of God's people. For this reason, Gog is regarded by many biblical scholars as a template for the New Testament antichrist figure."[14]

13 For a full discussion of Gog's identity and the battle outlined in Ezekiel 38, see chapters 6, 14–16 in *The Passover King*. These chapters also cover how Ezekiel 38–39, like Zechariah 14, compresses events that will occur over a three-and-a-half-year period into one short prophecy.

14 Michael S. Heiser, *The Unseen Realm: Recovering the Supernatural Worldview of the Bible* (Bellingham: Lexham Press, 2015), 365.

- Tractate *Avodah Zerah* in the *Babylonian Talmud* mentions how Gentile converts will see Gog fight against the Messiah. In this text, the Jewish sages correlated Ezekiel 38 and Psalm 2 (which speaks of the Messiah's victory over the Gentile nations). They stated: "When these converts see the war of Gog and Magog, every convert of this sort will say to Gog and Magog: For what purpose did you come? They [Gog and his armies] will say to him [the convert]: We came to fight against the Lord and against His Messiah, as it is stated: 'Why are the nations in an uproar? And why do the peoples mutter in vain. The kings of the earth stand up, and the rulers take counsel together, against the Lord, and against His Messiah' (Ps. 2:1–2)." As we can see, many of the early Jewish rabbis understood that Gog will be defeated by the Messiah, and that Gog is therefore the final archenemy of Israel (i.e., Antichrist).[15]

- Prophecy teacher Joel Richardson, in his book *Mideast Beast*: "In contrast to the popular Christian position, the Jewish rabbinic view identifies Gog as the final enemy of God's people. [...] While the Jews refer to the final evil dictator as Gog, the New Testament calls him by such titles as the Antichrist (1 John 2:22), the son of destruction (2 Thess. 2:3), the lawless one (2 Thess. 2:8), the Beast (Rev. 11:7), and other titles.[16]

Of course, we do not want to rely only on commentary traditions when determining Gog's identity. So it should also be stated that these traditions that equate Gog and the Antichrist rest on a very solid biblical foundation.

For example, there are many textual clues in Ezekiel 38–39 that prove Gog is the Antichrist. First, Ezekiel 38:20 says that when Gog is defeated the entire earth will "shake" at God's "presence" (panim). As noted earlier, the Hebrew word for presence here (panim) can also mean face, and it

15 *The William Davidson Talmud*, *Avodah Zerah* 3b, *Sefaria*, online.

16 Joel Richardson, *Mideast Beast: The Scriptural Case for an Islamic Antichrist* (Washington DC: WND Books, 2012), 62.

is often used to describe God's manifest presence in a physical form (cf. Gen. 30; Isa. 19). The use of this term implies that Gog is the enemy of Israel (i.e., Antichrist) who will only be defeated when Jesus, the physical manifestation of God, is back on the earth, not many years before.

Also, we should not ignore the parallelism between Isaiah 19:1 and Ezekiel 38:20. Both passages mention that the enemies of God will tremble and shake when they see His face (panim), and this is another clue that Ezekiel 38:20 is organically tied to the second exodus narrative outlined in the writings of the other Hebrew prophets. Whereas Isaiah 19:1 speaks of what will happen right at the beginning of the second exodus, Ezekiel 38:20 is the final chapter that details how it will end when the Messiah defeats Gog.

Isaiah 19:1	Ezekiel 38:8
"Behold, the LORD is riding on a swift cloud and is about to come to Egypt; The idols of Egypt will tremble at His presence (panim), and the heart of the Egyptians will melt within them."	"The fish of the sea, the birds of the heavens, the beasts of the field, all the creeping things that creep on the earth, and all the men who are on the face of the earth will shake at My presence (panim)."[17]

Second, Ezekiel 39:9 says that when Gog is defeated, the nations will know that God is "the Holy One in Israel." Notice that this verse does not use the phrase "Holy One of Israel." Instead, it says God will be "in Israel" after Gog is killed, which implies that God will be on the earth at this time. Remarkably, Ezekiel 39:9 is the only verse in the entire Bible that uses this precise phrase (Holy One in Israel) to describe God's presence in Israel, and this subtle detail in the text is another major clue that this passage describes events that will take place soon after the Second Coming but before the official start of the millennium.

17 Also notice how the order of created beings listed in Ezekiel 38:8, fish, birds, creeping beasts, and mankind, follows the created order in Genesis 1. This progression confirms that Ezekiel 38 is a new-creation text that outlines how the world will be renewed by God's presence after the second exodus is complete.

Many other pieces of evidence can be found in Ezekiel 38–39 that prove the defeat of the Antichrist is in view in this passage. But these two should suffice for now. The numerous statements in this text that indicate that God will be physically present on the earth when this prophecy is fulfilled point unambiguously to the Second Coming.

THE END-TIMES FULFILLMENT OF PASSOVER IN EZEKIEL 38

One of the main reasons it is so important to understand that Ezekiel 38–39 refers to events that will happen only after the Second Coming[18] is because this allows us to see (1) arguably the most dynamic picture of the Messiah's victory over the Antichrist in the entire Bible and (2) how the Passover story prophetically foreshadowed what the Messiah will accomplish when He returns. Regarding this second point, one of the most noteworthy features of Ezekiel 38 is the number of elements in this text that are drawn from the early chapters of Exodus, and it would not be a stretch to say that Ezekiel 38 gives one of the most detailed accounts in Scripture of what the end-times fulfillment of Passover, referenced by Jesus in Luke 22:15–16, will entail.

To briefly elaborate, in Ezekiel 38 Gog is presented as an end-times Pharaoh who oppresses God's people, hardens his heart, and suffers the consequences in the end. It is also no coincidence that when the fall of Gog is detailed in Ezekiel 38:18–23, we learn that the Messiah will defeat him with many of the same Passover plagues that first appeared in the book of Exodus. This passage describes Gog's demise in the following way:

> "It will come about on that day, when Gog comes against the land of Israel," declares the Lord God, "that My fury will mount up in My anger. In My zeal and in My blazing wrath I declare that on that day there will surely be a great earthquake in the land of Israel. The fish of the sea, the birds of the heavens, the beasts of the field, all the

18 Technically, Gog's invasion of Israel, which is referenced at the beginning of Ezekiel 38, will occur before the Second Coming, at the midpoint of the Seventieth Week. Most of the other events in these chapters, however, will occur after Jesus returns.

> creeping things that creep on the earth, and all the men who are on the face of the earth will shake at My presence; the mountains also will be thrown down, the steep pathways will collapse and every wall will fall to the ground. I will call for a sword against him [Gog] on all My mountains," declares the LORD God. "Every man's sword will be against his brother. With pestilence and with blood I will enter into judgment with him; and I will rain on him and on his troops, and on the many peoples who are with him, a torrential rain, with hailstones, fire, and brimstone. I will magnify Myself, sanctify Myself, and make Myself known in the sight of many nations; and they will know that I am the LORD." (Ezek. 38:18-23)

As noted earlier, Ezekiel 38:20 says that when Gog is defeated the nations will "shake" at God's "presence/face" (panim). This is a clear indication that it will be God in the flesh, the Messiah, who will defeat Gog after He comes "out of Egypt" (Num. 24:8; Isa. 19:1).

The next major feature in Ezekiel 38 that ties this passage into the second exodus narrative of the Hebrew Bible is the miraculous plagues that Ezekiel says Jesus will use to defeat the Antichrist. For example, Ezekiel 38:22 mentions how the Messiah will "enter into judgment" with Gog by sending "pestilence" and "blood" against him. It also says the Messiah will "rain on him and on his troops and on the many peoples who are with him, a torrential rain, with hailstones, fire, and brimstone."

The reference to these plagues in Ezekiel 38:22 evokes the original Passover story and implies that the Messiah will defeat the Antichrist as a miracle worker, just as Moses defeated Pharaoh. Furthermore, through this plague language, Ezekiel 38 builds on the second exodus prophecy in Habakkuk 3, which also mentioned how the Messiah will use "pestilence" and "plagues" against His enemies (Hab. 3:5).

Of course, not all of the original ten plagues from the book of Exodus appear again in Ezekiel 38:22. However, three of them do, including "pestilence" (*dever*), "blood" (*dam*), and "hail" (*elgaviysh*) and "fire" (*esh*) from heaven.

The plague of pestilence is what afflicted the Egyptian livestock in Exodus 9:3. The plague of blood corresponds to the plague on the Nile River and the entire Egyptian water supply in Exodus 7:17-21. And the torrential rain, hailstones, fire, and brimstone in Ezekiel 38:22 correspond to the plague of hail and severe weather in Exodus 9:18-26, which states:

> Now the LORD said to Moses, "Stretch out your hand toward the sky, that hail may fall on all the land of Egypt, on man and on beast and on every plant of the field, throughout the land of Egypt." Moses stretched out his staff toward the sky, and the LORD sent thunder and hail, and fire ran down to the earth. And the LORD rained hail on the land of Egypt.
>
> So there was hail, and fire flashing continually in the midst of the hail, very severe, such as had not been in all the land of Egypt since it became a nation. The hail struck all that was in the field through all the land of Egypt, both man and beast; the hail also struck every plant of the field and shattered every tree of the field. Only in the land of Goshen, where the sons of Israel were there was no hail (vv. 22-26).

Ezekiel 38 draws on this passage in Exodus and portrays the Messiah as both Israel's greater Moses and the Divine Warrior YHVH in the flesh, who will defeat the powers of evil through a supernatural display of miraculous signs and wonders. Just as Moses called down the Passover plagues against Pharaoh, Jesus will do the exact same thing to the Antichrist when He encounters him in the land of Israel.

Moreover, though the Messiah's victory in Ezekiel 38 is detailed in concise terms, we can use our imagination to fill in the picture. I suspect that Jesus will literally turn the water supply used by the Antichrist into blood, and then, when the Antichrist is foolish enough to confront Jesus on the battlefield, the Messiah will march out to meet him with sheer poise and confidence in His divine power.

With the hills of Jerusalem surrounding Him and His arms raised to the sky, Jesus will call down fire, lighting, and hail from the heavens, and the Antichrist and his armies will be left in utter disarray, confused, and fleeing in every direction before they are shattered by massive explosions bursting forth from above and consumed by pestilent plagues that will destroy them in a matter of minutes. As we read in Zechariah:

> Now this will be the plague with which the LORD will strike all the peoples who have gone to war against Jerusalem; their flesh will rot while they stand on their feet, and their eyes will rot in their sockets, and their tongue will rot in their mouth. It will come about that a great panic from the LORD will fall on them; and they will seize one another's hand, and the hand of one will be lifted up against the hand of another. [...] So also like this plague will be the plague on the horse, the mule, the camel, the donkey, and all the cattle that will be in those camps. (Zech. 14:12–15)

With one voice Israel's prophets emphasized how the Messiah will defeat the forces of evil with a terrifying sequence of killer plagues, and this element in the biblical narrative, along with the second exodus and Desert Warrior prophecies we looked at earlier, reveals that the events that take place in the first weeks after Jesus returns will follow the contours of the original Passover story. The biblical prophets knew that the Messiah would return and bring Passover to a glorious end-times fulfillment before any of the other biblical feasts.

THE PASSOVER PLAGUES IN REVELATION

Not surprisingly, the book of Revelation also describes the return of Jesus and His victory over the powers of darkness as a fulfillment of the Passover story. For example, the "bowl" judgments of wrath that God will pour out on the world at the end of the Seventieth Week replicate the Passover plagues from the book of Exodus (Rev. 16).

Revelation 16 says that when the first bowl of wrath is poured out on the earth, people who take the mark of the beast and worship "his image" will experience "loathsome and malignant" sores (Rev. 16:2). This plague corresponds directly to the plague of boils in Exodus 9:8-12.

When the second and third plagues are unleashed, the sea, rivers, and springs of the earth will be turned into blood, and all living creatures in the sea will die (Rev. 16:3-4). These plagues correspond to the plague that turned the Nile River and the entire Egyptian water supply into blood in Exodus 7:14-25.

With the fourth plague in Revelation 16, the earth will be scorched with fire and "fierce heat," which will be so severe that those left on the earth will blaspheme and curse God (Rev. 16:8-9). Interestingly, this particular plague does not have a direct parallel in the book of Exodus.

After this fourth plague, however, the fifth plague will bring "darkness" over the kingdom of the Antichrist, which will in turn cause men to gnaw "their tongues because of pain" (Rev. 16:10-11). This plague corresponds directly to the plague of darkness in Exodus 10:21-29.

When the sixth plague is poured out, the Euphrates River dries up and the Beast and the False Prophet send deceptive spirits like "frogs" out of their mouths to deceive the nations and gather them to Jerusalem to fight against Jesus (Rev. 16:12–14). This plague evokes the plague of frogs in Exodus 8:5–7.

Finally, the seventh plague in Revelation 16 is connected to the battle of Armageddon, which is spoken of in Revelation 16:13–21 and Revelation 19:11–21. This final battle between the Antichrist (i.e., the Beast) and Jesus is the same battle that was originally described in the Gog of Magog prophecy in Ezekiel 38–39.

Old Testament scholar Daniel Block clarifies this point regarding the relationship between these two passages and writes:

> Allusions to the Gog oracle appear in Christian apocalyptic tradition, probably as a result of Jewish influence. Most notable is John's portrayal of the eschatological conflicts in Rev. 19-20. The scene of the birds gathered for the great supper of God in 19:17-21 is clearly borrowed from Ezekiel's last frame (39:17-20). [...] Although this passage never

> mentions Gog by name, the beast [...] certainly represents him. In the prophecy John fills in several details missing from Ezekiel's prophecy.[19]

At this point, we should also note that when Revelation 16:13–21 says the Antichrist will gather the "kings of the whole world" to fight against Jesus in the "place which in Hebrew is called Har-Magedon, this locality designation implies the city of Jerusalem. Har-Magedon is often linked to the city of Megiddo in Israel. But the Greek text in Revelation 16:16 should be translated as "mountain of assembly," meaning Mount Zion or Jerusalem.[20]

Though many prophecy students do not know that Har-Magedon in Revelation 16 is God's holy mountain in Jerusalem, the idea that Jerusalem is in view in this passage makes the most sense both linguistically and theologically. Satan seeks to control Jerusalem because he knows the holy city will be the place of the Messiah's throne, and this is also why we are told in numerous places that the Antichrist will focus on Jerusalem and occupy this city for three and a half years during the final Tribulation (Lk. 21:24; Dan. 12:11).

Revelation 16 is simply the final chapter in the second exodus narrative that traces its roots to the Hebrew Bible. This text describes the final battle that will take place in the holy city after Jesus returns to Egypt, rescues the Jewish survivors in North Africa and the Middle East, and marches through the desert and into the land of Israel (Isa. 19:1; Num. 24:8; Isa. 10:24-27; 11:12-16; 27; Hab. 3; Isa. 63:1-6; Zech. 9:14).

THE FINAL BATTLE IN JERUSALEM

As we saw when we studied Ezekiel 38–39, Jesus will defeat the Antichrist

19 Daniel I. Block, *The New International Commentary on the Old Testament: The Book of Ezekiel Chapters 25–48* (Grand Rapids: Wm. B Eerdmans Publishing Co., 1998), 490–491.

20 Michael Heiser makes an excellent case that the Greek text of Revelation 16:16 refers to Mount Zion. See, Michael S. Heiser, *The Unseen Realm: Recovering the Supernatural Worldview of the Bible* (Bellingham: Lexham Press, 2015), 370–373.

(Gog) with hailstones, fire, and severe weather after he (the Antichrist) is foolish enough to confront Jesus in battle. This plague corresponds to the plague of hail and severe weather in Exodus 9:13–35, and Revelation 16:13–21 adds that the hailstones of judgment that will fall on the Antichrist and his armies will weigh one hundred pounds each:

> And I saw coming out of the mouth of the dragon and out of the mouth of the beast and out of the mouth of the false prophet, three unclean spirits like frogs; for they are spirits of demons, performing signs, which go out to the kings of the whole world, to gather them together for the war of the great day of God, the Almighty. [. . .] And they gathered them together to the place which in Hebrew is called Har-Magedon.
>
> Then the seventh angel poured out his bowl upon the air, and a loud voice came out of the temple from the throne, saying, "It is done. And there were flashes of lightning and sounds and peals of thunder; and there was a great earthquake, such as there had not been since man came to be upon the earth, so great an earthquake was it, and so mighty. The great city was split into three parts, and the cities of the nations fell. Babylon the great was remembered before God, to give her the cup of the wine of His fierce wrath. And every island fled away, and the mountains were not found. And huge hailstones, about one hundred pounds each, came down from heaven upon men; and men blasphemed God because of the plague of the hail, because its plague was extremely severe.

PASSOVER FULFILLED IN THE KINGDOM OF GOD

Earlier in this chapter, we studied how on the night before His crucifixion, Jesus spoke about a future fulfillment of Passover "in the kingdom of God" (Lk. 22:15–16). And now that we have covered the testimony of the Hebrew prophets and the Passover symbolism in Revelation, it should be much easier to understand why Jesus said this.

Jesus knew the writings of the prophets well, and as a result, He knew that Passover will only reach its ultimate prophetic fulfillment when He returns as the Divine Warrior and greater Moses, leads a second exodus out of Egypt, parts the Red Sea, rescues the Jewish nation from captivity, marches on a war path through the desert south of Israel, and finally travels up to Jerusalem to defeat the Antichrist and his armies with the Passover plagues from the book of Exodus. For Jesus, the relationship between Passover and the Second Coming was eschatology 101, and remarkably, He was actually thinking about this future fulfillment of Passover the night before He was crucified.

Perhaps Jesus was meditating on Numbers 24, Habakkuk 3, or Ezekiel 38 as He sat at the table and broke bread with His disciples at the Last Supper. Or perhaps He was thinking about how He will part the Red Sea a second time as this aspect of the Passover story was retold through the elements of the Passover meal.

In any case, and whatever Jesus had on His mind that night, His statement about a future fulfillment of Passover in the kingdom of God is without a doubt one of the most important yet widely overlooked statements about His Second Coming in the entire Bible. Right there at the Last Supper Jesus both invoked the second exodus prophecies of the Hebrew Bible and gave us a clue that the Passover story is the key to deciphering the mystery of His return to this earth. Passover, as it turns out, is a harbinger of how the God of Israel, the great Divine Warrior of the exodus, will eventually complete His plan of salvation for the entire world and bring His people into the glories of His new creation in the millennial kingdom.

WILL JESUS RETURN ON PASSOVER?

Now that we understand the second exodus prophecies in the Bible, as well as how Jesus Himself attached an eschatological meaning to Passover at the Last Supper, we must answer the inevitable question: Does all this mean Jesus will actually return on Passover?

As I mentioned in chapter 1, many prophecy teachers have taught that the return of Jesus will coincide with the fall feasts in the seventh month (September/October), whereas Passover is in the first month (March/

April). Despite the popularity of this view, the material in the Bible that reveals a future fulfillment of Passover at the time of the Messiah's Second Coming at the very least leaves room for some other alternatives.

With this future fulfillment of Passover in mind, in the rest of this chapter we will cover why a very strong case can be made that the return of Jesus and the establishment of His kingdom will coincide with Passover and the start of the spring season, not with the fall feasts. Then, in later chapters we will look at the possible timing of the fulfillment of the other feasts that occur later in the year (i.e., Weeks, Trumpets, Atonement, and Tabernacles).

As I make this case, however, please be aware that my goal is not to imply that Jesus must return in the spring. Rather, I only want to explain in more detail why He very likely could, and why this scenario makes a lot of sense from both a biblical and historical vantage point.

I hope to open people up to the possibility and beauty of a spring Second Coming, and to explain how it could lead to a natural and sequential fulfillment of every annual feast mentioned in Leviticus 23 after Jesus returns. Yet, I also hasten to add that the exact timing of the Messiah's return in relation to the feasts is not something we can be one hundred percent certain on. Though I do have my opinions and hunches on this matter, I still fully respect God's prerogative to do whatever He wants, whenever He wants to, and I also recognize that as of now, we all still "know in part and prophesy in part" (1 Cor. 13:9).

PASSOVER FULFILLED IN THE KINGDOM OF GOD

The first major reason why a spring Second Coming is possible, and perhaps likely, is because it is hard to imagine how the biblical texts related to the future fulfillment of Passover and the exodus could be fulfilled at some time other than the Passover season, in the spring. In the same way Passover reached an initial fulfillment when Jesus was crucified as our Passover Lamb on the literal day of Passover in the first century, it could be that for consistency's sake the final fulfillment of Passover when He returns will have to overlap in some way with the actual day of Passover on the calendar as well. Otherwise, Jesus' words in Luke 22:15–16 would be rendered meaningless.

Is it likely, or even possible, that in Luke 22:15–16 Jesus spoke of a future fulfillment of Passover that will be realized at some time other than the Passover season? I personally doubt it because with almost no exceptions Jewish people eat the Passover on Passover, and at the Last Supper this is what Jesus said He will do with His disciples in the kingdom.

With that said, Luke 22:15–16 does not have to mean that Jesus will return on the clouds of heaven on the exact day of Passover, because we know there are many events (i.e., those tied to the second exodus) that will have to happen before Passover can be "fulfilled in the kingdom of God," and there is no way all these events (i.e., the deliverance of Israel, journey through the desert, outpouring of the plagues, and defeat of the Antichrist) could happen in one day.[21] For this reason, I am inclined to think that Jesus will return a few weeks before Passover, close to the start of spring, sometime around the beginning of the first biblical month (March). This would allow the events associated with the second exodus, including the journey out of Egypt, the Red Sea crossing, and the prophetic plague sequence, to happen prior to the actual day of Passover so that Jesus and His disciples can then celebrate Passover in Jerusalem after it is fulfilled, "in the kingdom of God," as the inaugural feast of the millennial age.

Admittedly, this scenario rests on some speculation. But I outline it here because it shows how even though the events that transpire soon after the Second Coming will mirror those of the Exodus story, they may not necessarily follow the Exodus story precisely in terms of timing. We know Israel left Egypt right after Passover, on the fifteenth of Aviv, and that their journey through the desert and the parting of the Red Sea took place after Passover as well. But it seems unlikely that Jesus will come "out of Egypt" on the same day (i.e., the fifteenth of Aviv) when He returns, because in Luke 22:15–16 Jesus placed the fulfillment of

21 I personally believe these events will unfold over a period that will last close to a month.

Passover not in Egypt but "in the kingdom of God." This is why I can see the events of the second exodus taking place sometime around the start of the first month, before Passover, and then the Passover celebration of Luke 22:15–16 taking place on the fourteenth and fifteenth of the first month, only after Israel has been delivered, the second exodus has taken place, the Antichrist has been defeated, and the messianic kingdom has been formally established in Jerusalem.

In either case, the important point to take away here is that Jesus' statement in Luke 22:15–16, as well as the various texts in the Hebrew Bible that use Passover and Exodus symbolism to describe His return, could very well point toward a messianic redemption that will culminate in the spring, not the fall. Furthermore, the only reason the idea of a fall Second Coming became so popular in the 1970s was because most prophecy teachers did not understand the future prophetic implications of Passover. If they had, the various end-time scenarios that emphasize only the fall feasts, while ignoring the spring feasts, would never have gone mainstream.

KEY EVENTS IN THE FIRST MONTH

A second piece of evidence that could point to a spring Second Coming, is the pattern of events that are connected to the Passover season throughout Scripture. We already know Israel left Egypt in the spring. We also know the Messiah was crucified on Passover and raised from the dead during the Feast of First Fruits, just a couple days after Passover.

What is less well known, however, is that many other biblical events that foreshadow God's new-creation work also took place in the first biblical month (Aviv/Nisan). For example, the flood in the time of Noah ended at the start of the first month. We read in Genesis 8:13: "In the first month, on the first of the month, the water was dried up from the earth. Then Noah removed the covering of the ark, and looked, and behold, the surface of the ground was dried up."

We see in this text that the new creation in the days of Noah emerged in the spring, right before the time that would eventually coincide with

Passover on the biblical calendar. This could be a prophetic hint that the new creation after the return of Jesus will emerge at the same time, at the start of the first month, just as it did in the book of Genesis.

Likewise, in the time of Joshua, the Israelites miraculously crossed the Jordan River, entered the Promised Land, and began their conquest of Canaan in the first month, right before Passover. Joshua 4:19 states, "Now the people came up from the Jordan on the tenth of the first month and camped at Gilgal on the eastern edge of Jericho."

Notably, the crossing of the Jordan in Joshua 3–4 paralleled how the Israelites crossed the Red Sea under Moses in Exodus 14. Moreover, as we have seen in the last two chapters, crossing through the waters has clear new-creation significance in the Bible, because it summons the image of new life arising out of water and darkness in Genesis 1:2.

Just like in Genesis 8, in Joshua 4 new life in the Promised Land begins in the first month, during the Passover season. This too could be a prophetic hint that the Messiah, as the greater Joshua, will bring Israel back to their land in the first month, shortly after His Second Coming.

THE BIBLICAL PATTERN & THE FIRST MONTH

This survey of key biblical texts demonstrates that throughout the Bible major redemptive events connected to new life and new beginnings take place in the spring, often during or right before Passover. We see this with the exodus, the crucifixion and resurrection of the Messiah, the end of the flood in the time of Noah, and the Israelites' entrance into the land of Canaan. In light of these examples, it is possible that when Jesus returns God will simply follow this same pattern and save His people in the first month on the biblical calendar as a precursor to the total fulfillment of Passover "in the kingdom of God" (Luke 22:16).

Could it be that just as the earth comes out of dormancy and darkness in the spring, the light of the Messiah will rise upon Israel and the nations at the same time in the future? Could it be that just as the winter cold begins to thaw, the flowers come into bloom, and jubilant song birds announce the dawn of a new season, the Messiah will emerge as the ultimate sign of beauty and renewal within God's creation? Could it be that the regeneration and rebirth we witness every March and April in the natural world is nothing less than a prophetic foretaste of what we will experience when the Messiah returns, right before Passover?

Based on everything I see in Scripture, I would say this is a definite possibility, and one that is even likely. God works through patterns and seasons, and above all, it is the Passover season that celebrates the victory of God and the renewal of His world. Also, it simply makes a lot of sense that the reign of the Messiah will begin in the first month on the biblical calendar, rather than halfway through the year, in the fall (i.e., in the seventh month).

As noted earlier, not only was this the time when God chose to redeem Israel, but it also signified the first fruits of the barley harvest that took place two days after Passover (Lev. 23:9–14), which was also the day on which Jesus was raised from the dead (1 Cor. 15:20–23). Thus, it could be that even as this time was connected to new life and resurrection in the first century, it will again be connected to the first fruits and the very beginning of our new life in the kingdom of God in the future.

PASSOVER IN JEWISH AND CHRISTIAN ESCHATOLOGY

In addition to the biblical material, many Jewish and Christian traditions also link the glorious appearance of the Messiah to Passover, or to the spring season more generally. As a matter of fact, many people will be surprised to learn that most Jews and Christians prior to the modern period believed that the Messiah would set up His kingdom in the spring, sometime very close to Passover.

JEWISH ESCHATOLOGY AND PASSOVER IN THE TIME OF JESUS

On the Jewish side of the aisle, many historians have expanded on the relationship between Jewish end-times theology (i.e., eschatology) and Passover in the time of Jesus. For example, Jewish scholar Hayim Schauss writes:

> The highest point in the evolution of Pesach [i.e., Passover] came in the last century of the second Temple, when the Jews suffered from the heavy oppression of the Romans. It was during this period that the messianic hope flamed up, and in the minds of the Jews the deliverance of the future became bound up with the first redemption in Jewish history: the deliverance of Egypt. Jews had long believed that in the deliverance to come, God would show the same sort of miracles that He had performed in redeeming the Jews from Egypt. This belief gained added strength in the period of Roman occupation and oppression.
>
> Jews began to believe that the Messiah would be a second Moses [who] would free the Jews the self-same eve, the eve of Pesach. So Pesach became the festival of the second as well as the first redemption; in every part of the world where Jews lived, especially in [Israel], Jewish hearts beat faster on the eve of Pesach, beat with the hope that this night the Jews would be freed from the bondage of Rome, just as their ancestors were released from Egyptian slavery.[22]

In addition to Schauss, biblical scholar Geoffrey Wainwright also affirms that in the time of Jesus, the establishment of the messianic kingdom was closely linked to Passover in many sectors of the Jewish world. He writes:

> Now it is certain that a strong eschatological [or end-times] expectation, and that messianic, attached to the Jewish Passover at the time of Jesus. The high antiquity of the association between Passover and messianic expectation may be shown by the fact that the Samaritans also expected their Taheb (Messiah) to come on Passover in the same way as orthodox Judaism; but it is in any case clear from Josephus that messianic excitement reached fever pitch at Passover time, and there are hints to the same effect in the New Testament itself: John 6:6

22 Hayim Schauss, *Guide to Jewish Holy Days: History and Observance* (New York: Schocken Books, 1970), 46–47.

> and 15, Matt. 26:5, Luke 23:19, and Luke 13:1–3. We may therefore confidently suppose that in the time of Jesus the Jews looked for the coming of the Messiah in the same night as that in which the great deliverance from Egypt had been wrought. This messianic expectation would then mark the meal during which according to the gospels, Jesus instituted the eucharist [i.e., Lord's Supper].[23]

The comments offered by Schauss and Wainwright are valuable because they explain how the expectation of a second exodus, led by a greater Moses who would set the Jews free from slavery and oppression, permeated Jewish society in the first century. Their comments also highlight that the natural corollary to this second exodus theology in Judaism was the idea that the kingdom of God would be established on Passover or on "the eve of Pesach." During the time of Jesus, the common view within Judaism among both orthodox Jews (i.e., Pharisees), and even among marginalized groups (i.e., Samaritans), was that the season of the first redemption from Egypt would also be the season of the final redemption through the Messiah, and many Jews, including Jesus and the Apostles, understood that the events tied to this season of messianic redemption would mirror those recorded in the book of Exodus.

Of course, the irony here is that God actually did satisfy the Jewish hope for messianic redemption during Passover in the first century. He just did not do so in the way the Jewish people were expecting. In other words, God first gave the Jewish people a Passover Lamb instead of a Divine Warrior, which caused many of them to miss their Messiah.

However, contrary to the claims of many Christian scholars, the way God subverted some Jewish messianic expectations in AD 30 does not mean that He completely invalidated these expectations altogether. Rather, God simply postponed the fulfillment of the Divine Warrior aspects of Passover for a later time, as Jesus indicated in Luke 22:15–16. Furthermore, the fact that the messianic redemption began on Passover in

23 Geoffrey Wainwright, *Eucharist and Eschatology* (Epworth Press, 2003), 27.

the first century lends credibility to the idea that the messianic redemption will be completed on Passover when Jesus returns, in precisely the manner many religious Jews in the first century expected it would be.

JEWISH ESCHATOLOGY AND PASSOVER IN RABBINIC JUDAISM

After the death of Jesus, the connection between the establishment of the Messiah's kingdom and Passover continued showing up in a number of Jewish writings. For example, rabbi Joshua Ben Hananiah (c. AD 50–130), who was one of Judaism's most popular rabbis in the late-first and early-second centuries AD, predicted that the Messiah would deliver Israel in the first month, the month of Passover. The Talmud records that rabbi Joshua said:

> In Nisan [i.e., Aviv] the Jewish people were redeemed from Egypt; and in Nisan in the future the Jewish people will be redeemed in the final redemption.[24]

In this text, Rabbi Joshua establishes a clear link between Israel's first exodus from Egypt and their final redemption in the days of the Messiah, which consequently led him to suggest that the messianic age will begin in the month of Aviv (March/April).

Similarly, in a later Jewish text, known as Exodus Rabbah (c. AD 900-1100), the Jewish rabbinic writers also stated that the Messiah would set up His kingdom in the first month. Exodus Rabbah 15 states: "And the Messiah, who is called the first, will come in the first month."[25] In this passage from Exodus Rabbah, the Messiah is called "the first" because of His status as the preeminent messenger of God, which then leads to the idea that He will also come in the first month.

Moving beyond the ancient literature, in modern Judaism, there

---

24 *The William Davidson Talmud, Rosh Hashanah* 11a, *Sefaria*, online.

25 *Shemot Rabbah*, 15:1, *Sefaria*, online.

is still a well-established correlation between Passover and the appearance of the Messiah. Though we will not cover every element of the traditional Passover Seder meal now, in *The Passover King* I explain why the coming of the Messiah has been a major focus of the Passover Seder for over two thousand years in Judaism, and why it still is to this day, especially among Orthodox and ultra-Orthodox Jews.

All this to say, from a Jewish perspective, there is nothing novel or sensational about the idea that the Messiah will set up His kingdom right around the time of Passover, in the spring. For over two millennia this has simply been a common feature of Jewish messianic hope, and it is one that is deeply rooted in a careful reading of the second exodus prophecies in the Hebrew Bible, as well as the Passover story itself.

EARLY CHRISTIAN ESCHATOLOGY AND PASSOVER

Besides the Jewish sources, the writings of the early church fathers also confirm that most Christians in the first five hundred years of Church history expected Jesus to return on Easter Sunday, which occurred very close to Passover on the calendar.[26] As Wainwright notes, the Christian view that the Second Coming would occur in the spring was likely "carried over from the Jewish Passover...messianic eschatological expectations," and was also due to the importance of Resurrection Sunday within Christianity.[27] In other words, early Christians tied the Second Coming to the Passover season because they were influenced by Jewish theology and also because Easter was the most important day of the year for them.

26 Many early Christians celebrated Passover on the fourteenth of the first biblical month, at the same time as the Jewish people. However, others chose to celebrate the crucifixion and resurrection of Jesus on the first Friday and Sunday after Passover. Later, in the time of Constantine (AD 300s), the date of Easter Sunday was changed to coincide more closely with the vernal equinox, and thus, it was no longer observed on the first Sunday after Passover. But in any case, the point to note here is that from the beginning Easter Sunday was closely associated with Passover, and many early Christians considered Resurrection Sunday to be their way of observing Passover, which they called *Pascha* (i.e., the Greek word for Passover).

27 Wainwright, *Eucharist and Eschatology*, 27.

In the early church, many Christians attended a paschal vigil (i.e., a Passover service) on the day of the resurrection that lasted from late Saturday night to early Sunday morning, and the reason they did this was because they believed Jesus would return at this time. For example, according to Wainwright, the early church father Lactantius, writing in the AD 300s, "links both the resurrection of Christ and His coming *parousia* [i.e., return for the saints]" to the Easter vigil. Lactantius wrote:

> This is the night in which we keep vigil on account of the coming of our king and God. This night has a twofold meaning; in it Christ received life after death; and in it He will hereafter gain the kingdom over the whole earth.[28]

Likewise, the early church father Jerome (AD 400s) also spoke of the relationship between Passover, Easter, and the return of Jesus. Going one step further than Lactantius, Jerome added that his teaching on the Second Coming was rooted in earlier Jewish and apostolic traditions. Jerome wrote:

> For suddenly as at dead of night, when all are safely abed and deeply asleep, the shouts of angels and trumpets of the preceding forces will sound out the advent of Christ. Let us say something that may be useful to the reader. There is a Jewish tradition that the messiah will come in the middle of the night, in likeness of what happened in Egypt when the Passover was celebrated, and the angel of death came, and the Lord passed over them, and the doorposts were consecrated by lamb's blood. Whence I consider also the apostolic tradition to have been drawn, that it is not lawful to dismiss the people before midnight from the paschal vigil, for we expect the advent of Christ.[29]

28 Lactantius, *Divine Institutes*, Book VII.19; quoted in Wainwright, *Eucharist and Eschatology*, 28.

29 Jerome, *Commentary on Matthew*, 25.6; quoted in Wainwright, *Eucharist and Eschatology*, 28.

Notice how Jerome said that holding a Passover vigil past midnight on the day of the Messiah's resurrection was an apostolic tradition. If true, and we have no reason to doubt Jerome on this point, this means the celebration of the Passover vigil before Resurrection Sunday had origins in the first century, in apostolic times. Also, notice that Jerome said this tradition was instituted because on this night the early church expected "the advent of Christ," meaning His Second Coming, in the spring.

Finally, Isodore of Seville (AD 600s) also accepted the relationship between Passover, Easter, and the Second Coming. Isodore wrote:

> Vigil is kept on this night, on account of the advent of our king and our God, that at the time of His resurrection He may not find us sleeping but vigilant. There is a twofold reason for keeping this night: first because in it He received life after His passion and second because He will hereafter come for the judgment at the same hour as that in which He rose from the dead.[30]

THE EARLY JEWISH AND CHRISTIAN VIEW

When we look at the early Jewish and Christian sources that speak about the coming of the Messiah, a common theme emerges: Many of the most important Jewish and Christian teachers in ancient times taught that the glorious appearance of the Messiah, what we today call the Second Coming and the establishment of the messianic kingdom, will occur during the Passover season.

Some of these sources connect the coming of the Messiah to the first biblical month in a general sense, whereas others connect His coming to the actual day of Passover and/or Resurrection Sunday. But nuances aside, the Jewish and Christian sources reveal a strikingly coherent picture. For hundreds of years in both Judaism and Christianity, the idea that the Messiah will set up His kingdom sometime close to Passover was the mainstream, orthodox, and apostolic view, and that certainly has to count for something.

30 From Wainwright, *Eucharist and Eschatology*, 28.

PASSOVER & THE BLESSED HOPE

One of the most unfortunate trends in prophecy teaching since the 1970s has been the tendency to deny the relationship between Passover and the return of Jesus. Our goal in this chapter was to remedy this problem by exploring how the original Passover story paints one of most detailed pictures in all of Scripture of what will happen after the Messiah's Second Coming, and also quite possibly foreshadows that the Messiah will return, defeat His enemies, rescue Israel, and inaugurate God's new creation in the spring.

This study was deemed necessary because at the doctrinal level, we simply cannot understand many of the most important aspects of God's prophetic plan until we first reckon with the deeper prophetic meaning of Passover. At the same time, this study of Passover was also undertaken because it has important practical implications for the Lord's people today, as we await the "blessed hope" and the kingdom of God.

We might be tempted to read the stories in the Bible and think, "God did such great and miraculous things back then, but life today seems so normal and boring by comparison." Or we might think, "I wish I could have been there to see Moses calling down the plagues against Pharaoh or the parting of the Red Sea. It seems like all the epic events of redemptive history happened in the past, in Old Testament times."

While there can be no doubt that life in this world is often mundane, the Passover story is meant to serve as a reminder of the glorious future God has in store for us and the breathtaking events we will witness when Jesus returns. As a matter of fact, the things Jesus will accomplish for us when He returns will actually make the original Passover story look somewhat tame by comparison.

The Divine Warrior, Storm God, and greater Moses of the exodus is coming soon, and after we see Him vanquish His enemies on the battlefield, we will sit with Him at the Passover table and raise a glass in His honor. Then, as the new life of spring bursts forth into shouts of praise all around us, Israel and the nations will finally be brought out of the chaos and darkness of this world and into the glorious light of God's new creation.

Greater things indeed are yet to come.

CHAPTER SUMMARY

Below are the key points from this chapter that can help us restore the full prophetic meaning of Passover within the body of Messiah:

1. Though Passover, Unleavened Bread, and First Fruits were partially fulfilled through Jesus' first-century ministry, these spring feasts will not be completely fulfilled until His Second Coming. In Luke 22:15–16, Jesus placed the final fulfillment of Passover "in the kingdom of God," because numerous Old Testament prophecies describe the glorious appearance of the Messiah and His final victory over the powers of darkness in terms drawn from the book of Exodus. These texts reveal that at the time of His Second Coming, the Messiah will return to the land of the Pharaohs, rescue Israel from captivity, lead a second exodus out of Egypt, part the Red Sea, and march on a war path through Saudi Arabia and Jordan, before entering the land of Israel. They also predict that the Messiah will engage in the final battle with the Antichrist (i.e., Gog/the Beast) in Jerusalem and defeat him using many of the original Passover plagues (Isa. 19:1; Num. 24:8; Isa. 10:26; 11:15–16; Zech. 10:10–11; Hab. 3; Zech. 9:14; Ezek. 38:22; Rev. 16).

2. There is no way to know exactly when the Messiah will return to this earth. However, the biblical and historical evidence, as well as the fact that God has performed many of His most significant new-creation acts in the past in the first month, lends credibility to the idea that Jesus could return in the spring, sometime right before Passover (Gen. 8:13; Josh 4:19).

3. Many early Jewish and Christian traditions support the idea that Passover points forward to the glorious appearance of the Messiah. A number of early Jewish rabbis expected the Messiah to set up His kingdom in the first

month on the biblical calendar, and early Christians instituted a Passover vigil on the night before Resurrection Sunday because they expected the Second Coming in the spring, on the same day Jesus was raised from the dead. In Judaism, the Passover Seder was a way to anticipate the coming of the Messiah and the second exodus, and in Christianity the Passover vigil was meant to keep believers watchful and alert for the return of the Lord.

4. Based on Jesus' words in Luke 22:15–16, we can be confident that believers will celebrate Passover with Him "in the kingdom of God" after He completes the second exodus. Moreover, the first feast that we celebrate in the kingdom might be a Passover Seder, one that looks back not only to the first exodus, but also to the final victory of Jesus over the powers of darkness. As a result, every Passover Seder we celebrate today should anticipate the return of the Messiah and the time when He will fulfill this holy feast day in the future.

BIBLE STUDY QUESTIONS

1. How do you think Jesus' words in Luke 22:15–16 should change the way we think about and celebrate Passover?

2. What is your favorite second exodus prophecy and why?

3. Can you explain how the original Passover story is connected to many end-time events, as well as those that will occur after the Second Coming?

4. How does understanding Passover in its original historical context help us better grasp its future prophetic fulfillment?

4

THE FEAST OF WEEKS IN HISTORICAL CONTEXT

AFTER PASSOVER, the Feast of Unleavened Bread, and First Fruits in the first month (Lev. 23:4–11), the next appointed time on the biblical calendar is the Feast of Weeks (also known as *Shavuot* or Pentecost).[1] The Feast of Weeks was one of Israel's major harvest festivals and as we will see in this chapter and the next, it had important agricultural, religious, and prophetic significance.

THE FEAST OF WEEKS TIED TO EARLY FIRST FRUITS

Leviticus 23:15–16 places the Feast of Weeks seven sabbaths, that is, seven weeks or fifty days after the early First Fruits offering. We read in this passage:

1 The word *Shavuot* is the Hebrew form of "weeks," and Pentecost is derived from the Greek word meaning "fiftieth," because the Feast of Weeks took place fifty days after the second day of Unleavened Bread (Lev. 23:15–16).

> You shall also count for yourselves from the day after the sabbath, from the day when you brought in the sheaf of the wave offering; there shall be seven complete sabbaths. You shall count fifty days to the day after the seventh sabbath; then you shall present a new grain offering to the LORD. (Lev. 23:15–16)

In the last chapter we learned that the "sheaf of the wave offering" referenced in Leviticus 23:15 came from the first harvest of barley in the spring, which was offered in the Temple two days after Passover, on the second day of the Feast of Unleavened Bread (i.e., the sixteenth of Aviv).[2] Thus, the Feast of Weeks was celebrated seven weeks after the early barley offering (Lev. 23:10) as an extension of the harvest that began nearly two months earlier. As noted by biblical scholars Kevin Howard and Marvin Rosenthal, in Judaism "the time period from First Fruits to Shavuot is known as *Sefirah* (Heb. "counting")," and since this period began with the offering of the first-fruits sheaf of barley (Heb. *omer*) in the Temple, it is said that the forty-nine days between First Fruits and Weeks is the time for "counting the *omer*."[3]

2 The Sabbath referred to in Leviticus 23:15 is not the weekly Sabbath on the seventh day of the week. Rather, according to the Pharisees and Josephus, it is the first day of Unleavened Bread because Leviticus 23:7 says this day was also a day of rest. Thus, in the time of Jesus, First Fruits was celebrated on the sixteenth of the first month.

3 Kevin Howard and Marvin Rosenthal, *The Feasts of the Lord: God's Prophetic Calendar from Calvary to the Kingdom* (Orlando: Zion's Hope, 1997), 90.

THE COMPLETION OF THE WHEAT HARVEST

In contrast to First Fruits, however, the Feast of Weeks celebrated the "new grain" offering of wheat, not barley. This was because barley ripened before wheat, so it would be harvested and offered in the Temple nearly two months earlier (March-April). Then, sometime in May or June the wheat would ripen, and the Feast of Weeks would commemorate the conclusion of the grain harvest.

According to Jewish scholar Hayyim Schauss, "The grain harvest started with the reaping of the barley and after seven weeks ended with the cutting of the wheat, an occasion for a festive holiday."[4] Moreover, since the average Israelite would have taken over fifty percent of their calories from these two grains, the barley (March-April) and wheat (May-June) harvests were two of the most important events on their calendar.

THE FEAST OF WEEKS OFFERING

Unlike Passover, the Feast of Weeks did not include a prescribed festival meal for all Israelites. Instead, the rituals for this feast focused on the grain offering from the new wheat harvest, which is described in Leviticus 23:16–21:

> You shall count fifty days to the day after the seventh sabbath; then you shall present a new grain offering to the LORD. You shall bring in from your dwelling places two loaves of bread for a wave offering, made of two-tenths of an ephah; they shall be of a fine flour, baked with leaven as first fruits to the LORD. Along with the bread you shall present seven one year old male lambs without defect, and a bull of the herd and two rams; they are to be a burnt offering to the LORD, with their grain offering and their drink offerings, an offering by fire of a soothing aroma to the LORD. You shall also offer one male goat for a sin offering and two male lambs one year old for a sacrifice of peace offerings.

---

4 Hayyim Schauss, *Guide to Jewish Holy Days: History & Observance* (New York: Schocken Books, 1970), 86.

> The priest shall then wave them with the bread of the first fruits for a wave offering with two lambs before the LORD; they are to be holy to the LORD for the priest. On this same day you shall make a proclamation as well; you are to have a holy convocation. You shall do no laborious work. It is to be a perpetual statute in all your dwelling places throughout your generations.

In this passage, the Feast of Weeks offering is called "a new grain offering to the LORD." It is also described as "two loaves of bread for a wave offering, made of two-tenths of an ephah [...] of fine flour, baked with leaven as first fruits to the LORD."

Jewish tradition tells us that these two loaves were quite large: "four handbreadths wide, seven long, and four fingers high," and weighed about five pounds each.[5] For reference, a handbreadth was about four inches, so the loaves themselves were over two feet long and one foot wide.

Once they were prepared from the recently harvested wheat, the officiating priest would wave these two bread loaves before the Temple altar "forwards and backwards, then up and down."[6] Afterward, the two loaves would be shared as part of a festival meal among the other priests at the Temple.

THE HISTORICAL OBSERVANCE OF WEEKS

The Feast of Weeks was one of Israel's three major pilgrim festivals, and in order to observe this appointed time, every adult male was required to present an offering to the Lord at the Tabernacle or Temple (Exod. 23:17). As a result, during the days of the Second Temple, hundreds of thousands of Jewish pilgrims would travel to Jerusalem to observe the feast.

In his classic book on the Temple, Alfred Edersheim explains what the scene would have looked like in Jerusalem when the Feast of Weeks was celebrated in the time of Jesus. He writes:

5 Alfred Edersheim, *The Temple: Its Ministry and Services* (Peabody: Hendrickson Publishers, 1994), 209–210.

6 Howard and Rosenthal, *The Feasts of the Lord*, 91.

> On the day before Pentecost [i.e., the Feast of Weeks] the pilgrim bands entered the Holy City, which just then lay in the full glory of early summer. Most of the harvest all over the country had already been reaped, and a period of rest and enjoyment seemed before them. As the stars shone out in the deep blue sky [...] the blasts of the priests' trumpets, announcing the commencement of the feast, sounded from the Temple mount through the delicious stillness of the summer night. Already in the first watch the great altar was cleansed, and immediately after midnight the Temple gates were thrown open. For before the morning sacrifice all burnt- and peace-offerings which the people proposed to bring at the feast had to be examined by the officiating priesthood. Great as their number was, it must have been a busy time, till the announcement that the morning glow extended to Hebron put an end to all such preparations, by giving the signal for the regular morning sacrifice. [...]
>
> Then came the peculiar offering of the day—that of the two wave loaves, with their accompanying sacrifices. [...] As the [offering] for the 16th of Nisan [Aviv] was of barley, being the first ripe grain in the land, so the 'two wave-loaves' were prepared from wheat grown in the best district of the country. [...] Similarly, three *seahs,* or about three pecks and three pints of wheat, were cut down, brought to the Temple, thrashed like other [grain]-offerings, ground, and passed through twelve sieves. From the flour thus obtained two omers [...] were used for 'the two loaves;' the rest might be redeemed and used for any purpose. [...] The loaves were made the evening preceding the festival; or, if that fell on the Sabbath, two evenings before. In shape they were long and flat, [and weighed about five pounds each].[7]

Edersheim paints a fascinating picture of how the Feast of Weeks was celebrated in ancient Israel and captures quite well the sense of camaraderie that must have been experienced in Jerusalem as farmers

7 Alfred Edersheim, *The Temple,* 208–209.

from across the land gathered to offer their newly harvested wheat to the Lord. During this time the Jewish people acknowledged that God had carried them through the dark and cold months of winter, sustained their crops, and brought them into a season of harvest.

Thus, He commanded Israel: "Celebrate the Festival of Harvest with the firstfruits of the crops you sow in your field" (Exod. 23:16, NIV). And as they did, the Israelites honored God as their Provider and offered back to Him a portion of their sustenance with thanksgiving and praise for His blessings upon their nation.

THE LAW WAS (PROBABLY) NOT GIVEN ON PENTECOST

In later Jewish tradition, the Feast of Weeks (Pentecost) also became closely associated with the giving of the Mosaic Law, because Exodus 19:1–2 says Israel came to Mount Sinai, "in the third month after the sons of Israel had gone out of the land of Egypt, *on that very day*" (emphasis added). Based on this verse, it is often argued that Israel arrived at Mount Sinai on the first day of the third month, which would place them there just a few days before the Feast of Weeks, and also allow the giving of the Ten Commandments to take place in conjunction with this spring festival.[8]

The problem with linking the giving of the Law to the Feast of Weeks, however, is that Exodus 19:1 likely does not indicate the first day of the third month. Rather, it probably indicates that Israel reached Mount Sinai on the same day in the third month that they left Egypt in the first month (i.e., the fifteenth), which would place them at the holy mountain roughly ten days after the Feast of Weeks was later celebrated according to their calendar.

Notably, there are many verses in the Bible that specify the first day of a month, and these passages use much different language than what we find in Exodus 19:1 (cf. Gen. 8:13; Exod. 40:17). When these linguistic nuances are understood, it becomes almost impossible to defend

8 The NIV translation also adopts this interpretation and translates Exodus 19:1 as, "on the first day of the third month."

the idea that Israel arrived at Mount Sinai on the first day of the third month, and this also means that the giving of the Ten Commandments did not overlap with the Feast of Weeks.

Furthermore, when discussing the Feast of Weeks, Scripture never says anything about the giving of the Ten Commandments or any other laws. Though we have to be cautious not to build an argument from silence here, this silence still seems significant. If the giving of the Law to Israel took place during Shavuot, which was one of the biggest events in their national history, there would probably be some mention of this in the various biblical passages that speak of the Feast of Weeks. But there is not, and this is most likely the case because the giving of the Ten Commandments occurred after the Feast of Weeks.

Many Jewish scholars have recognized that there is no biblical connection between the Feast of Weeks and the giving of the Law, including Hayyim Schauss. He writes:

> Shovuos [Pentecost] [...] was considered no more than a continuation of and an epilogue to the Festival of Unleavened Bread. There was no effort made, even in later biblical times, to tie up the festival with a historic event; it remained, through all that time, an agricultural holiday, the festival of the completion of the grain harvest. In none of the books of the Bible is there any trace or mention of [the Feast of Weeks] in connection with the giving of the Torah.[9]

JEWISH TRADITION, THE LAW, AND THE FEAST OF WEEKS

The notion that the Law was given on Pentecost is a Jewish tradition that was only popularized by later Rabbinic authorities in the second century AD. After the destruction of the Second Temple in AD 70 and the exile of most Jewish people from Israel in AD 135, the Jewish rabbis were looking for a way to preserve the Feast of Weeks as an important holiday, even after it could no longer be observed as an agricultural harvest festival. As a result, they decided to make the Feast of Weeks

9 Hayyim Schauss, *Guide to Jewish Holy Days*, 87.

a celebration of the giving of the Torah, and in this way preserved its relevance to the worldwide Jewish community.

As noted in the last few chapters, Jewish traditions are often helpful when studying the biblical feasts, and this is certainly the case with Passover, because Jewish tradition has upheld the end-times significance of Passover much more than modern Christian teaching, which is certainly a good thing. However, in many other cases, Jewish traditions distract from the true meaning of a particular feast, and this is unfortunately what has happened with the Feast of Weeks.

Traditions of course are not inherently evil, so it is not wrong for us to commemorate the giving of the Torah during Shavuot. Nevertheless, since we are focused on the Second Coming of the Messiah, emphasizing a connection between Pentecost and the giving of the Torah is not very helpful. I say this because the future fulfillment of the biblical feasts will always be inseparably tied to what the feasts signified in their original historical context, not to how the feasts were later understood according to Jewish or Christian tradition, a point that will also become critical to remember when we look at the fall feasts.

THE GOD OF THE HARVEST

Therefore, if we want to know how the Feast of Weeks will be fulfilled when the Messiah returns, and really what this feast was pointing to all along, we need to understand it first and foremost as the climactic harvest festival of the spring. In ancient Israel, seeds for the coming harvest were sown in late fall and then as the rains continued to pour down the rest of the year, the barley and wheat would begin to emerge and ripen between March and June. As an agrarian society, Israel was completely dependent on this annual rhythm that led up to the spring harvest, and even though their spring feasts, especially Passover and Unleavened Bread, had deep historical and religious significance rooted in the events recorded in Exodus, each of the feasts were also closely tied to the agricultural cycle that represented their livelihood. Consequently, during the Feast of Weeks, Israel celebrated the Lord as the God of the Harvest.

CHAPTER SUMMARY

Below are three key points from this chapter that establish the historical meaning of the Feast of Weeks:

1. The Feast of Weeks was closely connected to the Feast of Unleavened Bread, which started on the fifteenth of Aviv, and the Feast of First Fruits, which was celebrated on the sixteenth of Aviv. The Feast of Weeks took place seven weeks later, after the barley harvest, and it signified the conclusion of the wheat harvest and the conclusion of the spring moedim (Lev. 23:15-22).

2. There is very little evidence that the Law was given on Shavuot (i.e., the Feast of Weeks or Pentecost). Israel probably arrived at Mount Sinai after the Feast of Weeks, and there is no biblical passage that links the giving of the Law to this holiday (Exod. 19:1).

3. The Bible defines the Feast of Weeks primarily in terms of the harvest, and this aspect of the festival unlocks not only its historical significance but its prophetic significance as well (Exod. 23:16).

BIBLE STUDY QUESTIONS

1. How was the Feast of Weeks related to the earlier spring feasts (Passover, Unleavened Bread, and First Fruits)?

2. What do you think is the most important thing to know about the Feast of Weeks?

3. Even though the Feast of Weeks was not tied to the events recorded in Exodus, why do you think God wanted the Israelites to celebrate this appointed time?

5

THE FEAST OF WEEKS & THE RETURN OF JESUS

IMAGINE THE SCENE IN JERUSALEM after Jesus returns and defeats the Antichrist: He has just led a second exodus through the desert, and as the greater Moses crushed His enemies with a series of Passover plagues and judgments. The nations who opposed Him have been obliterated, and a first-fruits remnant of Jewish people and Israelis have been brought back to the land of Israel. The new growth of spring is bursting forth throughout the land and believers and saints from across the ages have celebrated the fulfillment of Passover with Jesus "in the kingdom of God" (Lk. 22:15–16).

We have sat at the Master's table and experienced the Passover Seder led by none other than Jesus Himself. Passover has now reached its deepest level of prophetic significance, and every year henceforth we will celebrate this feast as a commemoration of the mighty victory of King Yeshua (the Hebrew name of Jesus) over the forces of evil. At long last, after the extremely dark days of the Tribulation, a new day has dawned and the millennial age has begun.

But what comes next?

To answer this question, one of the most important things to realize first is that when Jesus returns, He will not simply wave a magic wand and restore the earth in matter of minutes, days, or even weeks. Rather, after the Second Coming, a series of events will unfold over a period of many months that will gradually bring the world into the fullness of the messianic age. Even though Jesus will achieve victory over the powers of darkness soon after His return to earth, the fallout and remaining destruction from the end times will still be severe. As a result, in the early days of His millennial reign, Jesus will oversee a number of initiatives that will systematically lead to the total physical and spiritual restoration of God's good creation, and the Bible is clear that these initiatives will take at least half a year to accomplish, and even longer in some cases.

THE FEAST OF WEEKS IN THE KINGDOM OF GOD

In this chapter, we will explore how many of the redemptive events that will occur in the early days of Jesus' millennial reign will bring about the prophetic fulfillment of the Feast of Weeks. Indeed, just as Passover offers one of the clearest pictures in Scripture of how Jesus will redeem Israel and defeat the powers of darkness, the Feast of Weeks offers some amazing insights into how He will usher the world into the fullness of God's salvation after His kingdom has been established. Furthermore, because the Feast of Weeks is the next biblical feast on the calendar after Passover, Unleavened Bread, and First Fruits, this is our initial hint that after the Messiah returns to fulfill Passover as the victorious Divine Warrior of the exodus, He will then fulfill the Feast of Weeks as the great God of the Harvest.

To uncover the deeper prophetic layers of the Feast of Weeks, we will first look at how the day of Pentecost in the book of Acts foreshadows events that will take place when Jesus returns. Then we will turn our attention to the numerous passages in the Hebrew Bible that outline in more detail how the Feast of Weeks will be fulfilled in the millennium.[1]

---

1 As a reminder, the Feast of Weeks is called *Shavuot* in Hebrew and Pentecost based on its Greek name. In this chapter I will use these designations interchangeably.

THE FEAST OF WEEKS IN THE BOOK OF ACTS

After Jesus ascended to heaven, His disciples gathered in Jerusalem to await the outpouring of the Holy Spirit. At this time, Acts 2 tells us:

> When the day of Pentecost came they were all together in one place when suddenly a sound like a violent wind came from heaven and filled the whole house where they were sitting. And there appeared to them tongues as of fire distributing themselves, and they rested on each one of them. And they were all filled with the Holy Spirit and began to speak with other tongues, as the Spirit was giving them utterance. (Acts 2:1–4)

Because the Feast of Weeks was one of Israel's three major pilgrim festivals (Deut. 16:16), there would have been Jewish people "from every nation" in Jerusalem when the Spirit was poured out in Acts. As we read in Acts 2:9, at this time, "Parthians, Medes and Elamites, residents of Mesopotamia, Judea, Cappadocia, Pontus and Asia, Phrygia and Pamphylia, Egypt and parts of Libya near Cyrene; visitors from Rome (both Jews and converts to Judaism); Cretans and Arabs" (NIV) each heard the disciples "declaring the wonders of God" in their own tongue (Acts 2:11; NIV), and as a result, three thousand people were saved in one day (Acts 2:41).

Many scholars agree that the outpouring of the Spirit on Pentecost, when people from so many nations were present in Jerusalem, was the strategic mechanism that allowed the gospel to spread so rapidly in the first century. After the early converts to the messianic "Way" heard the gospel on Pentecost, they took the good news of the Messiah with them back to their nations—across Israel, Asia Minor, Europe, North Africa, Arabia, modern Iran—and beyond. Subsequently, they started small cell groups in their synagogues and local communities, which allowed the gospel to rapidly infiltrate the entire ancient world.

Furthermore, it was no coincidence that the ultimate harvest of souls into the kingdom of God started on Shavuot, the day that marked the completion of the spring harvest according to the biblical calendar. As we saw in the last chapter, on Shavuot there were two loaves of bread from the new wheat harvest that were waved before the Lord in the Jerusalem Temple, and we know from the timing of events in Acts 2 that this wheat offering in the Temple was made at the precise time the Holy Spirit was poured out on the early messianic community.

This correlation demonstrates that all along, the two wheat loaves of Shavuot prophetically symbolized Jew and Gentile, Israel and the nations, the two groups of people God planned to spiritually harvest and bring into the kingdom during this sacred time. Indeed, just as God aligned the Messiah's death and resurrection with Passover, Unleavened Bread, and First Fruits, He then continued following the biblical calendar by aligning the first spiritual harvest of souls in the New Testament with the Feast of Weeks forty-nine days later.

THE FEAST OF WEEKS & REVIVAL IN THE MILLENNIUM

Because of the consensus view on the feasts, which mistakenly maintains that the spring feasts were fulfilled through the Messiah's first coming, most teaching on the Feast of Weeks is built on the idea that the events recorded in Acts 2 exhausted the prophetic meaning of this harvest festival. However, just as this consensus view fails to properly explain the full prophetic depth of Passover, the same can also be said about the Feast of Weeks.

In other words, the Feast of Weeks was not entirely fulfilled in the first century AD. Rather, the historical events that took place on Shavuot in Acts 2 foreshadowed similar events that will occur in the early days of the Messiah's millennial reign.

The Hebrew prophets predicted that after the Second Coming, many people who survive the Tribulation will be physically gathered to Jerusalem and brought into the kingdom of God. Around this same time, a great outpouring of the Spirit upon Israel and the nations will take place, which in turn will lead to the full restoration of the earth during the millennium and the final prophetic fulfillment of the Feast of Weeks.

THE MIXED MULTITUDE IN THE MILLENNIUM

To paint a fuller picture of what will transpire when the Feast of Weeks is fulfilled in the future, we first need to understand the different types of people who will enter the millennial kingdom. Many Christians are under the impression that every person alive during the Tribulation who does not believe in Jesus will be killed either before He returns or shortly after His Second Coming. However, the Bible does not say that every nonbeliever will perish during the Seventieth Week, or when Jesus defeats the Antichrist and his armies. Instead, it indicates that some non-Christians will survive the end times and only come to saving faith in the days of the millennium.

For example, in Isaiah 13:12–13, God says this about the end times:

> I will punish the world for its evil, the wicked for their sins. I will put an end to the arrogance of the haughty and will humble the pride of the ruthless. I will make people scarcer than pure gold, more rare than the gold of Ophir. Therefore, I will make the heavens tremble; and the earth will shake from its place at the wrath of the Lord Almighty, in the day of His burning anger.

It cannot be denied that this text refers to harsh divine judgments that will be experienced on a worldwide scale during the end times (cf. Rev. 8–9, 16). However, notice that Isaiah also says some people will survive these days of judgment, like rare gold.

Similarly, Zechariah 14:16 speaks of "survivors from the nations" who will enter the millennial kingdom. So again, Scripture does not predict universal death on a worldwide scale during the end times. Rather, it predicts that there will be Jewish and Gentile nonbelievers (i.e., "survivors") who will be alive when Jesus returns and sets up His kingdom.

Therefore, just as many people did not believe in Jesus until they personally met Him at the time of His first coming, these Jews and Gentiles who survive the Tribulation will only experience messianic salvation after they encounter Jesus in the millennium, not before. God will preserve a remnant of Jews and Gentiles during the Tribulation and only bring them into a relationship with Himself after the Messiah returns.

THE FIRST AND SECOND RESURRECTION

Of course, we should also note here that those who place their faith in Jesus prior to His Second Coming (i.e., Old and New Testament saints) will have a much different experience in the millennium than those who get saved after He returns. For example, only people who believed in the Messiah before the Second Coming will live in their resurrection bodies during the millennium, because Scripture says "the first resurrection" (Rev. 20:6) is something that will only be experienced by existing believers and "the dead in Christ," who will be transformed and receive their glorified bodies when Jesus is revealed from heaven (1 Thess. 4:16–17; cf. Dan. 12:1–3).

However, the Bible also says that the Jewish remnant that survives the Tribulation and is rescued by Jesus at the time of the second exodus, as well as many other survivors from the nations, will still possess mortal bodies and experience an extended life followed by death during the millennium (Isa. 65:20). These people will be saved and receive the gift of eternal life in the long run. But they will not receive immortal resurrection bodies until the second resurrection, after the millennium (Rev. 20:4–6, 12–15).

THE FULFILLMENT OF THE FEAST OF WEEKS

The biblical material that specifies the different types of people who will enter the millennium is important, because it sets the stage for us to understand what will happen after the fulfillment of Passover in the kingdom of God, and more specifically, it is tied to the fulfillment of the Feast of Weeks. Whereas only a small remnant of Jewish Israelis will be delivered by Jesus and redeemed during the second exodus, the Feast of Weeks points forward to a broader gathering of survivors from the nations and a greater outpouring of the Holy Spirit that will occur in the early days of the Messiah's millennial reign, which will in turn result in the salvation of every nonbeliever still alive at that time and the complete renewal of every strata of society. Put simply, the Feast of Weeks foreshadows the epic spiritual and cultural revival that will launch the entire world into the glorious days of the millennium.

THE GATHERING OF JEWS AND GENTILES IN ISAIAH 66

Before the great outpouring of the Holy Spirit can take place in the millennium, many Jews and Gentiles from the nations will first have to be brought to the land of Israel after Jesus sets up His kingdom. For instance, Isaiah 66:18–21 says people from the nations will come to Jerusalem to see God's glory after the Second Coming, and this passage also uses the metaphor of the wheat harvest to describe these events. In this passage we read:

> "The time is coming to gather all nations and tongues. And they shall come and see My glory. I will set a sign among them and will send survivors from them to the nations: Tarshish, Put, Lud, Meshech, Tubal and Javan, to the distant coastlands that have neither heard My fame nor seen My glory. And they will declare My glory among the nations. Then they shall bring all your brethren from all the nations as a grain offering to the LORD, on horses, in chariots, in wagons, on mules and on camels, to My holy mountain Jerusalem," says the LORD, "just as the sons of Israel bring their grain offering in a clean vessel to the house of the LORD. I will also take some of them for priests and for Levites," says the LORD. (Isa. 66:18–21)

Notice how this passage refers to some type of "sign" the Lord will send to the nations after Jesus returns, which will reveal the truth of God to them. This sign will then be followed by evangelists who will go into these nations to preach the gospel of the kingdom.

Additionally, because these evangelists are called "survivors" in verse 19, these could very well be members of the Jewish remnant who survive the Seventieth Week and get rescued from captivity in the Middle East and North Africa during the second exodus. Thus, the picture here is one in which Jewish survivors who participate in the fulfillment of Passover then travel into the rest of the world to gather their scattered Jewish "brethren," as well as people from "all nations and tongues," so they too can meet the Messiah and see His glory in Jerusalem. With remarkable detail, Isaiah describes these newly harvested individuals from the nations being brought like a "grain offering" on "horses, in chariots, wagons, on mules, and on camels" to Jerusalem (Isa. 66:20), just as the wheat offerings were originally brought to the holy city for the Feast of Weeks in ancient times.

THE MILLENNIAL HARVEST IN ISAIAH 49 & ZECHARIAH 8

Another key text that refers to this millennial harvest of souls is Isaiah 49:22–23. These verses say that the peoples of the earth will bring the sons and daughters of the Jewish people "in their bosom" and "on their shoulders" back to Jerusalem, while kings serve as "their guardians" and princesses as their "nurses." In a divine turnaround, whereas the nations of the earth will seek to destroy Israel during the end times, in the future kingdom the royal families of the Gentile nations will serve as the elite security forces of God's chosen people, ensuring their safe passage back to the Promised Land.

As a result, Zechariah said that during the millennium, "old men and old women will again sit in the streets of Jerusalem, each man with his staff in his hand because of age, and [...] the city will be filled with boys and girls playing in the streets" (Zech. 8:4–5). Though this might seem like an absurd possibility during the final days of the Tribulation, God declares:

> "If it is too difficult in the sight of the remnant of this people in those days, will it also be too difficult in My sight?" declares the Lord of hosts. Thus says the Lord of hosts, "Behold, I am going to save My people from the land of the east and from the land of the west; and I will bring them back and they will live in the midst of Jerusalem; and they shall be My people, and I will be their God in truth and righteousness." (Zech. 8:6–8)

While promising that Jerusalem will experience peace and total security in the messianic age, the Hebrew prophets also spoke of the millennium as a time when the land of Israel will be blessed with agricultural abundance like never before. Consequently, we read in Joel 2:24 that "the threshing floors will be full of grain" after God saves Israel, and in Deuteronomy 33:28 Moses prophesied that in the days of messianic redemption the Jewish people will dwell securely "in a land of grain and new wine."

THE FULFILLMENT OF THE FEAST OF WEEKS

While it is true that there is no direct reference to the Feast of Weeks in these millennial-harvest passages in Isaiah and Zechariah, many of the concepts and themes in the above passages harmonize with what we see in other texts that deal more directly with Shavuot; namely, the harvest of souls from among the nations and agricultural abundance in the land of Israel. Also, because the harvested nations in Isaiah 66 are called a "grain offering," this passage does evoke the Feast of Weeks in some way, because even though grain was offered in the Temple at other times, the Feast of Weeks was the only appointed time that focused exclusively on the grain offering.

For this reason, because Paul said the biblical feasts are a "shadow of what is to come" (Col. 2:17), it is likely that when he pondered the Feast of Weeks, he had this gathering of Jews and Gentiles to Jerusalem in the millennial kingdom in mind, as well as how the Feast of Weeks prophetically foreshadows the abundant harvest of grain products from the earth in the future. In the same way the Feast of Weeks was an extension of the first-fruits barley harvest that began two days after Passover in ancient Israel (Lev. 23:15–16), it appears that in the kingdom the Feast of Weeks will also be an extension of the initial harvest of souls that will begin many weeks earlier, when Jesus returns to fulfill the Passover.

In God's mercy, Jews and Gentiles from the nations who survive the Tribulation will be brought to the holy city as part of a great harvest of souls that will take place very soon after Jesus returns. Imagine people from Africa with dark black skin, South Americans speaking multiple dialects of Spanish and Portuguese, and Asians from the most remote parts of the world wearing colorful silk garments, flocking to the Holy Land on horseback and camels with multitudes of Jewish people whose forefathers had lived in exile for over two thousand years. As they arrive in Jerusalem they are then greeted by believers and saints who are already in the city, who usher them into the presence of the great Divine Warrior they had up to that point only heard about through amazing tales in the early days after the Second Coming.

We may have to use our creative mind to fill in some of the details here, but this is precisely the type of harvest of souls that the biblical prophets envisioned at the dawn of the messianic age. And personally, I will not be surprised if this great gathering of sinners and saints to Jerusalem occurs sometime in the late spring, as part of an initial Feast of Weeks celebration in the kingdom of God.

Leviticus 23:16	Isaiah 66:20
"You shall count fifty days to the day after the seventh sabbath; then you shall present a new grain offering (*mincha*) to the Lord."	"Then they shall bring all your brethren from all the nations as a grain offering (*mincha*) to the Lord, on horses, in chariots, in litters, on mules, and on camels, to My holy mountain in Jerusalem."

THE OUTPOURING OF THE HOLY SPIRIT IN THE KINGDOM OF GOD

After the physical regathering of the nations to Jerusalem, God will then initiate the greatest outpouring of the Holy Spirit ever witnessed in the history of mankind. Indeed, though many people are not accustomed to thinking about the central role the Holy Spirit will play in world affairs in the future, the Spirit of God will in fact be the primary agent of renewal during the millennial age.

THE SPIRIT AND THE KINGDOM IN JOHN 3

There are many reasons why the Spirit will have to be poured out after the Second Coming, but the first has to do with something Jesus said about the nature of the kingdom in John 3. This passage records a conversation between Jesus and Nicodemus in which our Messiah said, "unless one is born again they cannot see the kingdom of heaven." In this same context, Jesus also clarifies that being born again is synonymous with being "born of the Spirit" (John 3:5).

In most cases when John 3 is discussed by believers today, the emphasis is placed on the need to believe in Jesus *before* He returns, which is definitely a good thing. However, Jesus' words here also have a broader application. They confirm that even those people who are harvested and brought to Jerusalem *after* Jesus returns will have to be born again of the Spirit of God, otherwise, based on the words of Jesus, they will not be able to live in the kingdom. As a result, since we know there will be many nonbelievers who will survive the Tribulation (cf. Isa. 13:12–13; Zech. 14:16), John 3 does implicitly point forward to a great spiritual awakening that will occur after the Second Coming.

THE OUTPOURING OF THE SPIRIT IN JOEL 2:28–29

Not surprisingly, there are many passages in the Hebrew Bible that speak of how God will pour out His Spirit upon Israel and the nations at the start of the millennium. For example, in Joel 2:28–29, Joel prophesied:

> It will come about after this, that I will pour out My Spirit on all mankind; and your sons and daughters will prophesy, your old men will dream dreams, your young men will see visions. Even on the male and female servants. I will pour out My Spirit in those days.

Usually when Joel 2:28–29 is referenced, it is interpreted as though it only predicts a coming revival before the return of Jesus. When read carefully, however, we can see that this text is concerned with an outpouring of the Spirit that will occur after Jesus returns, in the millennium.

Notice how verse 28 says, "It will come about *after this*, that I will pour out My Spirit on all mankind" (emphasis added). This language implies that the outpouring of the Spirit occurs subsequent to something else, which obviously reveals the timing of the spiritual revival referred to in verses 28–29.

In the immediately preceding context, in verses 18–27, God speaks of the time when He will bless Israel and dwell among the nation. For example, in verse 27 we read:

> Thus you will know that I am in the midst of Israel, and that I am the LORD your God, and there is no other; and My people will never be put to shame. (Joel 2:27)

Because the outpouring of the Spirit in Joel 2:28 occurs after these events in verse 27, we know Joel was focused here on a spiritual revival that will materialize during the millennium. After all, it will only be in the millennium that God will dwell in the midst of Israel and that Israel will know God and never again experience shame or persecution (vv. 18–27). The basic flow of events in Joel 2:17–29 can be outlined in the following way: God rescues Israel from their enemies, blesses the land, dwells in Jerusalem, and pours out the Holy Spirit on the entire world, after which all the inhabitants of the millennium will experience miracles, signs, wonders, supernatural dreams, visions, and the gift of prophecy as never before.

Of course, as we saw earlier, there was already a partial fulfillment of Joel 2:28–29 in the first century. This is why the Apostle Peter quoted Joel 2 when describing the first outpouring of the Spirit on the day of Pentecost in the book of Acts (Acts 2:14–21). Also, because we are called to pray for God's kingdom to come now (Matt. 6:10), it is certainly right for us to pursue the Spirit in this life and to work towards a last-days revival that will usher in another partial fulfillment of Joel 2:28–29.

Nevertheless, as important as the work of the Spirit is to us in this age, we must still accept that every outpouring of the Spirit prior to the return of Jesus points forward to the ultimate spiritual awakening that will only be realized after His Second Coming. Joel 2:28–29 was partially fulfilled in Acts 2, during the Feast of Weeks, and it has also been partially fulfilled many other times throughout history. But at the most basic level this prophecy is about the outpouring of the Spirit upon Israel and the nations in the kingdom of God.

Moreover, because the initial outpouring of the Spirit took place on Shavuot in the book of Acts, we have every reason to believe that the outpouring of the Spirit in the kingdom of God will take place at the same time as well, after the great harvest of Jews and Gentiles has been gathered to Jerusalem during the seven-week period that follows Passover (Isa. 66:18–21). In other words, I believe it is possible that the initial fulfillment of Joel 2:28–29 on the day of Pentecost in Acts 2 foreshadowed the final fulfillment of this prophecy on the day of Pentecost in the millennium.

The greatest spiritual revivals of the past will pale in comparison to the revivals we will witness when Jesus returns. The messianic age will indeed be the age of the Spirit.

THE OUTPOURING OF THE SPIRIT IN ZECHARIAH 12:10

Like Joel 2:28–29, Zechariah 12:10 also predicts the outpouring of the Spirit, particularly upon the Jewish remnant, in the kingdom. This verse states:

> I will pour out on the house of David and on the inhabitants of Jerusalem, the Spirit of grace and of supplication, so that they will look on Me whom they have pierced; and they will mourn for Him, as one mourns for an only son, and they will weep bitterly over Him like the bitter weeping over a firstborn. (Zech. 12:10)

Notably, this outpouring of the Spirit in Zechariah happens right after God destroys "all the nations that come against Jerusalem" (Zech. 12:9). Based on this language, we know we are looking here at a spiritual outpouring that will occur after the Antichrist has been defeated, in the early days of the millennium.

THE OUTPOURING OF THE SPIRIT IN EZEKIEL 39:28–29

One final text worth noting that details the role of the Spirit in the kingdom is Ezekiel 39:28–29. This text complements Joel 2:28–29 and Zechariah 12:10 and also speaks of how God will baptize Israel in the Spirit at the start of the millennium. We read:

> Then they will know that I am the Lord their God because I made them go into exile among the nations, and then gathered them again to their own land; and I will leave none of them there any longer. I will not hide My face from them any longer, for I will have poured out My Spirit on the house of Israel," declares the Lord God.

The flow of events in this passage is remarkably similar to the flow of events in Joel 2 and Zechariah 12. Ezekiel predicts that Israel will experience a time of discipline and exile in the last days, but then be gathered back to their own land, enter into a relationship with God, and experience an outpouring of the Spirit. Furthermore, because we know the preceding verses in Ezekiel 38–39 about the Gog of Magog war refer to the Time of Jacob's Trouble, the defeat of the Antichrist, and the final fulfillment of Passover, we can be confident that the outpouring of the Spirit referred to in Ezekiel 39:29 will take place after the Messiah returns, most likely as the kingdom fulfillment of the Feast of Weeks.

THE ROLE OF THE SPIRIT IN THE MILLENNIUM

When we survey these key passages in Joel, Zechariah, and Ezekiel, we can see that many of the Hebrew prophets understood the central role the Spirit of God will play in the salvation of Israel and the nations in the millennium. At one level, these passages speak of the Spirit's work in bringing Jews and Gentiles to saving faith in the kingdom of God.

For example, when Zechariah 12:10 says the Jewish people will look upon the pierced Messiah with eyes of faith and mourn for Him, he has in mind some type of saving faith encounter the Jewish remnant will have with Jesus after the Seventieth Week. When Joel mentions in Joel 2:28 that the Spirit will be poured out upon all mankind at the start of the millennium, this too implies that the Spirit will supernaturally reveal the essence of the gospel to those who survive the Tribulation, which will cause them to be "born of the Spirit" so they can enter the kingdom of heaven (John 3:5).

In other places, the Spirit's sanctifying work in the millennium is emphasized as well. Along these lines, in Ezekiel 36:27 God said to Israel: "I will put My Spirit within you and cause you to walk in My statutes, and you will be careful to observe My ordinances."

This verse in Ezekiel connects the Spirit's work not only to saving faith, but also to the sanctification of the Jewish nation. Here we see that in the messianic kingdom, the Holy Spirit will be the primary transformative agent who will enable Israel and the nations to walk righteously before the Lord.

THE SPIRITUAL ENVIRONMENT OF THE MILLENNIUM

Understanding that the Spirit will save and sanctify Israel and the nations after the Second Coming also clarifies some important points regarding the spiritual environment of the millennium. Many readers might wonder if people who are saved after Jesus returns will still be able to sin.

This question is raised because whereas people who believe in Jesus prior to His return will receive their resurrection bodies and experience moral perfection at the time of the Second Coming (1 Cor. 15:52), the survivors who get saved after the Second Coming will still possess mortal bodies subject to death during the millennium, and they also will not attain spiritual perfection until the second resurrection, which will occur only after the one thousand years of the millennium (Rev. 20:11–15). This all means that, at least in theory, some people could still be able to commit acts of sin after Jesus returns.

At the same time, however, the passages that speak of the spiritual outpourings that will occur during the millennium also imply that sin will be greatly reduced at this time, if not mostly eradicated. Paul says in Ephesians 5 that idolatry and immorality have no place in the kingdom of God (Eph. 5:5), so this indicates that the sanctifying work of the Spirit in the kingdom will be so potent that even those harvested after the Second Coming will, for all intents and purposes, be unable to fall into such sins. Additionally, Revelation 20:1–3 tells us that Satan will be bound for the thousand years of the millennium and unable to deceive the nations, which cancels out the possibility of widespread spiritual deception in the millennial kingdom as well.

Consequently, spiritual deception and personal sin, even among those who only get saved after Jesus returns, will be virtually nonexistent in the messianic age. Through the work of the Spirit, the millennium will be a time when righteousness prevails on the earth and over every sector of society. Imagine living in a world where everyone is saved, baptized in the Holy Spirit, and living for the Lord. That's the millennium.

OUR SPIRITUAL EXPERIENCE IN THE MILLENNIUM

In addition to the Spirit's general work that will cause many people to be born again and walk in righteousness after Jesus returns, it is important to note that Joel also highlights how the Spirit will lead the inhabitants of the millennium into an abundance of supernatural experiences. As noted earlier, Joel 2:28–29 says dreams and visions, as well as the gift of prophecy, will be experienced on a massive scale after the Second Coming.

This is a remarkable detail about the millennium that is too often overlooked. Joel makes clear that the millennium will not be a time when spiritual revelation from the Spirit decreases or disappears. Rather, the millennium will be a time when prophetic giftings and supernatural revelations from the Lord will be experienced to an even greater degree than they are now.

We have to assume that there will be at least tens of thousands of people, if not many more, who will survive the Tribulation and enter the kingdom of God after Jesus returns. Regardless of the exact number, what Joel hints at is that these people will have prophetic dreams and visions of Jesus, and as a result, they will traverse land and sea to meet Him in Jerusalem at the start of the millennium.

THE PROPHETIC AWAKENING IN THE MILLENNIUM

At this point, some readers might also wonder what need there will be for the gift of prophecy in the messianic kingdom. After all, won't most prophecies be fulfilled at this time?

To be sure, most prophecies will be fulfilled after Jesus returns, but the gift of prophecy concerns much more than simply predicting the future. More fundamentally, the gift of prophecy imparts a supernatural ability to explain and apply the Word of God for the present time. Thus, when Joel 2:28 says, "your sons and daughters will prophesy" in the messianic age, this implies that prophetic teaching and proclamation about God, His Word, and His plan of salvation will lead to the spiritual awakening that will materialize after the Second Coming.

Remember, the world will not be magically saved and renewed after Jesus returns. Instead, God will use many of the same instruments He uses today to do His work, though on a grander scale.

A multitude from among Israel and the nations will still have to be brought into the faith and discipled after Jesus returns, and the Spirit will be the primary agent of renewal who will aid God's people as they work to fulfill His redemptive plan. Through dreams, visions, and miraculous words of prophecy, the mystery of the gospel will be proclaimed throughout the world and the entire "earth will be filled with the knowledge of the glory of the LORD as the waters cover the sea" (Hab. 2:14). Throughout the messianic era, we will listen to the best sermons we have ever heard, and many of you reading this will be mighty prophetic preachers in the days of the kingdom.

On that note, I should also add that it will not only be those who are saved after the Second Coming who will receive this mighty baptism of the Spirit in the millennium. I mention this because there are hints in the New Testament that in the messianic age even glorified and resurrected believers will experience the Spirit in a more miraculous way than ever before. As a matter of fact, we will likely be the ones who will lead the spiritual awakening after the Second Coming, and we have every reason to believe that the dreams, visions, and gifts of prophecy mentioned in Joel 2:28 will be imparted not only to those who get saved after Jesus returns, but to us as well (more on this later).

THE HOLY SPIRIT AND PHYSICAL AND EMOTIONAL HEALING IN THE MILLENNIUM

Another aspect of the Spirit's work that is often emphasized in the Bible is His ability to effectuate physical and emotional healing for God's people. In Isaiah 61:1, for example, the Messiah is anointed with the Spirit, which enables Him to "bind up the brokenhearted" and proclaim "liberty to captives." According to Luke 4:18–19, Jesus quoted this passage at the start of His healing ministry because he understood that healing the sick and casting out demons was to be a central part of His Spirit-empowered outreach to the world.

Furthermore, while the healing ministry of Jesus in the first century was glorious and important, because the work of the Spirit is emphasized in so many prophecies that deal with the millennium, there is no reason to doubt that Jesus will continue to heal the sick and cast out demons in the early days of His millennial reign. After He returns, the Divine Healer from Nazareth will once again go to war against infirmity and spiritual oppression. He will lay His powerful hands on those afflicted with a multitude of diseases and health conditions, and bring the inhabitants of the earth into a place of holistic spiritual, mental, emotional, and physical well-being. The lame will walk, the blind will see, and the burdened and tormented masses will finally be at peace, as the prophecy in Isaiah 61 reaches its eschatological end goal through the work of God's Spirit-empowered Anointed One.

CULTURAL RENEWAL IN THE MILLENNIUM

In a fascinating way, the biblical prophets also reveal that the Spirit will play a central role in the renewal of governments, architecture, art, music, and broader society during the millennium. For example, throughout the Bible the Spirit is associated with political ability, and in Isaiah 11:1–5 the Messiah is said to have "the Spirit of the LORD," which gives Him "wisdom, understanding," "counsel," and the "ability to judge" righteously (cf. Judg. 3:10; 14:6). Furthermore, though Jesus will of course be the chief King who will rule in the power of the Spirit during the millennium, there are many other passages that indicate that He will delegate rule of the nations to His followers.

We see this in the famous parable of the talents in Luke 19, in which Jesus says His followers who use their gifts wisely in this fallen world will rule over various cities in the kingdom of God. Also, in Revelation 2:27 Jesus said that His followers who overcome temptation will be given "authority over the nations," and "rule them with a rod of iron" when He returns. In a remarkable way, this passage in Revelation applies a messianic Psalm not only to the Messiah Himself, but to His followers as well (cf. Ps. 2), and Revelation 20:6 adds that those who take part in the first resurrection will "reign with Him [Jesus] for a thousand years."

This collection of prophecies reveals that even as Jesus will rule in the power of the Spirit in the age to come (Isa. 11:1–5), so too will His followers. The Holy Spirit will give Christians and messianic Jews the ability to exercise righteous governmental rule over the nations in the kingdom of God, and even now the Lord is preparing us to be His co-regents in the age to come.

In terms of architecture, music, and art, these are aspects of society and culture that are frequently associated with the Holy Spirit in the Bible as well. Exodus 31:3 says that Bezalel, the chief architect of the Mosaic Tabernacle, was "filled with the Spirit of God," which enabled him to beautify God's sanctuary. Moreover, in Ephesians 5:18–19, Paul connects being "filled with the Spirit" to "singing and making music."

This connection between the Spirit and the arts, in both the Old and New Testaments, indicates that the most beautiful, Spirit-inspired music, architecture, and art ever seen in the history of mankind will be produced during the millennium. Though Scripture does not offer much detail on the particulars, I imagine that the activities of the Spirit in these areas during the millennium will be very surprising to many people.

The great artistic achievements of humanity are not reserved only for this current age of sin and darkness. Instead, the nations will be rebuilt during the millennium with the most breathtaking architecture ever seen, and we will enjoy a quality of food, music, and art that we cannot yet fathom. Various cultural styles will be preserved in each of these areas, from classical forms to tribal and ethnic varieties. People will live in houses and wear beautiful clothes and jewelry, cities will be constructed, fields will be planted, churches will be established, and concerts, worship nights, community meals, and art openings will be hosted. But all things will be done unto the Lord and sanctified by the imagination and inspiration of the Spirit.

Indeed, to grasp just how tangible and earthly our lives will be after the Second Coming, we must understand that the millennium will not be the age when we will fly off to heaven to float on a cloud forever. Rather, it will be the age when the Holy Spirit will reap a harvest from the earth, renew all things, and begin the process of building a completely new world.

As we read in Isaiah 61:4–7:

> They will rebuild the ancient ruins and restore the places long devastated; they will renew the ruined cities that have been devastated for generations. [...] You will feed on the wealth of nations, and in their riches you will boast. Instead of your shame you will receive a double portion, and instead of disgrace you will rejoice in your inheritance. And so you will inherit a double portion in your land, and everlasting joy will be yours.

Or in the words of Psalm 37:10:

> In a little while the wicked will be no more; though you look for them, they will not be found. But the meek will inherit the earth and enjoy peace and prosperity.

Beautiful architecture, the enjoyment of riches, good food, and other earthly delights that will be better than anything this world could ever offer is what the Spirit has prepared for us in the millennium. God may call us to endure poverty and affliction in this life. But His long-term plan is to make us all very rich, and to use us in diverse ways to renew every aspect of culture, society, and civilization after the Second Coming.

THE AGE OF THE SPIRIT

When Christians and messianic Jews today anticipate the Second Coming, we often focus exclusively on Jesus Himself. One reason for this is that it is easier to imagine a face-to-face relationship with Jesus than it is to imagine an intangible relationship with the Spirit.

As much as we all long to see Jesus face-to-face, however, there should be more emphasis on the person of the Holy Spirit and the role He will play in our lives in the millennial kingdom. Unfortunately, we often overlook that the Second Coming has just as much to do with the coming of the Spirit in fullness as it does with the coming of the incarnate Son of God.

In the millennial kingdom, we will not only see Jesus in the flesh, but we will also live our entire lives in intimate fellowship with the Holy Spirit to a greater degree than ever before. Even as the Spirit is given to us now to lead us through the darkness of this fallen world, He will also be given to us after Jesus returns in the fullest measure possible, in order to bring us into the deepest depths of our inheritance as children of God.

In Romans 8:23, Paul said that as long as we live in our mortal bodies we only have "the first fruits of the Spirit." Stop for a minute and consider the profound implications of this statement: Having only the "first fruits of the Spirit" now means there is a lot more to come.

Imagine the most powerful worship service you have ever been in, or the most enlightening time of Bible study you have ever experienced, or the most anointed preaching, or maybe even dreams, visions, and miracles from God that you have witnessed. Or maybe you are an artistic person who experiences the inspiration of the Spirit through writing, making art, or building and remodeling projects.

Everything you have experienced of the Spirit in some or all of these areas now is only the first fruits of what God has in store for His people. The biblical prophets reveal that in the age to come, the Holy Spirit will be so close to us that we will walk with Him, hear His voice, and sense His presence, His love, His power, and His kindness on a day-by-day, moment-by-moment, second-by-second basis. We will sit with fellow believers at the dinner table, break bread over a delicious meal, and experience the richest spiritual fellowship and delight in each other's company, as we talk about the Bible, nature, history, theology, food, music, and art. We will be led in praise and worship by the most artistically and spiritually-gifted musicians of all time, and our souls will be carried away to the heights of joy as we sing new songs, hear new instruments, and bow down before the King of kings. We will sit in beautiful silence and contemplation in nature as the peace of the Holy Spirit washes over us and removes every extraneous thought from our minds and centers our attention only on the love of God. We will plumb the depths of God's being as the Spirit reveals to us the most profound mysteries of the universe, on topics ranging from science, to mathematics, to theology. Like Ezekiel and Daniel, we will see open visions of God's glory and receive personal words of encouragement and direction from the Spirit daily. And perhaps most importantly, we will finally overcome our sin nature and never again rebel against the Lord, in thought, word, or deed.

Through the Spirit in the millennial kingdom, all of creation will be brought into union with the life of God, and through the Spirit, all of creation and every aspect of society will reflect His intelligence, beauty, joy, humility, and love. In many ways, the messianic age will be the age of the Spirit, and we must get the idea out of our heads that what we experience of the Spirit now somehow exhausts all that we ever could experience.

There is always more, and there will certainly be much more to come. Now we have the first fruits of the Spirit, but soon the final harvest.

THE FEAST OF WEEKS IN THE KINGDOM OF GOD

Like we saw with Passover, the future prophetic significance of the Feast of Weeks is often overlooked when believers are considering how the biblical feasts relate to the Second Coming of the Messiah. This is because the Feast of Weeks is a spring feast, which leads many to believe that it only has a past-tense prophetic fulfillment.

To be sure, the Feast of Weeks was partially fulfilled on the day of Pentecost in the first century (Acts 2). However, in this chapter we have seen that the Feast of Weeks also foreshadows many glorious events that will take place in the millennial kingdom, after the Messiah returns. In the words of messianic Jewish scholar Daniel Juster, "Shavuot is fraught with eschatological meaning and looks forward to the day when the Spirit is poured out on the whole world and the Age of the Spirit is fully established."[2]

Below are the four main points we covered in this chapter that outline the future fulfillment of the Feast of Weeks:

1. As the climactic harvest festival in the spring, the Feast of Weeks points forward to the abundant harvest of Jews and Gentiles who will survive the Tribulation and be gathered to Israel after Jesus returns (Isa. 66:18–21).

2. In addition, the Feast of Weeks also points forward to a great outpouring of the Holy Spirit upon Israel and the nations in the kingdom of God, which will mirror the original outpouring of the Spirit on the day of Pentecost in the book of Acts (Joel 2:28–29; Ezek. 39:29; Zech. 10:10–14; Ezek. 36:27).

3. After the Holy Spirit is poured out in the millennial age, He will serve as the primary agent of salvation, sanctification, and reconstruction among God's people. Through the Spirit, all the inhabitants of the kingdom will enter into a supernatural relationship with God and take part in the

2 Daniel Juster, *Jewish Roots: Understanding Your Jewish Faith* (Shippensburg: Destiny Image, 2013), 259.

renewal of the world through architecture, city planning, agriculture, music, food, the arts, etc. (Exod. 31:3–6; Eph. 5:19; Isa. 61:4).

4. The New Testament teaches that prior to the Second Coming, believers only have the first fruits of the Holy Spirit. This implies that after Jesus returns, we will experience the Spirit to an exponentially greater degree than we do now, on both an individual and corporate level (Rom. 8:23).

BIBLE STUDY QUESTIONS

1. What did you learn about the Feast of Weeks and the millennium?

2. Which biblical prophecies related to the Feast of Weeks encouraged you the most in your walk with God?

3. Why is Joel 2:17–29 so important as we seek to establish a sequence of events that will unfold in the millennium?

4. How do you think the work of the Holy Spirit in the millennium should impact our church and congregational life today?

6

THE FEAST OF TRUMPETS IN HISTORICAL CONTEXT

THE FEAST OF TRUMPETS is the first biblical feast that takes place in the fall, roughly four months after the Feast of Weeks. Typically, the Feast of Trumpets occurs near the beginning or middle of September on our modern calendars, but in the Bible, it is the appointed time that marks the start of the highly significant seventh month:

> Again the LORD spoke to Moses, saying, "Speak to the sons of Israel, saying, 'In the seventh month on the first of the month you shall have a rest, a reminder by blowing of trumpets [*zichron teruah*], a holy convocation. You shall not do any laborious work, but you shall present an offering by fire to the LORD.'" (Lev. 23:23–25)

There is less said about the Feast of Trumpets in Leviticus 23 than any of the other biblical feasts, and for this reason, the purpose and significance of this festival has often been established more through tradition and speculation than a close study of the Scriptures. Be that as it may, what we will discover in this chapter is that the Feast of Trumpets does have a core biblical meaning that is deeply rooted in Israel's national history.

To be more specific, the Feast of Trumpets was the commemoration of Israel's encounter with the Lord at Mount Sinai. This holy day was the annual reminder of the peoples' covenant with their God, and it was also closely tied to the Lord's enthronement as King of the Israelite nation.

THE FEAST OF TRUMPETS AND THE NEW YEAR (ROSH HASHANAH)

In modern Judaism, the Feast of Trumpets is synonymous with the Jewish New Year, which is called *Rosh HaShanah*, meaning, the head of the year. As a matter of fact, Jewish people today generally do not call the Feast of Trumpets by its biblical name (Heb: *Zichron Teruah)*[1] but will instead refer to this festival exclusively as Rosh HaShanah.

As we discussed in chapter 1, the biblical new year begins in the spring, fourteen days before Passover, on the first day of the first month (Aviv/Nisan). With this in mind, many readers might wonder how the Feast of Trumpets in the seventh month was eventually transformed into the Jewish New Year.

Various theories have been proposed to explain this development, and one of the most likely possibilities is that the Feast of Trumpets became Rosh HaShanah as a result of the Babylonian captivity of Judah, which began circa 605 BC. Like the Israelites, the Babylonians also used a twelve-month lunar calendar and had major festivals, called the Akitu, in the first and seventh months. And, like the Israelite moedim, the Babylonian Akitu was held close to the spring and autumnal equinox, as well as the spring and fall harvest.

The equinox occurs when there is twelve hours of daylight and

1 This Hebrew phrase literally means a "memorial of blasting or shouting," and we will soon analyze its significance in more detail.

twelve hours of nighttime in a twenty-four-hour period. In the northern hemisphere, the spring equinox marks the time when the days begin to grow longer, and the fall equinox marks the time when the days begin to grow shorter.

Many ancient cultures built their religious calendars around these two equinoxes, one which occurred in the spring, in the first month, and one which occurred in the fall, in the seventh month, because they both marked an important transition point in the year, and they were both connected to the harvest of key crops (barley in the spring and grapes, olives, and other fruits in the fall). In Babylon in particular, though the Babylonians had an important festival in the first month (Akitu 1), many scholars have noted that their festival in the seventh month (Akitu 2), which coincided with the fall equinox, took on greater importance and became closely associated with a time of new beginning for the people. As a result, the Babylonians essentially utilized what some scholars have called a "six-month equinox year" with a new beginning in the spring (in the first month) and a new beginning in the fall (in the seventh month).

In the words of historian Mark Cohen:

> In addition to the seasonal cycle and the lunar cycle, the Mesopotamians were affected by a third cycle—the cycle between the equinoxes, a period when the sun and the moon vied with each other for time in the sky. [...] This concept of the six-month equinox year appears to have been a major factor in the establishment of the cultic calendar throughout the Near East. In many locations there were parallel major festivals in the first and seventh month—suggesting that rather than considering one of these festivals as marking the beginning and the other the half-way point of the year, the ancients viewed each as a beginning, the onset of this six-month equinox year.
>
> This concept of two six-month periods defined by the equinoxes was further ingrained in the Mesopotamian psyche by the natural weather pattern of the seasonal year. The Babylonians divided the seasonal year into two periods, each beginning in the month of an

equinox. The summer [...], the hot season, or harvest season [...] began around March; the winter [...] or cold season [...] began around September."[2]

While there is nothing in the Bible that links the Feast of Trumpets to the New Year, because it occurred on the first day of the seventh month, right around the time of the fall equinox, it is not hard to see why this holiday became attached to celebrations of new beginning at some point in Israelite history. In addition, because so many Jewish people continued to live in Babylon from 605 BC onward, it is likely that as a result of Babylonian influence the first Israelite appointed time in the seventh month (i.e., the Feast of Trumpets) was eventually transformed into the Jewish New Year (Rosh HaShanah).

I should also add here that some scholars believe there were already New-Year elements linked to the seventh month in Israel prior to the Babylonian exile. This may or may not be true. But regardless, it is a verifiable fact that what we know of today as Rosh HaShanah did not exist until after the Babylonian exile, and it was probably Babylonian influence upon the Jewish religion that caused the merger of the Feast of Trumpets and the New Year (Rosh HaShanah). Notably, it is only in the Jewish literature written after the Babylonian exile, including the Babylonian Talmud, that we see this connection between the Feast of Trumpets and the New Year made in a direct way, which likely confirms that the Babylonian captivity formalized the observance of Rosh HaShanah in Judaism.

In any case, I hasten to clarify that the possible relationship between Babylonian traditions and Rosh HaShanah does not mean it is pagan or inherently wrong to celebrate the Jewish New Year in the seventh month. Traditions and cultural practices are not necessarily evil, and it is no more pagan to celebrate Rosh HaShanah in the seventh month

2 Mark E. Cohen, *The Cultic Calendars of the Ancient Near East* (Church: Capital Decisions, 1993), 6–7.

than it is to celebrate the modern New Year on January 1, or a person's birthday at another time of year. As long as one recognizes that celebrating the Jewish New Year at this time is a tradition, it is not a problem, and personally, I find many Rosh HaShanah traditions to be beautiful and harmless.

Yet still, one persistent problem created by this merger of Rosh HaShanah and the Feast of Trumpets is that it does often obscure the biblical meaning of the latter. In other words, because the "first day in the seventh month" has become so intricately interwoven with the New Year in Jewish tradition, there is usually very little thought given to what this day signified in its original historical context in ancient Israel. Additionally, when the historical significance of the Feast of Trumpets is marginalized, this in turn also stops people from understanding both the practical and prophetic implications of this festival, which leads to a whole new set of problems.

To help us avoid some of these common pitfalls, in the rest of this chapter we will take a closer look at how the ancient Israelites would have understood the Feast of Trumpets when it was first instituted thirty-five hundred years ago. Then, in the next chapter, we will explore how the Feast of Trumpets also foreshadows events that will unfold in the millennial kingdom.

A MEMORIAL OF TRUMPET BLASTS & SHOUTING

In Leviticus 23:23–25, the first day in the seventh month is called, "a reminder by blowing trumpets" (NASB). Interestingly, the word "trumpets" is not actually present in the Hebrew text, so a more literal rendering would be, "a reminder by blowing" or "a reminder by blasting" (Heb.: Zichron Teruah).

The term "blowing" or "blasting" is the Hebrew teruah, and in general this word denotes a very loud sound. In some passages teruah is used to depict the blast of a trumpet (Lev. 25:9; Num. 10:5–6; 31:6; Zeph. 1:16). However, in many other contexts teruah means to "shout" or to "raise an alarm" with one's voice in an extravagant manner (Josh. 6:5; 6:20;

1 Sam. 4:5–6; 2 Sam. 6:15; Ezra 3:11–13; Jer. 49:2).

The ambiguity surrounding the word teruah (i.e., blasting or shouting) in Leviticus 23:24, and the absence of the word "trumpets" in this verse, is interesting. It is probable that the blast (teruah) of the trumpet is implied here. However, it is also probable that the original Feast of Trumpets involved human shouting (teruah) in response to the trumpet blast (teruah) as well.

In his excellent article "Rosh HaShanah: The Original Meaning of Blowing a Teruah" Rabbi Shawn Ruby proves that the teruah on the first day of the seventh month in ancient Israel included not only the trumpet blast, but also "a sound people make in response to hearing the blast of a horn."[3] For example, he cites the story in Joshua that recounts Israel's experience outside of Jericho, and notes that when Israel surrounded the city they heard the trumpet sound and then let out a great shout (ruah) to implore the Lord's blessing before they invaded (Josh. 6:16). Similarly, in Numbers 10:9, God commanded Israel to "sound an alarm (ruah) with the trumpets, that you may be remembered before the LORD your God, and be saved from your enemies."

Joshua 6:16 and Numbers 10:9 use the verbal root of teruah, which is ruah, but this word means the same things as the word that appears in Leviticus 23:24 (teruah), and the interplay between these passages demonstrates that the teruah of Leviticus would have included both human shouting and trumpet blasts. Additionally, the series of events in Joshua and Numbers also indicates that the teruah of Leviticus would have operated in two directions. In other words, the teruah was directed at Israel and was meant to awaken their attention, but it was also directed at God and was meant to inspire Him to remember His people.

This bi-directional remembrance dynamic associated with the Feast of Trumpets is further confirmed when this festival is called a zichron in Leviticus 23:24. Zichron is derived from a Hebrew root that means

3 Rabbi Shawn Ruby, "Rosh HaShanah: The Original Meaning of Blowing a Teruah," *The Torah*, online.

"to remember," and it generally implies a memorial of some kind. Thus, the Feast of Trumpets is more technically the Memorial of Trumpet Blasts and Shouting according to Leviticus 23:24. This was a time to make a lot of noise in the presence of the Lord, not only with a trumpet or ram's horn but also with one's voice, and just as important, it was a time when both Israel and God entered into a time of remembrance in the presence of the other.

THE FEAST OF TRUMPETS AND THE SINAI COVENANT

With this background in mind, the next question that arises is, what did God want Israel to memorialize and what did Israel want God to remember during the Feast of Trumpets? Though seldom mentioned, the best answer to this question is that the Feast of Trumpets commemorates Israel's original encounter with the Lord at Mount Sinai.

Although the description of the Feast of Trumpets in Leviticus 23:23–25 is extremely concise, it is likely that not much detail is given here because the purpose of this holy day was so obvious to the Israelites that more elaboration was not needed. At the time the laws in Leviticus 23 were given, Israel was still camped at the base of Mount Sinai. They had just seen the glory of the Lord descend upon this mountain in a blazing fiery lightning storm, heard His thundering voice, and received His laws through Moses. Moreover, Exodus 19:16–20 states that one of the key features of Israel's encounter with the Lord at Sinai was the blasting sound of a ram's horn trumpet (*shofar*). In this passage we read:

> So it came about on the third day, when it was morning, that there were thunder and lightning flashes and a thick cloud upon the mountain and a very loud trumpet [shofar] sound, so that all the people who were in the camp trembled. And Moses brought the people out of the camp to meet God, and they stood at the foot of the mountain.
>
> Now Mount Sinai was all in smoke because the Lord descended upon it in fire; and its smoke ascended like the smoke of a furnace, and the whole mountain quaked violently. When the sound of the

> trumpet [shofar] grew louder and louder, Moses spoke and God answered him with thunder. The LORD came down on Mount Sinai, to the top of the mountain; and the LORD called Moses to the top of the mountain, and Moses went up. (Exod. 19:16–20; cf. Exod. 20:18)

Prior to Leviticus 23:24, the only other reference to a trumpet in the Torah is found in the Sinai narrative in Exodus 19–20, which refers specifically to the ram's horn trumpet, called a shofar, that Israel heard while camped at Sinai. Thus, when God told the Israelites in Leviticus 23:23–25 to have a holy convocation and a "reminder" by blowing trumpets every year, it is logical to assume that they would have understood this commandment in light of their Mount Sinai experience.

To briefly elaborate, when Israel blew the trumpet every year at the start of the seventh month, they were commemorating the events at Sinai and renewing the Sinai covenant. The Feast of Trumpets was the annual memorial of Israel's miraculous encounter with God at the holy mountain, and on this day, through the blast of the trumpet and responsive shouts of praise (teruah), both the people and God Himself were reminded of their covenant obligations one to the other.

MOUNT SINAI & THE FEAST OF TRUMPETS IN JEWISH TRADITION

It is true that many Jewish traditions surrounding the Feast of Trumpets focus on the New Year, which is not always helpful. But thankfully, there are many other Jewish traditions and practices that highlight how the Feast of Trumpets was meant to be a memorial (zichron) of the events that unfolded at Mount Sinai.

Among these traditions, one of the most important is a series of readings called the *Shofarot* that are part of the Rosh HaShanah synagogue liturgy in modern Judaism. Shofarot is the plural form of the Hebrew word for a ram's horn trumpet (shofar), and these readings link the Feast of Trumpets to Exodus 19–20 in a very clear way.

For example, the Shofarot readings during the Feast of Trumpets begin with Exodus 19:6, 19:19, and 20:18, which are the three verses from the Sinai narrative that speak of the ram's horn trumpet (shofar). While the importance of these readings may not be fully appreciated by the casual synagogue attendee, the inclusion of Exodus 19–20 in the Rosh HaShanah liturgy is significant. This aspect of the Rosh HaShanah service indicates that the Feast of Trumpets commemorates the original Sinai encounter, and it also proves that for thousands of years many Jewish rabbis have understood this. Furthermore, the emphasis placed on the ram's horn trumpet (shofar) during the Feast of Trumpets in modern Judaism, rather than a man-made silver or brass trumpet, further establishes the link between Sinai and this appointed time, because it was at Sinai that Israel first heard the shofar blast (Exod. 19:16–19).

In the same way Israel heard the sound of the shofar at Mount Sinai and accepted God's covenant, saying, "All that the LORD has spoken we will do, and we will be obedient!" (Exod. 24:7), when the shofar is sounded on the Feast of Trumpets today, this is an invitation to again respond to God's trumpet blast and covenant words with a willing and obedient heart. As noted by Rabbi Noson Gurary, the shofar blast "represents the outcry of the return to God from the deepest part of the soul, deeper than words."[4] It "awakens a feeling of trembling, as did the blowing of the shofar at the revelation at Sinai," and is meant to bring about a renewal of Israel's covenant relationship with God.[5]

At the same time, however, in ancient Israel, the Feast of Trumpets would also have included responsive shouts (teruah) from the people, imploring God for His mercy and acknowledging His lordship. When Israel heard the trumpet and God heard the voice of His people, both parties were reminded of their covenant relationship through the sound of teruah (i.e., trumpet blasting and shouting).

On this last point, Rabbi Rudy elaborates on how the Feast of Trumpets originally had just as much to do with Israel reminding God

4 Noson Gurary, *The Jewish Holy Days in Chasidic Philosophy* (Northvale: Jason Aronson Inc., 2000), 31.

5 Gurary, *The Jewish Holy Days in Chasidic Philosophy,* 34.

of His promises as it did with God reminding Israel of their obligations. He writes, "the term *zichron teruah* [reminder by blasting/shouting] in Leviticus emphasizes how, on this day, Israel wants to make enough noise to get God's attention, and remind God of the covenant with Israel."[6]

THE FEAST OF TRUMPETS & MARRIAGE RENEWAL

Many scholars have also recognized that the Sinai covenant itself is presented as a marriage contract in Exodus, and this is an important point. At Sinai, the Lord took Israel to be His lawfully wedded wife and pledged to be the husband of the nation even as they agreed to be His bride (Exod. 19:8; 24:7).

Therefore, in the same way husbands and wives celebrate a wedding anniversary in modern times, Israel and the Lord held their anniversary ceremony during the Feast of Trumpets. When the events at Sinai were commemorated on the first day of the seventh month, both parties recommitted to walk in covenant fidelity with the other.

THE FEAST OF TRUMPETS AND ISRAEL'S LAWGIVER KING

Along with the themes of covenant and marriage, the theme of God's kingship is also prominent in the Sinai narrative. This kingship motif is seen most clearly when the Mosaic Law is given, because in the ancient world kings would frequently issue law codes to their people to both establish their sovereignty and delineate the parameters of the king-subject relationship. Also, when God came down to physically dwell on Mount Sinai, He actually established His throne in the midst of Israel, first on the holy mountain (Exod. 24:10) and then in the Mosaic Tabernacle (Exod. 25:8).

This kingship theme in the Sinai narrative also sheds more light on why God appeared at Mount Sinai with trumpet blasts. As many of us have probably seen in various movies, coronation ceremonies for kings and queens in the ancient world often included the blast of trumpets

6 Ruby, "Rosh HaShanah: The Original Meaning of Blowing a Teruah."

and human shouting (teruah/ruah), and this is a pattern that we also find in the Bible.

For example, in 1 Kings 1:34 the coronation of King Solomon is announced with trumpet blasts, and Psalm 98:6 says, "With trumpets and the sound of the horn [shofar] shout [ruah] joyfully before the King, the LORD." Numbers 23:21 also says the "shout (teruah) of the King" is among Israel, and in 1 Samuel 10:24 the verbal root of teruah is used when the people shout, "Long live the king!"

In each of these passages, we see the link between the sound of the trumpet, human shouts, and the enthronement of Israel's king, whether a human king or the Lord Himself. Based on this connection, we can conclude that the reason the trumpet blast was such a central part of Israel's encounter with God at Sinai was because at this time God was officially enthroned as the King of the Israelite nation. The mighty shofar blasts in Exodus 19 announced the formal reign of the Warrior King of the exodus, whose kingship Israel acknowledged for the first time after they crossed the Red Sea (Exod. 15:17–18).

Furthermore, because the Feast of Trumpets was a memorial of these events at Sinai, we can also conclude that even as the sound of teruah on the Feast of Trumpets was meant to inspire a renewal of the Sinai marriage covenant, it was also meant to re-enthrone God as King of the Israelite nation on an annual basis. In essence, the Feast of Trumpets was a coronation ceremony that was held every year in the seventh month, and it is probable that during this time the people acknowledged God's kingship with mighty trumpet blasts and extravagant shouts of praise (teruah), proclaiming: "Great is our King, YHVH!" During the Feast of Trumpets, Israel's relationship with her bridegroom God and sovereign Lord was reestablished for another year.

JEWISH TRADITION AND THE ENTHRONEMENT OF ISRAEL'S KING

Like we saw with the Shofarot synagogue readings, other Jewish traditions associated with Rosh HaShanah also emphasize how this holy day commemorates God's enthronement at Mount Sinai. For example, in modern Judaism, the Rosh HaShanah morning service begins with the chanting of a beautiful melody called *HaMelech*, and also includes another important song called *Avinu Malkeinu*. The Hebrew phrase HaMelech means "the King," and Avinu Malkeinu translates as "Our Father and King."

According to orthodox rabbis, these songs highlight that the dominant theme of Rosh HaShanah "is our coronation of God as king of the universe and our submission to His sovereignty."[7] Or, as stated by Rabbi Noson Gurary:

> The key spiritual event of Rosh HaShanah [i.e., Feast of Trumpets] is the renewal of God's Kingship which we bring about through [...] the coronation of the King. This means we submit ourselves to God with our total being and entreat Him to reveal His Kingship "below," in the physical world. Our request that God reveal His Kingship is the constant theme of the liturgy of Rosh HaShanah since we seek to elicit God's will to reign and His delight in being King for the whole year.[8]

In addition to the songs of Rosh HaShanah, key biblical passages called the *Malkhuyot* (meaning "kings") are also recited during this time, many of which are Psalms that declare God's kingship (e.g., Ps. 22:28; 93:1; 24:7–8).[9] For example, the Malkhuyot reading from Psalm 24 declares:

> Lift up your heads, O gates, and be lifted up, O ancient doors, That the King of glory may come in! Who is the King of glory? The LORD strong and mighty, the LORD mighty in battle (vv. 7–8).

7 "The King and I; Hamelech," from the Chassidic Masters, online, *Chabad*.

8 Gurary, *The Jewish Holy Days in Chasidic Philosophy*, 9–10.

9 Rabbanit Gloria Nusbacher, "The Rosh HaShanah Musaf," online, *Sefaria*.

By singing these two songs (HaMelech and Avinu Malkeinu) during the Feast of Trumpets and reciting the Malkhuyot Psalms, the Jewish people invite God to reign in their midst and confirm that above all, this appointed time is focused on the coronation of the Lord and His kingship. Additionally, because God's kingship is emphasized on Rosh HaShanah, this day has also become closely tied to the concept of repentance and judgment in modern Judaism. Jewish tradition upholds that Rosh HaShanah is also "the day of judgment," when a person's sins are presented before God in a court case that will only culminate with forgiveness on the Day of Atonement ten days later.[10] In the words of Rabbi Iscah Waldman, beginning on the Day of Trumpets, "we sing of the king, judge, and awesome sovereign who sits in judgment over us, while at the same time, we appeal to God's mercy and longstanding tradition of forgiveness."[11]

APPLICATIONS FOR MESSIANIC JEWS AND CHRISTIANS

Even though messianic Jews and Christians today are not living by every law of the Sinai covenant, the Feast of Trumpets can still teach us many important lessons in the New Covenant era. This is because the author of Hebrews compares the spiritual encounter we have with the Messiah now to the physical encounter Israel had with God at Mount Sinai, and believe it or not, he also says that what we experience in the Messiah now is greater and more terrifying that what Israel experienced in the wilderness:

> You have not come to a mountain that can be touched and that is burning with fire; to darkness, gloom and storm; to a trumpet blast or to such a voice speaking words that those who heard it begged that no further word be spoken to them, because they could not bear what was commanded: "If even an animal touches the mountain, it must

10 Rabbi Iscah Waldman, "Manzoor Contents: A Guide to the High Holiday Prayers," My Jewish Learning, online.

11 Waldman, "Mahzor Contents."

> be stoned to death." The sight was so terrifying that Moses said, "I am trembling with fear."
>
> But you have come to Mount Zion, to the city of the living God, the heavenly Jerusalem. You have come to thousands upon thousands of angels in joyful assembly, to the church of the firstborn, whose names are written in heaven. You have come to God, the Judge of all, to the spirits of the righteous made perfect, to Jesus the mediator of a new covenant, and to the sprinkled blood that speaks a better word than the blood of Abel.
>
> See to it that you do not refuse Him who speaks. If they did not escape when they refused Him who warned them on earth, how much less will we, if we turn away from Him who warns us from heaven? (Heb. 12:18–25)

Because we have come not to a physical mountain, but to "Mount Zion," "the city of the living God," and "the heavenly Jerusalem," and because we have been cleansed by the most precious blood of the Messiah Himself, God calls us to a life of covenant love and obedience that far surpasses anything that was ever required of Israel under the Sinai Covenant. For this reason, the author of Hebrews says that if Israel responded to God's covenant offer with fear and trembling, so too should we. If Israel had to be careful to honor the Lord, we should be exponentially more careful not "to refuse Him who speaks" to us through the Spirit and warns us from heaven.

Furthermore, for those of us who want to heed this admonition in Hebrews 12, the Feast of Trumpets offers a great opportunity to do so. When we hear the sound of the shofar in the fall, we should think not only of Israel's encounter with God at Sinai, but also of how the Lord calls us even now to the heavenly Mount Zion and into covenant with Himself through the Messiah. During the Feast of Trumpets, we do not hear the blast (teruah) of the shofar in a passive sense. Rather, we also give back to God a shout (teruah) from the deepest depths of our souls and bind ourselves to Him as subjects who are committed to willingly serving our righteous King. In the words of Rabbi Gurary, at this time of year we must trust that our "cry from the depths of the soul reaches the essence of God and causes God to accept kingship and allows us to be His servants once again."[12]

Therefore, let the sound of the trumpet during this memorial season awaken your heart to God's covenant with us in the Messiah, and also use this time to declare back to God your love for Him, your desire to repent of your sins, and your willingness to walk in covenant obedience with Him as your Bridegroom and King. On the Memorial of Trumpet Blasts and Shouting (Zichron Teruah), blow the shofar and raise a shout to the Lord. Let Him awaken your heart with His teruah, and let your voice of teruah awaken His heart as well. Hear the trumpet that enthrones the King of kings and respond as in the days of old: "Long live our glorious King and Messiah! "All that the LORD has spoken we will do, and we will be obedient!" (Exod. 24:7). Renew your marriage vows to the Lord and coronate God as the only Sovereign of your life. To do these things is to touch the spiritual essence of the Feast of Trumpets, because on this day God calls to us and we call back to Him as our hearts are turned one towards the other just as in the days at Sinai.

THE APPOINTED TIMES AND THE EXODUS

In this chapter, we have seen that the Feast of Trumpets at the start of the seventh month is in many ways an extension of the spring feasts that begin with Passover, in the sense that both the spring and fall feasts are tied to the events recorded in Exodus, though in different ways. As noted in chapter 2, the first half of Exodus is a warfare text that portrays the Lord as a mighty Divine Warrior and Storm God. In this text, the Lord becomes the King of the Israelite nation only after He has first vanquished their enemies on the battlefield.

Subsequently, the next major scene in Exodus centers around God's marriage covenant with Israel and official enthronement ceremony at

12 Gurary, *The Jewish Holy Days in Chasidic Philosophy*, 33.

Mount Sinai. From Exodus 19 onwards, the great Storm God of the exodus is presented as One who will dwell on His throne in Israel and rule the nation with His righteous laws, which is precisely why in this context we also see the same storm-god elements from earlier in Exodus, particularly when the Lord appears at Sinai in a thunder and lightning storm with fire and thick smoke.

With the exodus narrative in mind, if we zoom out and consider the overall outline of the appointed times in Leviticus 23, we can see that they follow this trajectory of events in Exodus 1–24 quite beautifully. They begin by commemorating the exodus in the first month with Passover and Unleavened Bread. Then, at the start of the seventh month, there is a transition to focus on the Sinai encounter during the Feast of Trumpets. In this way, the spring and fall feasts complemented each other perfectly and continually brought Israel back to the God who delivered them from Egypt and then met with them at His holy mountain.[13]

CHAPTER SUMMARY

As we prepare to move on in the next chapter to study how the Feast of Trumpets will be fulfilled when Jesus returns, below are some key points from this chapter that summarize the original historical meaning of this appointed time:

---

13 Note: The relationship between the events at Sinai and the Feast of Trumpets does not mean the entire Law was given in the seventh month, because we know the Law was given over a period of time that lasted nearly a year. Also, the fact that the Feast of Trumpets commemorates the original Sinai encounter in Exodus 19–20 does not mean that the events in these chapters necessarily took place in the seventh month. It only means that because the Sinai encounter lasted for an extended period, the first day of the seventh month was chosen by God as the time to memorialize these events, most likely because the seventh month was also an important time from an agricultural point of view (more on this in chapter 11).

1. In Jewish tradition, the Feast of Trumpets is synonymous with the New Year (Rosh HaShanah). Originally, however, the Feast of Trumpets was not tied to the New Year, and it only became known as Rosh HaShanah after the Babylonian captivity of Judah (c. 500s BC), likely as a result of Babylonian influence upon Israelite religion.

2. In Hebrew, the Feast of Trumpets is simply called Zichron Teruah, which implies a memorial marked by trumpet blasts and human shouting before the Lord. At the most basic level, the name of this appointed time indicates that during this festival both God and Israel were attempting to make enough noise to get the other's attention, and to remind each other of their covenant obligations (Lev. 23:23–24; Josh. 6:16; Num. 10:9).

3. More specifically, however, the trumpet blast during the Feast of Trumpets commemorates Israel's original encounter with the Lord at Mount Sinai. It was at Sinai that Israel first heard the sound of the trumpet (shofar), entered into a marriage covenant with the Lord, received His righteous laws, and enthroned Him as the Sovereign of their nation (Exod. 19-20).

4. When the events of Exodus 19–24 are understood as the background to the Feast of Trumpets legislation in Leviticus 23:23–25, it becomes clear that this appointed time was instituted to help Israel renew their marriage vows to the Lord and recommit to living under His sovereign rule, according to His laws. In essence, the Feast of Trumpets was a covenant renewal and coronation ceremony which mirrored other coronation ceremonies in Scripture. When this festival was celebrated, God asserted His kingship through the blast of the shofar, just like at Sinai, and Israel responded in kind with shouts and trumpet blasts that acknowledged God's reign and petitioned His mercy (1 Kings 1:34; Ps. 98:6; 1 Sam. 10:24).

BIBLE STUDY QUESTIONS

1. What was the purpose of the Feast of Trumpets within its original historical context in ancient Israel?

2. Why is the biblical name of the Feast of Trumpets, Zichron Teruah, so important to understand?

3. What does the Hebrew word teruah mean and how does its meaning shed light on what would have been taking place during the Feast of Trumpets?

4. How do you think the Feast of Trumpets can positively impact your relationship with God?

7

THE FEAST OF TRUMPETS & THE RETURN OF JESUS

MOST TEACHING ON THE BIBLICAL FEASTS in the last fifty years has maintained that the Feast of Trumpets will be fulfilled at the time of the Rapture. As a brief reminder, the Rapture will take place when believers from across the ages are raised from the dead, and those who remain alive until this time are "caught up together with them in the clouds to meet the Lord in the air" (1 Thess. 4:17).

Put simply, the Rapture will mark the time of our ultimate redemption and transformation as children of God. When Jesus gathers us together to meet Him in the sky, we will receive our glorified resurrection bodies, enter into the fullness of eternal life, and then return with Him to the earth to rule and reign during the millennium.

Many readers will also be aware that there are intense debates within the messianic community over the timing of the Rapture. However, we do not need to delve into these debates now.

We only need to understand that in many places we are told that the Rapture will be announced with the sound of a very loud trumpet, and for this reason the Rapture is often linked to the Feast of Trumpets. For example, in 1 Thessalonians 4:16 Paul associated the Rapture with "the trumpet of God," and in 1 Corinthians 15:52 he connected the Rapture to "the last trumpet." Likewise, in Matthew 24:31 Jesus spoke of a "great trumpet" that will sound when His elect are gathered by angels "after the tribulation" (Matt. 24:29).

Because the Rapture is so clearly tied to a trumpet blast in these passages, and because most people believe the spring feasts were already fulfilled through the first coming of the Messiah, they naturally land on the idea that the Rapture must represent the fulfillment of the Feast of Trumpets. After all, this seems obvious enough.

According to them, the next feast to be fulfilled on the biblical calendar is the Feast of Trumpets, and right there in the Gospels and the writings of Paul we see that at the exact same time the Rapture takes place a great trumpet blast will be heard in all the earth. Thus, in their view, it must be that the Feast of Trumpets was pointing forward to the Rapture all along, and that this event will bring the Feast of Trumpets to its final prophetic fulfillment.

Due to the popularity of this view, it is also common to hear the argument that the Rapture itself and the Second Coming of Jesus to the earth will happen at the same time the Feast of Trumpets was celebrated in ancient Israel, on the first day of the seventh month, in the fall. Many prophecy teachers have been dogmatic on this point, even going so far as to develop complex Rapture timelines and predictive theories centered around the Feast of Trumpets (i.e., Rosh HaShanah).

In this chapter, we will see why this popular theory that upholds an intrinsic connection between the Rapture and the Feast of Trumpets is not as sound as it first appears. Put simply, we will unpack the reasons why the Rapture trumpet may not have anything to do with the Feast of Trumpets at all. Then, in later sections, we will study the events that will transpire in the millennial kingdom, after Jesus is already back on the earth, that will bring the Feast of Trumpets to a glorious prophetic fulfillment in the kingdom of God.

Through this deeper study of many of the events that will unfold in the millennium, it will become clear that the Feast of Trumpets points forward not so much to the Rapture, but to the enthronement ceremony that will be held for Jesus on Mount Zion after He has defeated the Antichrist and gathered the Jewish and Gentile remnant from the nations back to Jerusalem. In other words, the Feast of Trumpets will be fulfilled when Jesus is officially crowned King of the messianic age on God's holy mountain, just as the Lord was crowned King of all the earth at Mount Sinai.

THE BIBLICAL FEASTS AND THE TRUMPET BLAST

There are three primary reasons why we should not assume that the Rapture will take place at the same time as, or prophetically fulfill, the Feast of Trumpets. The first is that trumpet blasts were a major feature of every single festival celebration mentioned in the Bible, and we also know trumpets were used at many other times of the year in biblical Israel as well.

To briefly elaborate, in Numbers 10:10 God tells the Israelites:

> Also in the day of your gladness and in your appointed feasts [moedim], and on the first days of your months, you shall blow the trumpets over your burnt offerings, and over the sacrifices of your peace offerings; and they shall be as a reminder of you before your God. I am the LORD your God.

In this passage, God commands Israel to blow the trumpet on the day of their gladness, on the first day of every month, and at the time of their appointed feasts (moedim), which would have included the weekly Sabbath as well as the spring and fall feasts. Additionally, in other places in Scripture the trumpet blast is associated with warfare (Num. 10:9) and special gatherings (Joel 2:15–16).

From these passages we can deduce that (1) trumpet blasts were heard at many different times of the year in ancient Israel and (2) trumpets were utilized for various reasons. This in turn also implies that the New Testament Rapture passages that mention the sound of a trumpet (e.g., 1 Thess. 4:16; 1 Cor. 15:52) do not necessarily speak of the prophetic fulfillment of the Feast of Trumpets. According to Numbers 10:10, the Rapture trumpet could coincide with any of the biblical feasts, and because trumpets were used at other times of the year as well, the Rapture trumpet may not even be connected to one particular feast at all.

Trumpet blasts signify important events in the Bible, which is why a trumpet will be used to announce the Rapture. However, there is no biblical proof that the Rapture trumpet is synonymous with the shofar that was used during the Feast of Trumpets in ancient Israel. Scripture simply does not tell us what time of year the Rapture will occur, and none of the prophecies that speak of the Rapture ever mention the seventh month or the Feast of Trumpets from Leviticus 23:24.[1]

PASSING OVER PASSOVER AND THE SPRING FEASTS

The second reason we should not be too quick to establish an intrinsic connection between the Rapture and the Feast of Trumpets is because

1 Some prophecy teachers have argued that Jesus' statement that "no one knows the day or hour" (Matt. 24:36) of His return implies that His return and/or the Rapture will take place at the same time as the Feast of Trumpets/Rosh HaShanah. This suggestion is made because the Feast of Trumpets was celebrated on the first day of the seventh month, which would have started the day after the sighting of the first visible crescent of the new moon. Generally, the Jewish religious authorities did not know exactly which day the new moon would appear, and thus, the assumption is made that because Jesus said "no one knows the day or hour of His return" He was using a Jewish idiom in this verse to state that He will rapture His saints and return on Rosh HaShanah. Though this interpretation of Matthew 24:36 has a lot of popular appeal, it is unsound and misleading to say the least. For one, none of the Jewish literature from the time of Jesus speaks of the Feast of Trumpets using the "day or hour" language from Matthew 24:36. In other words, this was not a common or idiomatic way for Jews in the first century to speak of the starting time of Rosh HaShanah, and those who say otherwise are merely making things up to support a theory. Second, and most important, Jesus' statement in Matthew 24:36 should be taken at face value. The Messiah was saying here that no one knows exactly when He will return. There is no cryptic reference to Rosh HaShanah in this verse, and we should certainly not use a passage that cautions against date-setting to set an exact day of the year when the Rapture/Second Coming must occur!

this entire approach is built on the mistaken idea that Jesus already fulfilled the spring feasts and will thus only fulfill the fall feasts in the future. In other words, people wrongly believe the spring feasts relate only to the first coming of the Messiah, so when they come to one of the next big events on the prophetic calendar, namely, the Rapture, they think this event must overlap with the next biblical feast that is set to be fulfilled on *their* timeline, namely, the Feast of Trumpets. Also, because they see a trumpet in these Rapture passages, they think this further verifies the connection between the Rapture/Second Coming and the Feast of Trumpets.

Though this might all sound very compelling, it should be clear by this point why this entire line of reasoning is so dubious; not only is it poor methodology to connect every trumpet we see in the Bible to the Feast of Trumpets (unfounded assumption No. 1), it is equally as problematic to build one's entire doctrine of Rapture timing and significance on the idea that only the fall feasts will be fulfilled at the time of the Messiah's Second Coming (unfounded assumption No. 2).

THE FEAST OF TRUMPETS IN HISTORICAL CONTEXT

The third reason I question the relationship between the Rapture and the Feast of Trumpets is because the prophecy teachers who link these two things never discuss what the Feast of Trumpets originally celebrated in ancient Israel. Put another way, they do not sufficiently account for how the prophetic fulfillment of each feast, including the Feast of Trumpets, will be intricately tied to its original historical meaning.

In the last chapter, we discovered that the Feast of Trumpets is technically called Zichron Teruah in Leviticus 23:24, which indicates a memorial time (zichron) of human shouting, praises, and trumpets blasts (teruah) that was instituted so Israel and the Lord could commemorate their Sinai encounter and renew their covenant with one another. When this historical background is understood, it becomes clear that when trying to ascertain how the Feast of Trumpets will be fulfilled after Jesus returns, we should not simply be looking for New

Testament passages that mention a trumpet. Instead, we should be looking for prophetic passages that describe future events in the millennial kingdom in terms drawn from the Sinai narrative, and more specifically, we should be looking for prophetic passages that use the teruah language of Leviticus 23:24 to describe these future millennial events (more on this later).

After all, the Feast of Trumpets (Zichron Teruah) does not actually include the word "trumpets" in its title, which again, illustrates why it is not a good idea to casually link this holy day to every New Testament Rapture passage that uses the word trumpet. Rather, we should go back to what the Feast of Trumpets signified in its original historical context, and then move from there to how the earthly enthronement of God at Mount Sinai foreshadowed events that will take place in the millennial kingdom.

THE RAPTURE AND THE FEAST OF TRUMPETS

As someone who has been involved in the messianic Jewish world for twenty years, I understand that when many people celebrate the Feast of Trumpets and hear the blast of the shofar every fall, their hearts are captivated with thoughts of the Rapture. At one level, I do not think this is all bad, and it is not my intention to deflate anyone's sense of longing for the time when we will hear the great trumpet blast and meet the Lord in the air. Personally, I long for this day as much as anyone.

I also do not have a firm position on when exactly the Rapture will happen in relation to the biblical calendar, because again, trumpets were utilized at many times of the year in the Bible and for many types of gatherings (Num. 10:10). So, in theory, I am open to the idea that the Rapture could possibly take place in the seventh month, if God so decides, and I am also open to the idea that, at most, the Rapture could represent a partial fulfillment of the Feast of Trumpets, at least at one level.[2]

At the same time, I still find it unfortunate that the Rapture has overshadowed celebrations of the Feast of Trumpets within the modern Christian and messianic Jewish communities for so long, because this emphasis obscures the true prophetic fulfillment of this important biblical holy day. While the Rapture may or may not be connected in some way to the Feast of Trumpets, what we can be sure of is that this first fall festival does point forward to future events in the millennium and God's salvation plan for Israel and the nations.

As a result, these millennial events should be our primary focus when studying the Feast of Trumpets and thinking about our future. We should emphasize the prophetic layers of the Feast of Trumpets that are made clear in Scripture, and not spend so much time speculating on the timing of the Rapture in relation to this biblical feast day (because this is less clear), which is exactly what we will attempt to do in the rest of this chapter.

THE LORD OF THE RINGS AS A WINDOW

To understand how the Feast of Trumpets will be fulfilled after the Second Coming, it will be helpful to use one of my favorite book and movie trilogies, *The Lord of the Rings* by J. R. R. Tolkien, as a window into the early days of the messianic age. This epic story of how a band of four small Hobbits (Frodo, Sam, Pippin, and Merry) and their allies defeat the powers of evil and usher in a new age of peace for the entire world offers many illustrative insights into how Jesus will conquer the forces of darkness and set up His kingdom in the age to come.

2 My personal views on the Rapture fall within the category known as "pre-wrath," which is a modified form of the post-Tribulation Rapture theory. According to proponents of pre-wrath, the Rapture could happen at any number of points in time after the Great Tribulation is "cut short" for New Testament saints (Matt. 24:22) and will involve Jesus taking believers into God's dwelling place in heaven before we return with Him to the earth (possibly right before Passover). Based on the details of this scenario, the Rapture could theoretically occur at any time on the biblical calendar, including, but not limited to, the start of the seventh month. For more on pre-wrath, see: Alan Kurschner, *Antichrist Before the Day of the Lord* (Eschatos Publishing, 2013) and Travis M. Snow, *The Passover King* (Shiloh Media, 2020), chapters 18–20.

Those familiar with the final installment of *The Lord of the Rings*, which is titled *The Return of the King,* will remember that at the end of the trilogy a series of final battles between the forces of good and evil are fought in Middle Earth. One occurs outside the gates of Mordor, which is the stronghold of the dark lord Sauron, and another takes place outside the gates of Minas Tirith, which is a city on the cliff of a mountain held by the allies of the Fellowship of the Ring (i.e., the good guys).

After these battles are over and the Fellowship of the Ring is victorious, the righteous inhabitants of Middle Earth are gathered to Minas Tirith to witness the coronation and crowning of the man who will lead them into the future: the valiant warrior Aragorn, who is also renamed King Elessar.

At the crowning ceremony, one of Aragorn's commanders, Faramir, stands up and issues a proclamation that is saturated with prophetic significance. Faramir declares:

> '[H]ear now the Steward of this Realm! Behold! One has come to claim the kingship again at last. Here is Aragorn son of Arathorn […] Captain of the Host of the West, bearer of the Star of the North, wielder of the Sword Reforged, victorious in battle, whose hands bring healing, […] Elessar of the line of Valandil, Isildur's son […] Shall he be king and enter into the City and dwell there?' And all the host and all the people cried "yea" with one voice.[3]

After the people agree to have Aragorn as their king, the Hobbit Frodo then takes the designated crown from Faramir and gives it to the White Wizard Gandalf. Then we read:

> And Aragorn knelt, and Gandalf set the White Crown upon his head, and said: "Now come the days of the King, and may they be blessed while the thrones of the Valar endure!" […]

3 J.R.R. Tolkien, *The Return of the King*, Book 6, chapter 5.

> But when Aragorn arose all that beheld him gazed in silence, for it seemed to them that he was revealed to them now for the first time. Tall as the sea-kings of old, he stood above all that were near; ancient of days he seemed and yet in the flower of manhood; and wisdom sat upon his brow, and strength and healing were in his hands, and a light was about him.
>
> And then Faramir cried: "Behold the King!" And in that moment all the trumpets were blown, and the King Elessar went forth [...] and amid the music of harp and of viol [stringed instruments] and of flute and the singing of clear voices the King passed through the flower-laden streets, and came to the Citadel, and entered in; and the banner of the Tree and the Stars was unfurled upon the topmost tower, and the reign of King Elessar began, of which many songs have told.[4]

With his kingship established, King Elessar (Aragorn) then enters his throne room and begins to act as ruler and judge of the nations. Toward the end of *The Return of the King*, the beginning of his reign is also described in the following way:

> In the days that followed his crowning the King sat on his throne in the Hall of the Kings and pronounced his judgements. And embassies came from many lands and peoples, from the East and the South, and from the borders of Mirkwood, and from Dunland in the west.[5]

THE FEAST OF TRUMPETS AND THE CORONATION OF THE KING

As we read these passages from *The Return of the King*, it is not hard to see why this story has captured the hearts and minds of so many people. We all long to live in a land ruled by a righteous king, even if most people do not realize that it will be Jesus Himself who will satisfy

4 J.R.R. Tolkien, *The Return of the King*, Book 6, chapter 5.

5 J.R.R. Tolkien, *The Return of the King*, Book 6, chapter 5.

these deepest longings of the human heart for His elect at the time of His Second Coming.

But beyond the basic theme of kingship in *The Return of the King*, there is also a lesson here that illuminates how the biblical feasts will be fulfilled after Jesus returns. In *The Return of the King*, we see that Aragorn's official coronation ceremony takes place only after the final battles against evil have been won and the nations have been gathered into his presence at a later time. It is this sequence of events that enables him to be accepted and proclaimed as king with great trumpet blasts, a verbal declaration by the people, and musical celebrations, which subsequently allows him to sit on his throne and rule the nations.

Furthermore, though Tolkien's tale is fictional, it aligns well with the prophetic storyline of Scripture and reveals how the fulfillment of the biblical feasts in the kingdom of God could move from Passover in the first month, to the Feast of Weeks fifty days later, to the Feast of Trumpets at the start of the seventh month. Just like we see with the inhabitants of Middle Earth in *The Return of the King*, the first thing Jesus will do when He returns is fight a series of battles against the forces of darkness. At this time, Passover will be fulfilled when Jesus leads His people through a second exodus, defeats the Antichrist at the battle of Armageddon (Rev. 16:16–21; 19:17–21; Ezek. 38:17–23; 39:1–6), and celebrates the Passover feast among existing believers in the kingdom of God (Lk. 22:15–16). Then, the Jewish and Gentile remnant from the nations will be gathered to Jerusalem and experience a great outpouring of the Holy Spirit that will initiate the renewal of the entire world (Isa. 66:19–21; Joel 2:28–29). As noted in chapter 5, this harvest of souls from the nations could unfold during the forty-nine days after Passover and culminate with the outpouring of the Spirit during the Feast of Weeks, which will bring about the ultimate prophetic fulfillment of what started in Acts 2. Then, a little over three months later, at the start of the seventh month, when the Feast of Trumpets takes place, all the peoples of the earth could very well assemble on Mount Zion, where Jesus will be officially crowned and enthroned King of the messianic age with trumpet blasts, music, and shouts of praise.

Though again, we can only speculate on the exact timing of each of these events in relation to the biblical calendar. But regardless, the most important point to note here is that when we understand the Feast of Trumpets in its original historical context, including how it was primarily connected to the enthronement of Israel's King (YHVH) at Mount Sinai, then the deeper prophetic meaning of this feast and how it will be fulfilled after the Second Coming naturally begins to emerge. The Feast of Trumpets always pointed forward not so much to the Rapture, but to the formal enthronement and coronation ceremony that will be held for the Jesus *in the millennium.*

Even as the fictional characters of Middle Earth were gathered to the mountain stronghold of Minas Tirith to witness the coronation of King Elessar, to hear the blast of the trumpet, and to proclaim "Behold the King!" all the inhabitants of the world will be gathered to Mount Zion in the age to come, where they will then hear the trumpet blast (teruah) proclaiming the kingship of Jesus and will respond in kind with their own shouts of praise (teruah), saying, "Long live our glorious Messiah! All that He speaks to us we will do!" At this time, the nations will enter into a covenant with the Lord, become His holy people, and agree to live by His righteous laws for the one thousand years of the millennium.

Just like the original Passover story, Israel's Sinai encounter in the book of Exodus is also a prophetic harbinger of "things to come" (Col. 2:17). In due time, the crown of authority will be placed on the head of the Messiah, and He will then set up a central government in Jerusalem and rule and judge the nations.

THE FEAST OF TRUMPETS AND THE MESSIANIC AGE IN JEWISH TRADITION

In his book *The Jewish Holy Days in Chasidic Philosophy*, Rabbi Noson Gurary explains how at the deepest level the Feast of Trumpets foreshadows how the Messiah will be enthroned as king of all the earth in the millennium. He writes:

> In the prayers of Rosh Hashanah, when we refer to God in terms of Kingship and ruling, we are not simply referring to the spiritual renewal of His Kingship [in our own lives]. We say, "And you shall rule" and "Rule over the whole world," and from the depths of our hearts we cray out "Hamelech"—"the King." We are asking for an extension of the scope of His kingship until "every created thing will understand that You created it." Thus, the ultimate expression of the theme of kingship on Rosh Hashanah is our request that God's kingship will reach the ultimate revelation of the days of *Mashiach* [Messiah].[6]

Gurary's point here is that the Feast of Trumpets (Rosh Hashanah) is the first taste of the Messiah's ultimate enthronement in the messianic age. When we hear the trumpet blast at the start of the seventh month, we are supposed to enthrone Jesus as the King of our personal lives now because we know He will someday reign as the King of all the earth in the future. In essence, during the Feast of Trumpets, we are calling upon the Messiah to return to His holy mountain and to extend His rule over all the earth.

This first festival in the seventh month is not only a remembrance (zichron) of God's enthronement at Mount Sinai. It is also a reminder (zichron) of the Messiah's future reign from Mount Zion. In a very real way, the Feast of Trumpets is a dress rehearsal for the messianic age, and we have good reasons to believe that in the early days after Jesus returns the nations will meet with Him on His holy mountain in the seventh month, as part of an initial Zichron Teruah celebration in the kingdom of God.

JERUSALEM: CAPITAL CITY OF THE MILLENNIUM

Not surprisingly, there are numerous texts in the Old and New Testaments that refer to Jerusalem and Mount Zion as the location

6 Noson Gurary, *The Jewish Holy Days in Chasidic Philosophy* (Northvale: Jason Aronson Inc., 2000), 38.

where the Messiah will be enthroned as King at the start of the millennium. Before we look at these texts, let us first note that Mount Zion refers to an actual hill located just outside the modern Old City of Jerusalem. However, in the Bible, Mount Zion can also refer to the entire city of Jerusalem, including the modern Temple Mount, because all of Jerusalem sits on mountainous terrain about twenty-five hundred feet above sea level, which rises rapidly and dramatically compared to the surrounding area (including the Dead Sea region, which at one thousand feet below sea level is the lowest point on earth).

Time and again we are told in Scripture that God has chosen Mount Zion as the place of His throne. For example, Psalm 132:13–14 says:

> For the LORD has chosen Zion; He has desired it for His habitation. "This is My resting place forever; Here I will dwell, for I have desired it. [...] There I will cause the horn of David to spring forth; I have prepared a lamp for Mine anointed. His enemies I will clothe with shame, but upon Himself His crown shall shine.

In this Psalm, Zion is called the habitation and resting place of God's "anointed," the "horn of David," meaning, the Messiah. Moreover, we are told that when the Jesus gathers the peoples of the earth to Mount Zion, He will be formally crowned as King of Israel and the nations. Notice in particular how this Psalm refers to the "crown" that will "shine" forth from above the Messiah's brow (v. 14).

Likewise, in Psalm 2:2, God says, "But as for Me, I have installed My King upon Zion, My holy mountain." This Psalm points forward to the era when God's Anointed One will reign over the entire world from Jerusalem. At this time, verse six also says the nations will be given as His "inheritance" and the "ends of the earth" as His "possession."

Outside of the Psalms, the prophet Zechariah also spoke of the centrality of Zion and God's holy mountain in the millennium. For example, in Zechariah 8:3 God says:

> I will return to Zion and will dwell in the midst of Jerusalem. Then Jerusalem will be called the City of Truth, and the mountain of the LORD of hosts will be called the Holy Mountain.

Similarly, in Zechariah 2:10–12 God encourages the inhabitants of Jerusalem with these words:

> "Sing for joy and be glad, O daughter of Zion; for behold I am coming and I will dwell in your midst," declares the LORD. "Many nations will join themselves to the LORD in that day and will become My people. Then I will dwell in your midst, and you will know that the LORD of hosts has sent Me to you. The LORD will possess Judah as His portion in the holy land, and will again choose Jerusalem.

Many commentators have argued that these Psalms and prophetic passages that emphasize the centrality of Jerusalem and Mount Zion are only concerned with the role this city played in God's plan in Old Testament times, or at the time of Jesus' first coming. Others have postulated that these verses refer primarily to the spiritual experience of the Church. A closer study of these texts, however, reveals that they depict a future era of peace and righteousness that has not yet arrived.

Zechariah, for example, envisioned the day when Jerusalem will be called "the City of Truth" and a "Holy Mountain" (Zech. 8:3–8), at a time when its inhabitants will "know the LORD of hosts has sent" them the Messiah (Zech. 2:11) and will be God's people "in truth and righteousness" (Zech. 8:8). None of these details in the text have been fulfilled yet, and we know this to be the case because in the past only a very small remnant of Jewish people honored God and recognized the Messiah, whereas Zechariah implies that the entire nation will know the Lord when He takes possession of Judah and the city of Jerusalem for Himself in the future (v. 12).

Moreover, the specific focus on the "holy land" in Zechariah 2:12 also negates the possibility that this passage could be referring only to a spiritual fulfillment in the Church, or to some generalized eschatological reality not tied to the territory promised to Abraham and his seed. After all, when the prophets used these place names (i.e., the holy land, Judah, and Jerusalem), as well as terms like the "daugher of Zion," they were referring quite simply to the people of Israel and various locations within their land.

SINAI TO ZION THEOLOGY

These prophecies about Jerusalem and Mount Zion are the natural extension of the Mount Sinai and Feast of Trumpets theology that was already present in Exodus and Leviticus. The Israelites knew that God's ultimate plan was to establish His throne not in the wilderness at Sinai, or in the Mosaic Tabernacle, but on His holy mountain in the Promised Land. They even proclaimed after crossing the Red Sea:

> You will bring them and plant them in the mountain of your inheritance, the place O LORD, which You have made for Your dwelling, the sanctuary O LORD, which your hands have established. The LORD shall reign forever and ever! (Exod. 15:17–18)

Throughout the Bible, the Hebrew prophets build on this promise in Exodus 15:1–18 and continually demarcate Mount Zion as the site where the Messiah will be crowned as king, establish His throne, and build His sanctuary (Ps. 2; 132; Zech. 2; 8). In the future, Mount Zion will become the capital city of the entire world and the New Mount Sinai.

THE ELEVATION OF THE HOLY MOUNTAIN

Notably, when Mount Zion does become the capital city of the entire world in the millennium, Zechariah also says the city will be elevated above its current altitude, while at the same time some of the surrounding regions will be flattened into a plain. Zechariah 14:10–11 describes the change in Jerusalem's topography in this way:

> All the land will be changed into a plain from Geba to Rimmon south of Jerusalem; but Jerusalem will rise and remain on its site from Benjamin's Gate as far as the place of the First Gate to the Corner Gate, and from the Tower of Hananel to the king's wine presses. People will live in it, and there will no longer be a curse, for Jerusalem will dwell in security.

According to biblical scholar Matthew Ervin, "Geba is located approximately six miles NE of Jerusalem, while Rimmon is thirty miles SW." This detail indicates that when the Messiah returns, all the land within a five to thirty-mile radius of Jerusalem will be "changed into a plain." Though we are not told how high Jerusalem itself will rise at this time, the broader point is that the city's elevation will emphasize that it is "the center of world authority."[7]

THE KING JUDGES THE NATIONS AND GIVES US HIS LAW

Like Zechariah, Isaiah also highlights how Jerusalem will be elevated above its current height in the messianic age. Additionally, Isaiah fills in this picture with more detail and speaks of how the nations will stream to Jerusalem to receive the righteous laws and judgments of the Messiah. He writes:

> In the last days the mountain of the LORD's temple will be established as the highest of the mountains; it will be exalted above the hills, and all nations will stream to it. Many peoples will come and say, "Come, let us go up to the mountain of the LORD, to the temple of the God of Jacob. He will teach us His ways, so that we may walk in His paths."
>
> The law will go out from Zion, the word of the LORD from Jerusalem. He will judge between the nations and will settle disputes for many peoples. They will beat their swords into plowshares and their spears into pruning hooks. Nation will not take up sword against nation, nor will they train for war anymore. (Isa. 2:2–4, NIV)

7 Matthew Bryce Ervin, *One Thousand Years with Jesus: The Coming Messianic Kingdom* (Eugene: Resource Publications, 2017), 47.

Isaiah 2:2–4 gathers together many themes and motifs from the Exodus narrative and uses them as a prophetic backdrop to highlight how the peoples of the earth will submit to God's reign and receive His law during the millennial age. According to Isaiah, our encounter with the Messiah on Mount Zion in the future will in many ways mirror what Israel first experienced at Mount Sinai thirty five hundred years ago, and this is one of the core prophecies that emphasizes the centrality of Jerusalem in the kingdom of God. As Matthew Ervin states:

> This uplifted mountain symbolizes the center of the world's government and worship in several places, including Isaiah 2:2–4. [...] Pilgrimages to Jerusalem are to become so dense that it will appear as if the nations are flowing toward the mountain like water (v. 2; Mic 4:1). Numerous people will travel to the mountain because it is where they shall receive instruction from the Lord and become His followers (v. 3; Mic 4:2). Think of this as the Great Commission in reverse. It is atop this mountain where Jesus will be the supreme judge, settling disputes between distant countries, and determining the course for many peoples. Under the Messiah's governance, nations will finally be at perfect peace with one another (Mic. 4:3)."[8]

THE GREAT TRUMPET BLAST AND THE GATHERING OF THE NATIONS

One of the primary clues that the gathering of the nations to Mount Zion in the millennium will lead to the prophetic fulfillment of the Feast of Trumpets, can be seen when we consider how Isaiah emphasizes the shofar (i.e., ram's horn trumpet) blast that the peoples of the earth will hear at this time. For example, Isaiah 27:13 builds on Isaiah 2:2-4 and says that in the early days of the messianic age, "a great trumpet [shofar] will sound" and those who were formerly exiled and experienced tribulation in the last days "will come and worship the Lord on the holy mountain in Jerusalem." Isaiah 18:3–7 also says the nations of the

8 Ervin, *One Thousand Years with Jesus*, 80–81.

world will hear the blast of the "trumpet" (shofar) and will come "to the place of the name of the LORD of hosts, even Mount Zion" (v. 7).

We learned in the last chapter that the Feast of Trumpets was a memorial (zichron) of Israel's Sinai encounter, and that the shofar has been used to celebrate this appointed time for thousands of years precisely because the giving of the Law at Mount Sinai was initiated with the shofar blast in Exodus 19. With this in mind, it becomes clear that Isaiah 27:13 and 18:3–7 emphasize the mountain of the Lord and the shofar because the prophetic fulfillment of the Feast of Trumpets is in view in these passages. Isaiah foresaw the Feast of Trumpets being fulfilled not at the exact moment the Messiah returns to the earth (or at the time of the Rapture), but instead, many months later, after the nations have been harvested and called to God's holy mountain with the mighty blast of the ram's horn trumpet.

THE GREAT CORONATION CEREMONY ON MOUNT ZION

Once the nations are finally harvested and gathered to Jerusalem, the Bible tells us there will then be a great coronation and enthronement ceremony for Jesus on Mount Zion. And not surprisingly, Psalm 47:5–9 even describes this ceremony using the precise Feast of Trumpets language from Exodus and Leviticus. In this passage we read:

> God has ascended with a shout [teruah], The LORD, with the sound of a trumpet [shofar]. Sing praises to God, sing praises; Sing praises to our King, sing praises. For God is the King of all the earth; Sing praises with a skillful psalm. God reigns over the nations, God sits on His holy throne. The princes of the people have assembled themselves as the people of the God of Abraham, for the shields of the earth belong to God; He is highly exalted.[9]

9 Note: this Psalm is part of the Feast of Trumpets liturgy in modern Judaism, which shows how the Feast of Trumpets is meant to enthrone God as King in anticipation of events that will take place on Mount Zion in the millennium.

Though this Psalm only refers to God in a general sense, we know we are looking at a picture of the Messiah's enthronement here because many of the other details in this text match what we find in prophecies about the millennium. Also, Jesus is God in the flesh, so there is definitely a messianic application here.

But most importantly, notice how this Psalm incorporates both the shofar language from Exodus 19:6–19 and the teruah language from Leviticus 23:24 to give us a more detailed picture of how the Feast of Trumpets will reach its eschatological end goal in the kingdom of God. Whereas the various passages in Isaiah related to the Feast of Trumpets speak more broadly of the nations going up to Jerusalem to receive the Messiah's law (Isa. 18:3–7; 27:13), Psalm 47 speaks more specifically of how Jesus will first ascend His holy mountain as the "princes of the people" assemble before Him and proclaim His kingship with shouts of praise (teruah) and the sound of the shofar. This Psalm reveals how the coronation of Israel's King (YHVH) at Mount Sinai, and the coronation of other kings in the Old Testament, both of which were associated with verbal proclamations and trumpet blasts (Exod. 24:7; 1 Kings 1:34), always foreshadowed the coronation of the Messiah on Mount Zion in the age to come.

IMAGINE THE GREAT CORONATION CEREMONY

To picture what will happen during this coronation ceremony on Mount Zion, just imagine standing in Jerusalem in the future, on God's holy mountain elevated far above its current height, as peoples of every skin color and language, and Israelites from all the twelve tribes, bow down before Jesus, and a great shofar blast announces the beginning of His reign. Then one of the Messiah's chief commanders brings forth the royal golden crown studded with precious jewels and gemstones, and says with a mighty voice, "Will you, peoples of the earth, take this man, Yeshua of Nazareth, to be your King?" To which all the nations respond with a shout (teruah): "Yes! All hail our glorious King and Savior!"

When this enthronement ceremony takes place, there will no

doubt be coronation Psalms read by the servants of the Messiah as well, including Psalm 47, but perhaps also Psalm 98, which reads:

> Shout [ruah] joyfully to the LORD, all the earth; break forth and sing for joy and sing praises. Sing praises to the LORD with the lyre, with the lyre and the sound of melody. With trumpets and the sound of the horn [shofar]. Shout [ruah] joyfully before the King, the LORD. (vv. 4–6)

As these Psalms acknowledging God's kingship are read before Jesus in the millennium, the Feast of Trumpets, this Memorial of Trumpet Blasts and Shouting (Zichron Teruah), will be fulfilled in the kingdom of God. Perhaps on the first day of the seventh month, in the first year of the Messiah's millennial reign, we will attend the greatest coronation ceremony in human history, Jesus will be formally crowned and enthroned King of the new creation, and all the nations of the earth will submit to living by His righteous laws.

Then, according to Isaiah:

> There will be no end to the increase of His government or of peace. He will reign on David's throne and over His kingdom, establishing and upholding it with justice and righteousness from that time on and forever. (Isa. 9:7, NIV).

And of course, just as in the days at Sinai:

> The LORD will create over all of Mount Zion and over those who assemble there a cloud of smoke by day and a glow of flaming fire by night; over everything the glory will be a canopy. (Isa. 4:5; NIV)

CHAPTER SUMMARY

Below are the major points from this chapter that summarize how the Feast of Trumpets will be fulfilled in the millennium.

1. The Feast of Trumpets is often linked exclusively to the Rapture. However, there may not be such a clear connection between the Rapture and the Feast of Trumpets for three reasons. First, trumpets were used throughout the year in biblical times, and for many different purposes (i.e., during all of the appointed times, at the start of every month, on the battlefield, and to signal other gatherings (Num. 10:10). Thus, we cannot be certain that the Rapture trumpet we see in the New Testament will be sounded during the Feast of Trumpets in the seventh month. Second, the Feast of Trumpets-Rapture connection has become popular only because the future prophetic implications of the spring feasts are widely overlooked. And third, linking the Feast of Trumpets primarily to the Rapture requires us to ignore what this holy day signified in its original historical context in ancient Israel. Though the Rapture could occur at the start of the seventh month, there is no clear proof that it must, and regardless, the Feast of Trumpets will only be completely fulfilled in the kingdom, not at the time of the Rapture.

2. Fundamentally, the Feast of Trumpets foreshadows a messianic enthronement and coronation ceremony, which will be held for Jesus on Mount Zion after He is already back on the earth. Numerous prophecies use Feast of Trumpets and Mount Sinai language when describing the establishment of the Messiah's throne and governmental control center in Jerusalem. And collectively, these texts reveal that just as Israel was called to Mount Sinai to enter into a covenant with the Lord and enthrone Him as their King, all the nations of the earth will be gathered to Mount Zion to enter into a covenant with the Messiah and enthrone Him as King of the millennium. From that point forward, Jerusalem will serve as the capital city of the millennial kingdom and the place from which Jesus will rule the nations as their righteous Lawgiver and Judge (Exod. 15:17–18; Isa. 2:1–5; 18:3–7; 27:13; Ps. 2:2; 132:13–14; 47:5–9; 98:1–6; Zech. 8:3).

3. Christians and messianic Jews can celebrate the Feast of Trumpets today looking forward to the great coronation ceremony that will take place on God's holy mountain in the future. We can recognize the Messiah's kingship in the seventh month now as a foretaste of the day when He will reign as King of the messianic age.

BIBLE STUDY QUESTIONS

1. Why have many prophecy teachers viewed the Rapture as the fulfillment of the Feast of Trumpets, and why should we be cautious about definitively linking these two things?

2. How does the historical meaning of the Feast of Trumpets shed light on how this appointed time will be fulfilled in the millennium?

3. What prophecies in the Bible that reveal a future fulfillment of the Feast of Trumpets did you learn the most from, or find the most compelling?

4. In what ways can studying and celebrating the Feast of Trumpets today encourage us in our walk with God and ground us in the hope of His kingdom?

8

THE DAY OF ATONEMENT IN HISTORICAL CONTEXT

TEN DAYS AFTER THE FEAST OF TRUMPETS, the Day of Atonement, called *Yom Kippur* in Hebrew, is observed according to the biblical calendar. In Leviticus 23:26–27, a basic overview of this appointed time is given in the following terms:

> The LORD spoke to Moses, saying, "On exactly the tenth day of this seventh month is the Day of Atonement; it shall be a holy convocation for you, and you shall humble your souls and present an offering by fire to the LORD."

Also, in Leviticus 16–17, the Day of Atonement is outlined in more detail when God says:

> This shall be a permanent statute for you: in the seventh month, on the tenth day of the month, you shall humble your souls and not

> do any work, whether the native, or the alien who sojourns among you; for it is on this day that atonement shall be made for you to cleanse you; you will be clean from all your sins before the LORD. (Lev. 16:29–30)

As modern Christians and messianic Jews, we understand the importance of atonement, and we also have many ideas about what exactly atonement means and/or accomplishes. Although many of these ideas are good and useful, the purpose of this chapter is to take a step back from our New Testament framework of thinking so that we can understand the meaning of the Day of Atonement in its original historical context. Thus, in this chapter, we will focus on questions such as: "How would the average ancient Israelite have viewed the Day of Atonement?" "What did this day accomplish from their perspective?" "And why was the Day of Atonement necessary for these people whom God had miraculously delivered from the land of Egypt?"

Approaching the Day of Atonement with these questions in mind will reveal that the purpose of the Day of Atonement was to preserve a holy space for God's glory so that He could continue to dwell among His people. From a strictly historical vantage point, the Day of Atonement had less to do with what those of us living in the twenty-first century might call "individual salvation," and more to do with giving Israel a way to maintain their corporate relationship with God at His holy Tabernacle or Temple.

In the next chapter, we will also see how this connection between the Day of Atonement and the sacred space inhabited by the glory of God has implications related to what will take place after Jesus sets up the millennial kingdom. But to start, in the sections that follow, we will leave the messianic and eschatological layers of the Day of Atonement on the back burner and look only at how this day is described in the core passages in Leviticus that speak of its observance in ancient Israel.

GOD'S SANCTUARY IN ISRAEL

The laws in Leviticus that stipulate a Day of Atonement are rooted in the twenty-fifth chapter of Exodus. In this passage, God expresses His desire to once again dwell on the earth among His people, just as He had done with Adam and Eve in the garden of Eden. Consequently, as Israel camps at the base of Mount Sinai, God tells Moses to have the people build Him a sanctuary on the earth, which would later become known as the Mosaic Tabernacle. We read:

> Let them construct a sanctuary for Me, that I may dwell among them. According to all that I am going to show you, as the pattern of the tabernacle and the pattern of all its furniture, just so you shall construct it. (Exod. 25:8)

Modern readers might be prone to view the Tabernacle as the same thing as a contemporary worship space, such as a church or synagogue. However, a more accurate view is that the Tabernacle was the place of God's throne on the earth. It was the singular location where God chose to take up residence so that He could rule His redeemed nation, enjoy fellowship with His people, and continue to mediate His blessings, presence, and commandments to them after they left Mount Sinai.

Old Testament scholar John Walton elaborates on how the Tabernacle functioned as both God's personal house and throne room. He writes:

> [A] temple is built in the ancient world so that a deity can have a center for his rule. The temple is the residence and palace of the gods. Like the American White House, it is the hub of authority and control. It is where the work of running the country takes place. When a newly elected president looks forward to taking up his residence in the White House, it is not simply so he can kick off his shoes and snooze in the Lincoln bedroom. It is so he can begin the work of running the country. [...] This is far from relaxation. The turmoil

> and uncertainty of the election is over, and now he can settle down to the important business at hand.
>
> The role of the temple in the ancient world is not primarily a place for people to gather in worship like modern churches. It is a place for the deity—sacred space. It is his home, but more importantly his headquarters—the control room. When the deity rests in the temple it means that he is taking command, that he is mounting to his throne to assume his rightful place and his proper rule.[1]

GOD'S TABERNACLE BRINGS HEAVEN TO EARTH

To build on Walton's point here, we should also note that in the Bible there is an intricate relationship between God's Tabernacle on the earth and His Tabernacle in heaven. The earthly Tabernacle was patterned after a heavenly prototype, and this parallel highlighted that the earthly Tabernacle was intended to bring the heavenly rule of God to the earth.

We can see this connection between God's heavenly dwelling place and the Tabernacle perhaps most clearly if we consider the ark of the covenant that sat inside the holy of holies (Exod. 25:10–22). On top of the ark there were two cherubim with outstretched wings covering the mercy seat. These cherubim represented the holy angels that are stationed before the Lord in heaven (cf. Isa. 6:1–2), and their presence in the holy of holies confirms that the inner sanctum of the Tabernacle was God's throne room on the earth, which was modeled after the heavenly original.

In a sense then, when we call the Tabernacle "sacred space," really what this means is that the Tabernacle was heavenly space on the earth. It was both a portal to the heavenly realm and a place where God's heavenly presence and sovereign rule touched the earth and extended outwards from one primary location.

---

1 John H. Walton, *The Lost World of Genesis One* (Downer's Grove: IVP Academic, 2009), 75.

GOD'S PRESENCE AND HUMAN SIN

As important as it was for God to rule the Israelite nation from His Tabernacle, this situation also created liabilities. Human contact with the Lord was not something to be taken lightly, and in certain cases this contact could even result in death.

For example, in Leviticus 10:1–3, Nadab and Abihu, the sons of Aaron the high priest, were consumed by fire that came "from the presence of the LORD" because they tried to offer sacrifices that were not prescribed in the Mosaic Law. These sacrifices are called strange fire, and God further specifies that Nadab and Abihu were destroyed because they did not treat Him as holy in the sight of the people (Lev. 10:3).

Similarly, in 1 Samuel 6:19 more than fifty thousand men from Beth-shemesh were killed because they "looked into the ark of the LORD." According to the Torah, only the high priest was allowed to enter the holy of holies to see the ark once a year, and even then he was not allowed to look inside it.

Finally, in Isaiah 6:1–7, after Isaiah is taken into the heavenly Temple, he cries out, "Woe is me, for I am ruined! Because I am a man of unclean [*tame*] lips, and I live among a people of unclean lips; for my eyes have seen the King, the LORD of hosts." At this point, one of the angels in the Temple purifies Isaiah's lips with a "burning coal" from the heavenly altar and assures him that his iniquity has been taken away and his sins forgiven (Isa. 6:6–7).

These passages demonstrate the biblical principle that sinful and unclean humans cannot directly contact the Lord without incurring death. As mysterious as this principle is, there is something in the holy nature of God that prevents Him from having unmitigated and unregulated fellowship with His people, and as a result, He must remain set apart and distant to some degree.

CLEAN AND UNCLEAN

In the Mosaic Law, this unique and holy aspect of God's nature, which separates Him from humans, is driven home through the various regulations that outline clean and unclean practices and states of being. At the most basic level, uncleanness did not have anything to do with moral sin. A woman was unclean for seven days after giving birth to a child (Lev. 12:2), and therefore, not allowed to approach the Tabernacle during this time. In addition, a person was pronounced unclean if they had a certain type of skin infection (Lev. 13), contacted a dead body (Num. 19:11–22), ate an unclean animal (Lev. 11), had intercourse (Lev. 15), and much more.

In each of these cases, it was not that the person who became unclean had committed a moral transgression. They had not sinned in the sense that we define sin today. Rather, they had experienced something that the Mosaic Law wanted to keep separate from God's holy presence in the Tabernacle.

Scholars have debated why the Torah regards certain things as unclean, and one likely reason for this categorization is that "though not sinful in themselves" these unclean practices "still reflect sin's damage and pollution of the earth, and therefore require ritual cleansing." In other words, there is a sense in which unclean things were so tied to the "physical imperfection" of the fallen world that they needed to be kept distant from God.[2] The clean/unclean distinction in the Torah highlighted the otherworldly nature of God, His holiness, and the extent to which He is distinct from His creation.

Things which make a person unclean are associated with very human and earthly experiences: childbirth, death, infections, intercourse, bodily fluids, eating certain foods, and the like. Each of these things relate to the human experience of life on earth, yet none of them are experienced by God. As a result, we can deduce that the clean and unclean categorization was a way to remind the Israelites that although God had taken up residence in their midst, He was still completely other, completely holy, and completely set apart from them. He exists in a

2 L. Michael Morales, *Who Shall Ascend the Mountain of the Lord: A Biblical Theology of the Book of Leviticus* (Downer's Grove: Intervarsity Press, 2015), 161.

category all His own, and He is first and foremost to be identified with the heavenly realm.

For this reason, those in a state of uncleanness could not approach the house of the Lord. The unclean had to submit to certain protocols that restored ritual purity (e.g., Lev. 13), which often culminated with various sacrificial offerings at the Tabernacle (Lev. 5; 14).

HUMAN SINFULNESS AND MORAL TRANSGRESSIONS

In comparison to ritual uncleanness, human moral sins did more damage to the relationship between the Lord and His people and often carried greater consequences. For example, many sins in ancient Israel made the sinner subject to the death penalty or excommunication (Num. 15:30). More minor sins, on the other hand, could be atoned for through the priesthood and sacrificial system, particularly through the sin and guilt offerings (Lev. 4–5).

To complete these offerings, the sinful party would place their hands on the head of the sacrificial animal to symbolically transfer their sin to the animal. Then the animal would be sacrificed, its blood would be sprinkled (or poured out) (1) in front of the curtain that separated the holy place from the holy of holies, (2) on the altar of incense in the holy place, and (3) at the base of the bronze altar that was used for burnt offerings.[3] Finally, the inner organs of the sacrifice would be offered in smoke on the bronze altar and the rest of its body would be burned "outside the camp" (Lev. 4:1–35).

THE PURIFICATION OF SACRED SPACE

As we think about these purification and sacrificial laws in the Torah, one key point to keep in mind is that these laws were primarily concerned with keeping God's sanctuary pure and removing uncleanness and sin from the Israelite community in a physical sense so that God's

3 After the blood of the sacrifice was sprinkled in the holy place, the remainder was poured out at the base of the large bronze altar where burnt offerings were made (Lev. 4:7).

manifest glory could continue to dwell in the Tabernacle. In other words, being unclean or committing sin brought physical pollution into the community and into God's sacred space, which had to be physically washed away and purged through the various ritual practices and sacrificial offerings prescribed in Leviticus.

The reason it is important to note that the Levitical system dealt only with physical contamination is because as modern Christians and messianic Jews we tend to think about atonement, cleansing, and forgiveness in exclusively spiritual terms, and in relation to our eternal salvation. We know we need to be forgiven for our sins in order to escape God's judgment and to have a relationship with Him (both now and after death), so we view atonement as the primary answer to our personal sin problem. Atonement, in our view, is the primary means through which we will escape God's punishment for our rebellion against His laws, and thereby be granted a place in His eternal kingdom.

To be sure, modern Jews and Christians have different beliefs about how atonement is achieved. Many in the mainstream Jewish community believe atonement is achieved through prayer, fasting, repentance, and good works. In contrast, most modern Christians and messianic Jews understand that atonement has already been achieved through the sacrifice of the Messiah, which means we only need to trust in His work (not our own) in order to receive God's forgiveness and to have our sins atoned for. But even though many Jews and Christians disagree on the source of atonement, both groups still focus primarily on individual spiritual cleansing when thinking about the need for atonement.

In their original historical context, however, the ritual purity and sacrificial laws in the Torah did not secure eternal forgiveness for the individual. Nor did they accomplish some kind of spiritual transformation that led to a change in one's eternal standing with God. When the Israelites observed these laws, they were not thinking, "I did these immoral things or became unclean, so I need atonement so I can get right with God and not go to hell."

Instead, when the Israelites observed the ritual cleansing and sacrificial atonement laws in Leviticus they were thinking more in terms of: "God's house is literally right down the street, and He cannot mix with sin and human uncleanness. Therefore, these laws are necessary because they provide a way to remove the stain of human uncleanness and sin from the physical space where God lives, so that He can continue to dwell among us and so that we can continue to approach Him when we bring our sacrifices." Again, the observance of these laws resulted in the purification of the physical domain where God lived and the ritual cleansing of the individual. But nothing in the laws of Leviticus enabled the Israelites to improve their spiritual or moral status, much less their eternal standing with God.

In the words of Old Testament scholar Michael Heiser:

> The emphasis in Leviticus and, largely, all of the sacrifices (at least the ones that are "sin and guilt offerings"), is not to apply the blood to the individual person who committed the wrong and extend forgiveness to them on some moral basis. The blood is never applied to the sinner; the one who is bringing the offering. Rather, the blood is applied to the sanctuary to purge it of pollution. The priesthood in Leviticus is about purifying sacred space that has been polluted and making it fit for the Lord's presence again after it has been violated.[4]

Though Heiser does overlook that the Levitical sacrifices made both God's house and the people themselves clean, his emphasis on the tangible realm is still important. After all, even when a purification offering did accomplish something positive for the individual, it did so only at the level of outward ritual purity (e.g., Lev. 14:19–20) so that the individual could once again access sacred space.

Of course, the limited types of problems that the Levitical system could deal with (i.e., physical rather than spiritual contamination) do not imply that it is wrong for people to think about their spiritual state

4 Michael Heiser, *Notes on Leviticus* (Blind Spot Press, 2017).

or eternal standing with God. Quite the opposite, we should never deny the primary importance of such things, and in a very direct way the inherent weaknesses of the Levitical system highlight our need for a much better priesthood and sacrifice for sins (one that offers complete moral and spiritual purification), which is only available through the work of the Messiah (cf. Heb. 10:3–5).

But still, our goal at present is not to understand how the New Covenant priesthood and sacrifice of Jesus is superior to what the Levitical system offered (as important as that topic is). Rather, our goal is to understand the Levitical system in its original historical context so that we will have the right foundation in place to later see how the Day of Atonement will be fulfilled when Jesus returns.

The Levitical system did not get the Israelites "saved" in the Billy Graham altar-call sense. Instead, the purification rituals and the sprinkling of sacrificial blood within the Tabernacle did just enough to remove the physical pollution that human sin and uncleanness left behind in God's house. Additionally, these laws extended grace to the ritually impure individual and enabled them to be made clean, so they would not be deemed a source of permanent contamination in the broader territory where God had chosen to make His home.

The main idea of Leviticus is that certain purification and sacrificial laws have to be followed because the otherworldly God of the universe lives in the midst of Israel. The contents of this book center around the question of how to practice hospitality towards the Lord.

THE DAY OF ATONEMENT MADE EVERYTHING CLEAN

The physical pollution created by human uncleanness and sinfulness could be dealt with to a limited extent through the rituals that were observed and the sacrifices that were offered throughout the biblical year. However, Leviticus still reiterates that these regular rituals and sacrifices were not enough to deal with the pervasive nature of the problem.

For this reason, God commanded Israel to observe the annual Day of Atonement on the tenth day of the seventh month. This holy day provided a more comprehensive solution to the problem of human sin and uncleanness, especially in terms of purifying the holy space occupied by God in the Tabernacle.

Importantly, the word we translate as "atonement" is the Hebrew word *kaphar*, which literally means "to purge." Therefore, the ceremonies associated with the Day of Atonement purged, washed away, and removed the contaminating residue created by human sin and uncleanness from both the people themselves and God's Tabernacle, so that His holy space and His holy presence would not be violated.

The detailed descriptions of the Day of Atonement in Leviticus 16 also confirm that this appointed time was primarily concerned with preserving a holy space where God could dwell. This passage states that on the tenth day of the seventh month atonement was made "for the tent of meeting and for the altar," as well as "for the priests and for all the people of the assembly" (Lev. 16:33). Leviticus 16:16 adds that a Day of Atonement was necessary because God "abides" with Israel "in the midst of their impurities [or uncleanness]."

THE DAY OF ATONEMENT AND GOD'S TEMPLE ENTHRONEMENT

In chapter 6, we learned that during the Feast of Trumpets Israel reenthroned God as the King of their nation and recommitted to honor Him as their sovereign Lawgiver, in commemoration of the events at Mount Sinai. We also learned in chapter 7 that the coronation of God at Mount Sinai foreshadowed the great enthronement ceremony that will take place in the millennium when Jesus is enthroned King of Israel and the nations on Mount Zion (Ps. 98; 47).

Because the first fall feast in the seventh month (i.e., the Feast of Trumpets) revolves around God's kingship and enthronement, it should not surprise us that the Day of Atonement was closely tied to the enthronement of God as well. As a matter of fact, we could even say that the purpose of the purification ceremonies that took place on the Day of Atonement was to preserve the place of God's throne, which implies that the Day of Atonement solidified the enthronement of God among His people that was first initiated ten days earlier during the Feast of Trumpets.

On the first day of the seventh month Israel accepted God's kingship and renewed their covenant with Him through trumpet blasts and shouts of praise (teruah), but it was not until the tenth day of the seventh month that God's enthronement was fully effectuated, after the place of His throne (i.e., the Tabernacle) was purified on the Day of Atonement. The general idea of Leviticus 16 is that the Day of Atonement reestablishes the Tabernacle as the place of God's throne and reinvites the King of kings to dwell in the holy of holies.

Biblical scholar John Bergsma is one of the few who has recognized this close and important connection between the purification ceremonies of the Day of Atonement and God's enthronement. He writes:

> The presence of uncleanness in the tabernacle/temple was understood to prevent or impede YHVH from inhabiting it; thus, the necessity of periodic purgations and—quintessentially—*yom kippur* [the Day of Atonement]. If therefore *yom kippur* removes that which drives YHVH away from the sanctuary and thus His people, there must have existed a sense that following *yom kippur*, the presence of YHVH among His people had been renewed in a particular way.[5]
>
> [In other words] it may be argued that *yom kippur* does suggest some sort of re-assertion or renewal of YHVH's presence in the tabernacle/temple, and therefore also His rule as King over Israel.[6]

As Bergsma notes, when the Day of Atonement was complete the result was not so much that every individual Israelite would have believed they were "saved" in a modern Christian sense. Rather, the result was that every individual Israelite would have been able to rest assured that God was still on His throne and ruling their nation. This

5 John Stetze Bergsma, *The Jubilee from Leviticus to Qumran: A History of Interpretation* (Leiden: Brill, 2007), 32.

6 Bergsma, *The Jubilee from Leviticus to Qumran*, 31–32.

holy day was all about preserving an appropriate throne room for God, so that He could maintain His kingship and continue to govern the Israelite nation from the holy of holies, the very place where His glory had come to dwell on the earth.

THE DAY OF ATONEMENT RITUAL

In terms of specifics, the Day of Atonement ritual involved three main elements: (1) a bull for a sin offering that accomplished atonement for the high priest himself, (2) a goat for a sin offering that accomplished atonement for the people, and (3) "a scapegoat" that would have the sins of the people confessed over it before it was sent away into the wilderness.

According to Leviticus 16, the high priest was commanded to cast lots at the doorway of the Tent of Meeting to determine which of the two goats would become the sin offering for the people (Lev. 16:7–10). When this was decided, the high priest would sacrifice the bull and the first goat, enter the holy of holies to burn incense before the Lord, and then sprinkle the blood of the offerings on top and in front of the mercy seat of the ark of the covenant (Lev. 16:14–15).

Next, the high priest would enter the holy place, just outside the holy of holies, and sprinkle the blood of the sin offerings in front of the curtain that separated the holy of holies from the holy place (Lev. 16:16–17). While in the holy place, the high priest would also sprinkle the blood of the sin offerings on the incense altar that stood next to the golden lampstand and the table that held the bread of God's presence (Exod. 25; 30). Then finally, the high priest would leave the holy place and sprinkle the blood of the sin offerings on the bronze altar stationed in the outer court, where the people presented their sacrifices (Lev. 16:18–19).

This progression from the holy of holies to the holy place and then finally to the outer court of the Tabernacle on the Day of Atonement signified a complete cleansing of the entire sanctuary, to the point that all contamination caused by human sin and uncleanness was purged (kaphar) from God's holy house. With this part of the service complete, the high priest would then lay his hands on the scapegoat and "confess over it all the iniquities of the sons of Israel and all their transgressions in regard to all their sins" (Lev. 16:20–22). Next, the goat would be sent away "into the wilderness" and "bear all their iniquities into a solitary land" (Lev. 16:21–22). Once the scapegoat had been sent into the wilderness, the high priest would change his clothes and sacrifice another series of burnt offerings, after which the bodies of the bull and goat that were used for the sin offerings would be taken "outside the camp" and burned with fire (Lev. 16:27).

At this point, the Tabernacle was pronounced clean and therefore fit to remain the place of God's throne for another year. Additionally, after the Day of Atonement services, the priesthood and the people were also regarded as clean and therefore fit to serve the Lord and fellowship with Him at His primary dwelling place on the earth, which is precisely what God always intended when He brought the Israelites out of Egypt (Exod. 25:8; 3:18; 8:27; Lev. 16:30).

CHAPTER SUMMARY

As we prepare to study in the next chapter how the Day of Atonement will be fulfilled when Jesus returns, below are the most important points to review from this chapter:

1. When God brought the Israelites out of Egypt, He expressed His desire to establish His dwelling place in their midst. In the ancient Near East, a sanctuary for a deity functioned as both their house and their throne room. Thus, God's Tabernacle was His base of operations in the same way the White House is the base of operations for the American president. It was the place where God's heavenly rule touched the earth and extended outwards over His entire creation (Exod. 25:8; 29:44–46).

2. According to Leviticus, if common human uncleanness and sin mingled with God's presence, the results could be catastrophic judgment and death.

For this reason, the Torah prescribed that a complex set of ritual purity laws had to be observed relating to clean and unclean practices and states of being, so that God's unique and holy nature would not be violated (Lev. 10:1–3; Lev. 11–15).

3. The ritual purity and sacrificial laws helped to remove the physical pollution created by sin and uncleanness to a certain degree. However, the Day of Atonement provided a more comprehensive solution to the problem. On the Day of Atonement, the entire sanctuary was cleansed of contamination. In addition, the sin and uncleanness of the people and the priesthood was also completely removed for another year through the two sin offerings and the scapegoat that was sent into the wilderness. Notably, however, none of these atonement or purity practices in Leviticus improved the moral or spiritual status of the people, let alone their eternal standing with God. Instead, they only dealt with the physical pollution that sin and unclean practices created in the physical space where God lived (Lev. 16).

4. Because God's throne room was purified on Yom Kippur, the rituals performed on this day completed the enthronement process that began ten days earlier during the Feast of Trumpets (Yom Teruah). Israel acknowledged God as their King on Yom Teruah and then made a place for Him to dwell on Yom Kippur.

BIBLE STUDY QUESTIONS

1. Why is it important to understand the Levitical system within the framework of hospitality towards the Lord?

2. What did the Day of Atonement accomplish in ancient Israel?

3. How did the laws in Leviticus extend grace to the people? Also, what were the limitations of these laws?

9

THE DAY OF ATONEMENT & THE RETURN OF JESUS

IN THE LAST CHAPTER, we discovered that the main purpose of the Day of Atonement was to purify the sacred space in the Tabernacle, as well as the Israelites themselves, so that God could continue to dwell in the midst of His people. We also learned that God's presence in the Tabernacle was closely linked to His enthronement and rule over the nation of Israel; the holy of holies was the place of God's throne, and every year on the Day of Atonement, when the sanctuary was purged of sin and uncleanness, His kingship was renewed.

After the Day of Atonement ended, the process of coronating God as the King of Israel and creating a suitable place for Him to dwell, which had begun during the Feast of Trumpets ten days earlier, was complete. Through the first two fall feasts, the King of glory was acknowledged, exalted, and invited to rule His people for another year.

With this historical background in mind, you may already get a sense of where we are headed in this chapter and of how the Day of

Atonement will be fulfilled when Jesus returns. What we will see is that the Day of Atonement always pointed forward to the physical purification of the sacred space where the Messiah will establish His throne in Jerusalem, as well as to the complete physical and spiritual purification of Israel and the nations. At the deepest prophetic levels, the Day of Atonement foreshadows how Jesus will create a purified people who can live in God's presence, and a sanctified place where God's glory can dwell, during the millennium.

To fully unpack the messianic and eschatological implications of the Day of Atonement, we will begin by looking at how the Messiah already brought about a partial fulfillment of Yom Kippur through His first-century ministry. Then we will branch out from there to analyze the events that will take place both before and after the Messiah's coronation ceremony during the Feast of Trumpets, which will bring the Day of Atonement to its final prophetic fulfillment in the messianic age.

THE MESSIANIC FULFILLMENT OF THE DAY OF ATONEMENT

Christians and messianic Jews have recognized that the Day of Atonement reveals many important lessons about the work of the Messiah and even the core of the gospel message itself. For example, the book of Hebrews says that whereas the high priest entered the holy of holies of the earthly Tabernacle once a year with the blood of bulls and goats, Jesus entered the "more perfect tabernacle" in heaven, "not through the blood of goats and calves, but through His own blood," and in this way He "obtained eternal redemption" and forgiveness of sins for His people (Heb. 9:11–12).

The point made in Hebrews is that Jesus is both the perfect sacrifice and the perfect High Priest that the Day of Atonement rituals always typologically prefigured. According to Hebrews, the Levitical system only offered a "shadow of the good things to come" through the Messiah (Heb. 10:1), and it also constantly reminded the people of their "sins year by year" (Heb. 10:3), which resulted in a sense of "condemnation" (2 Cor. 3:9). However, Jesus accomplished for us something that the

Levitical system never could: not temporary outward cleansing, but a total purification of body, soul, and spirit so that we can serve God according to "a new and living way" (Heb. 10:20) and abide fully in His presence forever, both now and in the age to come.

At the practical level, the relationship between Yom Kippur and the work of the Messiah can help us if we ever struggle with sin and condemnation in this life. I remember when I was a new Christian back in 2004, I thought I might be condemned for my past sins of drug use and immorality. Then I read a book called *The Normal Christian Life* by Watchman Nee.

In this book, Nee draws from the Day of Atonement passages in Leviticus and emphasizes that to have a clear conscience and be free from condemnation we must accept how valuable the blood of Jesus truly is in the eyes of God. According to Leviticus, the primary element that accomplished atonement for the people was the blood of the sacrifice sprinkled inside and outside the Tabernacle. When God saw the blood, He was satisfied, because the blood made everything clean.

Therefore, as followers of the Messiah, to have peace in our hearts and peace with God, we must shift our focus from our own works and meditate on the value that God Himself places on the blood of the Messiah. We often struggle with condemnation because we believe our past sins carry more weight with God than the blood of His own Son. But this is simply not true.

As Nee explains:

> The Blood is therefore not primarily for us but for God. If I want to understand the value of the Blood I must accept God's valuation of it, and if I do not know something of the value set upon the Blood by God I shall never know what its value is for me.[1]
>
> We have to believe that the Blood is precious to God because He says it is so (1 Peter 1:18–19). If God can accept the Blood as a payment for our sins and as the price of our redemption, then we

1 Watchman Nee, *The Normal Christian Life* (Tyndale House Publishers, 1957), 7.

> can rest assured that the debt has been paid. [...] Our valuation of the Blood is only according to His valuation [...] and He is holy and righteous and has the right to say that the Blood is acceptable in His eyes and has fully satisfied Him. [...] Oh, what an emancipation it would be if we saw more of the value in God's eye of the precious Blood of His dear Son![2]

On the Day of Atonement, it was the blood, and only the blood, that effectuated atonement for Israel. As a result, if you believe in Jesus and trust in His sacrifice, you can be one hundred percent confident that atonement has been made for you and that God regards you as clean. 1 Peter 1:2 says you have been "sprinkled" with the blood of the perfect sacrifice and purified from all sin and spiritual uncleanness. Furthermore, to fully confirm that Jesus is the perfect Yom Kippur sacrifice, God made sure that He was crucified outside the city of Jerusalem, just as the Day of Atonement sin offerings were burned "outside the camp" (Lev. 17:27). As the author of Hebrews says: "Therefore Jesus also, that he might sanctify the people through His own blood, suffered outside the gate" (Heb. 13:12).

Understanding the power of the Messiah's atoning sacrifice offers us dynamic protection against the lies of the Devil. Indeed, the accusations of Satan can only gain a foothold in our lives to the extent that we diminish the value of the Messiah's blood in the eyes of God. Yom Kippur teaches us about the value of the blood from God's perspective, so that we can draw near to Him "with a sincere heart in full assurance of faith, having our hearts sprinkled clean from an evil conscience and our bodies washed with pure water" (Heb. 10:22).

Though repentance and good works should certainly have a place in our lives, in and of themselves these things cannot secure our salvation. Only the blood of the Messiah can do that, and because Jesus has gone before us as our great Yom Kippur sacrifice and High Priest into the

2 Nee, *The Normal Christian Life,* 10–11; 21.

heavenly Tabernacle, we can be at peace knowing our salvation is secure. In addition, now that the Messiah has been "offered once to bear the sins of many," His followers can be confident that He will "appear a second time for salvation, without reference to sin, to those who eagerly await Him" (Heb. 9:28).

THE DAY OF ATONEMENT & THE RETURN OF JESUS

There should be no doubt that the sacrifice of Jesus and His high priestly ministry allow us to experience a spiritual fulfillment of the Day of Atonement now. Nevertheless, the prophetic nature of the spring and fall feasts also implies that there will be a final fulfillment of this appointed time when Jesus returns.

Since the 1970s, the most popular view has maintained that the Day of Atonement will be fulfilled in the future when the Jewish people and Israelis who survive the final Tribulation are saved after the Second Coming. In other words, the Day of Atonement has generally been linked to the salvation of the Jewish remnant right at the beginning of the messianic age.

Others have also connected the Day of Atonement to various judgment events and the defeat of the Antichrist, which will transpire very soon after Jesus returns. But in both cases, whether a person places the emphasis on the salvation of Israel, the judgment of evil, or both when considering the deeper prophetic meaning of the Day of Atonement, this day is almost always linked to events that will happen almost immediately after the Second Coming. As noted in chapter 7, the popular theory maintains that Jesus will return during the Feast of Trumpets and then save Israel and defeat the Antichrist within ten days, thereby fulfilling the Day of Atonement.

MAPPING THE FULFILLMENT OF THE DAY OF ATONEMENT

In the rest of this chapter, we will explore why the Day of Atonement will not be fulfilled immediately after Jesus returns, and how it points forward not so much to the initial salvation of Israel and the defeat of the Antichrist, but rather to a longer process of spiritual and physical purification that will unfold over an extended period of time. To briefly elaborate, the biblical prophets reveal that the salvation and cleansing of Israel will not be complete until many months after the Second Coming, which means a stronger case can be made that the Day of Atonement, like the Feast of Trumpets, will only be fulfilled sometime later in the first year of the Messiah's millennial reign, not in the first week and a half after He returns.

Moreover, we will also discover how the fulfillment of the Day of Atonement will be closely tied to the cleansing of the land of Israel itself, which will take seven months to accomplish and lead to the consecration of a holy allotment for the millennial Temple. We will see that just like in Leviticus, the fulfillment of the Day of Atonement in the messianic age will involve a dual reality of cleansing the Israelite people and cleansing a sacred space within the land, so that the millennial Temple can be established as the place of the Messiah's throne, and the place where God's glory will physically dwell on the earth in the days of the kingdom.

THE CLEANSING OF ISRAEL IN EZEKIEL 36

Ezekiel 36 uses language from the Day of Atonement passages in Leviticus to describe the salvation and cleansing of Israel after the Second Coming. For example, in Ezekiel 36:24–25 God tells the Jewish nation:

> For I will take you out of the nations; I will gather you from all the countries and bring you back into your own land. I will sprinkle clean water on you, and you will be clean; I will cleanse you from all your impurities and from all your idols.

The Hebrew words used for "clean" (*tehor*) and "cleanse" (*taher*) in Ezekiel 36 are the precise words used in Leviticus 16:30 when God describes the end goal of the Day of Atonement: "On this day atonement will be made for you to cleanse [*taher*] you. Then, before the LORD you will be clean [*tehor*] from all your sins" (NIV).

Also, on the Day of Atonement the high priest and those involved in the ceremony would undergo multiple ritual washings with clean water (Lev. 16:4, 26–28) before and after the Yom Kippur service. For example, before the high priest could put on his white linen garments and officiate the atonement ceremony, we read in Leviticus 16:4 that he first had to "bathe his body with water."

These linguistic and thematic parallels in Ezekiel 36:24–25 and Leviticus 16 are not a coincidence. The emphasis on cleansing (*taher*) and water (*mayim*) in both passages indicates that Ezekiel derived his atonement theology from Leviticus 16, and offered a picture of how Yom Kippur will reach its deepest level of prophetic fulfillment when God spiritually cleanses the Jewish nation after the Second Coming.

PURIFICATION AFTER THE SECOND EXODUS

Because Ezekiel 36, and many other passages, use this atonement and cleansing language to describe the salvation of Israel after the Second Coming, many prophecy teachers have concluded that this must mean Jesus will return in the seventh month, save Israel, and fulfill the Day of Atonement in short order. However, notice that Ezekiel 36:24 says Israel will be spiritually cleansed after God gathers the Jewish remnant back to Israel "from all the countries" of their exile.

We saw in chapters 3 and 5 that when Jesus returns, an initial remnant of Israeli exiles will be saved at the time of the second exodus, likely in the first days and weeks after the Second Coming. But we also know that many other Jewish people living in the distant nations will only come back to Israel weeks and months later, when the harvest of Jews and Gentiles from the four corners of the earth takes place (cf. Isa. 66:19–20), as a prophetic fulfillment of the Feast of Weeks.

Since we know this gathering of the Jewish remnant back to Israel will unfold for at least a month and a half after the Messiah returns, and possibly longer, this implies that the Day of Atonement will not be fulfilled until many months after the Second Coming. After all, for the Day of Atonement to be prophetically fulfilled in the way Ezekiel

36:24–25 describes, all Israel will have to be saved and cleansed of their impurities, iniquities, and uncleanness, and this is not something that could happen within ten days after the Messiah is back on the earth. Instead, the prophets outline a longer series of events that will involve the gathering of the Jewish remnant from the ends of the earth, the outpouring of the Spirit, and the spiritual cleansing of Israel and the nations, which will then culminate with the fulfillment of the Day of Atonement at a later time, likely after the Feast of Trumpets coronation ceremony in the seventh month.

It is also worth noting here that the idea that Jesus will return in the fall and immediately fulfill the Day of Atonement is rooted in the faulty notion that the spring feasts have already been fulfilled. However, once we understand that every feast relates to the return of Jesus in a different way, it becomes harder to imagine that the Second Coming will occur very close to the Day of Atonement on the calendar.

Additionally, from a historical vantage point it was always Passover, not the Day of Atonement, that was most closely associated with the initial redemption of Israel, the victory of God on the battlefield, and the establishment of God's new creation. This is another reason why the complete spiritual salvation of Israel and the Gentiles that the Day of Atonement prophetically foreshadows will probably not be complete until the spring feasts are fulfilled first.

THE SEVEN MONTHS OF CLEANSING IN EZEKIEL 39

Another text in Ezekiel that supports the idea that the Day of Atonement will be fulfilled many months after the return of Jesus can be found in Ezekiel 39. This prophecy uses the same atonement language as Ezekiel 36 and Leviticus 16. In Ezekiel 39, however, Ezekiel emphasizes how the land of Israel itself will be cleansed after the defeat of the Antichrist (i.e., Gog).

To understand the context of Ezekiel 39, we can recall that Ezekiel 38 says the Messiah will defeat the Antichrist with many of the same Passover plagues that Moses used to defeat Pharaoh in the book of Exodus (Ezek. 38:22). Ezekiel understood that the Messiah will be a greater Moses who will lead his people through the wilderness, part the Red Sea, and then confront the Antichrist and his armies in a final battle (i.e., Armageddon), which will then bring the Passover story to fulfillment in the kingdom of God (Lk. 22:15–16).

After the battle of Armageddon takes place, Ezekiel 39 also says there will be so many rotting corpses and leftover bones in Jerusalem and the surrounding areas of Israel that it will take the Jewish remnant seven months to bury the remains of those who sided with the Antichrist against the Messiah:

> On that day I will give Gog a burial ground there in Israel [...] So they will bury Gog there with all his horde, and they will call it the valley of Hamon-gog. For seven months the house of Israel will be burying them in order to cleanse the land. Even all the people of the land will bury them; and it will be to their renown on the day that I glorify Myself," declares the Lord God. "They will set apart men who will constantly pass through the land, burying those who were passing through, even those left on the surface of the ground, in order to cleanse it. At the end of seven months they will make a search. As those who pass through the land pass through and anyone sees a man's bone, then he will set up a marker by it until the buriers have buried it in the valley of Hamon-gog. [...] So they will cleanse the land. (Ezek. 39:11–16)

CLEANSING AND ATONEMENT LANGUAGE IN EZEKIEL 39

There are a number of clues in Ezekiel 39 that shed light on how the Day of Atonement will be fulfilled after the Messiah's Second Coming. First, the word "cleanse" (taher), which is repeated three times in Ezekiel 39:11–16, is the primary word used in Leviticus 16 to describe the cleansing of God's sanctuary, as well as the Israelite people, on the Day of Atonement (Lev. 16:19, 30).

With this connection in mind, it is not hard to see that the cleansing of the land referred to in Ezekiel 39 will lead to the fulfillment of the Day of Atonement in the millennium, not when the battle of Armageddon takes place, but some time later, after the Messiah has already fulfilled the spring feasts. Furthermore, because the Day of Atonement is the most holy day of the year on the biblical calendar, it cannot be fulfilled until the purification of both the individual Israelites (Ezek. 36:24–25) and their land (Ezek. 39:11–16) is complete, which Ezekiel says will take seven months to accomplish after the defeat of the Antichrist.

On that point, let me also note that the more I have read Ezekiel 39 and considered how polluted the land of Israel will be after the battle of Armageddon, the less sense it has made to me that this battle will coincide with the Day of Atonement. Above all, the Day of Atonement was associated with purity. It was the day that made everything clean. Thus, it is hard to imagine how this appointed time could be fulfilled immediately after Jesus returns, when the land is still defiled with rotting corpses and many members of the Jewish remnant from the nations have not even yet been saved and brought back to Israel. Such a scenario contradicts everything the Day of Atonement originally signified in the book of Leviticus, which is another reason why it seems more logical to me that the Day of Atonement will not be fulfilled and celebrated in the millennium until both the people and the land of Israel are cleansed, seven months or so after the defeat of the Antichrist.

As always, I leave precise timelines to the Lord. But it is still worth pointing out that what we are told about the on-ground conditions in Israel in the early days after the Second Coming does pose problems for those who argue that Jesus will return in the seventh month and immediately fulfill the fall feasts.

THE SEVEN MONTHS

In addition to the cleansing language in Ezekiel 39, the seven months designated to purify the land may also imply that this cleansing process will be completed sometime in the seventh month and thereby bring the Day of Atonement to fulfillment in the kingdom. Admittedly, this idea rests on some speculation. However, we do know that Ezekiel uses a lot of Passover symbolism in Ezekiel 38 when describing the Messiah's victory over Gog, which means this final victory may take place sometime right before Passover is fulfilled in the kingdom of God.

If this is the case, then it is not unreasonable to suggest that the seven months referred to in Ezekiel 39 could span the time between the spring feasts in the first month and the fall feasts in the seventh month. In other words, if we hypothetically assume for the sake of argument that the Antichrist will be defeated sometime right before Passover (March), and that believers will then eat the first Passover meal with Jesus in the kingdom shortly thereafter (March/April), then the cleansing of the land, which would start right after the defeat of the Antichrist (March), would last through September. This would then bring us to the start of October, which is the precise time when the Day of Atonement is often celebrated.

Of course, there is no explanation attached to the seven months in Ezekiel 39, so I am not dogmatic on the idea that the seven months will conclude at the exact moment the Day of Atonement is fulfilled. Seven is the number of completion in the Bible, so it is possible that this time designation in Ezekiel 39 was chosen only to imply the completion of the cleansing process in a general sense.

At the same time, however, there is an interesting element of flow and transition in Ezekiel 38–39. At the beginning of this prophecy, we see a concentration of Passover motifs and at the end we see overt cleansing and atonement language. This could be a hint that we are looking here at Ezekiel's version of how the biblical feasts will be fulfilled when the Messiah returns, beginning with Passover in the first month and culminating with the fall feasts seven months later.

CLEANSING A SPACE FOR THE MILLENNIAL TEMPLE

The idea that the events outlined in Ezekiel 39 will lead to the fulfillment of the Day of Atonement in the millennium is further confirmed by the fact that the building of the millennial Temple in Ezekiel 40–48 occurs immediately after this cleansing process is complete (Ezek. 39). As we learned in the last chapter, the purpose of the Day of Atonement was to maintain a holy space where God could live, and because this is exactly what Ezekiel concentrates on at the end of his prophecy, this is another clue that in these chapters he is painting us a picture of events that will lead to a great Yom Kippur celebration in the first year of the messianic age.

According to Leviticus, God's holy presence cannot mingle with uncleanness and death. Therefore, Ezekiel emphasizes the meticulous burial of the dead after the battle of Armageddon in Ezekiel 39 because this is the prerequisite that has to be met before the land for God's house can be consecrated. Moreover, the way these final chapters in Ezekiel incorporate the cleansing and sanctuary themes from the Day of Atonement passages in Leviticus proves that they revolve around the deeper eschatological realization of what this festival always pointed forward to in the first place; namely, the time when Israel and the nations, as well as the holy space for God's sanctuary, will be completely cleansed and purified after the Messiah returns, so that construction of the millennial Temple can begin and God can once again dwell among His people.

WHY THERE WILL BE A FUTURE MILLENNIAL TEMPLE

Many Christians are against the idea that there will be an actual Temple in the millennium because they do not accept that there will be a need for animal sacrifices now that Jesus has already died for our sins, and, in their view, "fulfilled the sacrificial system." However, there are two reasons why there will have to be a millennial Temple with an operational system of sacrifices after the Second Coming.

First, as we saw in the last chapter, the physical sacrifices in the Temple accomplished ritual purification of sacred space in a physical sense, whereas the sacrifice of Jesus purifies us in a spiritual sense. This means that the physical sacrifices in the Temple and the sacrifice of Jesus are concerned with two separate things: the former physical realities and the latter spiritual realities, so one does not necessarily nullify the need for the other.

Consequently, physical sacrifices will be required in the millennium because God's physical presence will again dwell with imperfect and unclean humans during this time. Remember, many people will be saved after Jesus returns, and these people, though they will experience the Holy Spirit in miraculous ways, will remain in their pre-resurrection bodies until after the millennium. This means that death and other bodily practices associated with ritual uncleanness will still be present during the millennium, which will in turn necessitate some type of sacrificial system so that the place of God's sanctuary can remain clean.

In the words of biblical scholar Ian Bacon:

> The very nature of the New Covenant makes it a unique relationship in which God will be present with Israel in the Millennial Kingdom. The sacrifices in Ezekiel 40-48 afford Israel the opportunity to keep the temple cleansed and purified as God's glory resides in their midst. It has been shown that the animal sacrifices in Ezekiel 40-48 will take place in a literal future temple for outward purification purposes in the presence of Christ Jesus glorified who resides over His theocratic

kingdom operating under the New Covenant in the Millennial temple. Thus, Ezekiel 40-48 is best interpreted literally.[3]

Second, there will have to be an actual Temple in the millennium because this sanctuary will serve as the place of the Messiah's throne during the messianic age. As noted in the last chapter, in the ancient world, a temple was not the same thing as a modern worship space, such as a church or synagogue. Rather, a temple functioned as the command center for a deity; God's Temple was the place from which He extended His heavenly rule over the entire earth.

Once we understand the intrinsic relationship between sacred temple space and the kingship of God, it becomes much easier to understand why the Hebrew prophets place so much emphasis on the millennial Temple. The worldview of the prophets was not characterized by the modern Christian prejudice against a future physical Temple. Instead, they were more concerned with the rule and reign of God, which is why they regarded it as an obvious fact that there will have to be a millennial Temple constructed when the Messiah sets up His kingdom. The prophets understood that the Messiah's throne will be placed in the future Jerusalem sanctuary, and that from there He will judge and rule the nations (Ezek. 43:7).

3 For an excellent summary of the ritual purification view of millennial sacrifices, which is distinct from the memorial and Mosaic covenant views, see: Ian S. Bacon, *The Plausibility of Animal Sacrifices in Ezekiel 40–48 Literally Operating in the Millennial Kingdom Under the New Covenant*, Liberty University, 2018, online. Quoted selection from p. 59 of this work. To briefly elaborate on the point here, even though Ezekiel says God will make Israel clean after the Second Coming, the word clean is applied in a moral/spiritual way in Ezekiel 36:24–25. It implies that Israel will no longer worship idols or commit major moral transgressions in the millennium. However, because only people who believe in Jesus prior to His Second Coming will receive their fully perfected and immortal resurrection bodies at the time of the Rapture/Second Coming, those who place their faith in Him after these events, during the messianic age, will still experience a number of things tied to ritual uncleanness (e.g., sexual relations, childbirth, death, bodily emissions) in the days of the millennium, which will make physical sacrifices a necessity once God resides again in His Temple.

THE MILLENNIAL TEMPLE ACCORDING TO EZEKIEL AND DANIEL

In addition to Ezekiel 40–48, many other prophecies also speak of the millennial Temple. For example, in Ezekiel 37:26–28 God makes a general statement about the millennial Temple when He says:

> I will make a covenant of peace with them; it will be an everlasting covenant with them. And I will place them and multiply them, and will set My sanctuary in their midst forever. My dwelling place also will be with them; and I will be their God, and they will be My people. And the nations will know that I am the LORD who sanctifies Israel, when My sanctuary is in their midst forever.

The broader context of these verses describe the time when the Messiah will be King in Israel. Consequently, there should be no doubt that the reign of the Messiah will also be linked to the reestablishment of God's "sanctuary" and "dwelling place" in Israel (cf. Isa. 66:20).

Likewise, Daniel's famous seventy-weeks prophecy in Daniel 9:24–27 says that after the final Tribulation, the Jewish people will "anoint a most holy place" (v. 24). This phrase, "most holy place," is only used in the Hebrew Bible to designate sacred space or sacred objects in the Tabernacle/Temple. Thus, the linguistic details here confirm that after Daniel's Seventieth Week a new holy place will be anointed in Jerusalem, which will then become the site of the millennial Temple (cf. Dan. 8:14).

And perhaps most important, in Ezekiel 43:7 God describes the millennial Temple as "the place of My throne and the place of the soles of My feet, where I will dwell among the sons of Israel forever." Just as the Lord expressed His desire to live among the Israelites after they left Egypt, He again promises that He will make His dwelling place among them in the messianic age. The Feast of Trumpets and Day of Atonement ceremonies that formally establish the Messiah's kingship in the first year of the millennium will naturally lead to the building of the Lord's holy sanctuary at the top of Mount Zion.

In this vein, Zechariah 6:11–15 adds that the Messiah will "build the Temple of the Lord," serve as a "priest on His throne," and unite the "two offices" of King and Priest when He reigns on the earth. As a result, in the words of Bible teacher David Barron, there should be no doubt that a literal millennial Temple will be constructed after the Second Coming. Barron writes:

> But, we may ask, what Temple is it that the Messiah, according to this and other predictions, was to build? In answer to this question we would say first of all that we cannot exclude from this prophecy the reference to a literal Temple in Jerusalem, which shall, after Israel's national conversion, be built under the superintendence of their Messiah-King, and which will, during the millennial period, be "the House of the Lord" on earth, to which "the nations will flow" and many peoples will go, in order that they may be taught His ways, and learn to walk in His paths, and which will be literally "A House of Prayer and worship for "all the nations." [...] Whatever fulfillment of the words we may already see, the full realization of them will not be until Messiah sits and reigns as 'priest upon His throne' over Israel."[4]

THE DAY OF ATONEMENT AND THE JUBILEE

Besides its purification aspects, the future fulfillment of the Day of Atonement will also include a fulfillment of the biblical Jubilee. As many readers will be aware, the Jubilee took place after every forty-nine years in ancient Israel (at least under ideal circumstances), and during this time Israelite slaves were set free and land that had previously been sold was returned to the original tribal family to whom it belonged.

In a nutshell, the Jubilee was a mechanism that preserved freedom within Israelite society and stopped any one family from becoming too powerful through the excessive acquisition of land and slaves. Prior to the Jubilee, if a person fell on hard times, they could temporarily "sell" their land to a creditor to pay off debt, or they could sell themselves

4 David Baron, *Zechariah: A Commentary on his Visions and Prophecies* (Grand Rapids: Kregel, 1918), 195; 204.

or a family member into temporary servitude to accomplish the same purpose. At the Jubilee, however, the land would be given back to the original owner and slaves would be set free, which helped preserve justice and equilibrium between the different members of society.

One important thing to know about the Jubilee was that it was proclaimed on the Day of Atonement:

> You shall then sound a ram's horn [shofar] abroad on the tenth day of the seventh month; on the Day of Atonement you shall sound a horn all through your land. So you shall consecrate the fiftieth year and proclaim a release throughout the land to all its inhabitants. It shall be a jubilee for you, and each of you shall return to his own property, and each of you shall return to his family. (Lev. 25:8–10)

Many scholars have noted that the Jubilee was proclaimed on the Day of Atonement because of the close connection between this holy day and the kingship of God. In the ancient Near East, it was the responsibility of the king of a nation to preserve justice within his realm. Therefore, at the same time God's kingship was acknowledged and renewed during the Feast of Trumpets and on the Day of Atonement, His justice was also enacted after every forty-ninth year through the Jubilee.

THE PROPHETIC FULFILLMENT OF THE JUBILEE

Given the prophetic nature of the biblical feasts, we can assume that when the Day of Atonement is fulfilled in the future there will be a fulfillment of the Jubilee at the same time as well. Although this fulfillment of the Jubilee will have multiple layers, at its core it will involve the return of the Israelite tribes to their ancestral land because this is what the Jubilee was always concerned with from the very beginning: physical real estate belonging to the twelve Israelite tribes.

Not surprisingly, there are many texts in the Hebrew Bible that indicate that after the Messiah returns and purifies the land of Israel, He will then designate the tribal allotments for the nation of Israel, in the territory that was originally promised to Abraham, Isaac, and Jacob in the book of Genesis. For example, in Ezekiel 37:25 God promised the Israelites that when the Messiah sets up His kingdom, they "will live on the land that I gave to Jacob My servant, in which your fathers lived; and they will live on it, they, and their sons and their sons' sons forever; and David My servant will be their prince forever." Likewise, in Ezekiel 47:13 we read: "Thus says the LORD God, 'This shall be the boundary by which you shall divide the land for an inheritance among the twelve tribes of Israel.'" Then, the remaining verses in Ezekiel 47–48 describe in detail the land that will be given to the Israelite tribes after the Second Coming.

These passages that speak of the Israelite tribes returning to their land in the messianic age are tied to the fulfillment of the biblical Jubilee, which also leads to another important point about when the Day of Atonement and the Jubilee will be fulfilled in relation to the return of Jesus. Notice that Ezekiel gives the most detail regarding the return of the Jewish tribes to their land in chapter 47 of his prophecy, after the earlier segments that speak of the fulfillment of Passover, the second exodus, and the cleansing of the land after the defeat of the Antichrist (Ezek. 38–39). This placement of the prophetic material confirms that the Jubilee, and by correlation the Day of Atonement, will only be fulfilled many months after the Messiah returns. After all, just as the fulfillment of the Day of Atonement will require a seven-month period of cleansing before the holy space for the Temple can be consecrated, so too the Jubilee will require the same seven-month period of cleansing because the land cannot be divided among the tribes until the prerequisite purification takes place.

THE DAY OF ATONEMENT IN THE KINGDOM OF GOD

We must use our imaginations to surmise what precise events will take place when the Day of Atonement is fulfilled in the millennium. But I envision a Day of Atonement ceremony taking place on Mount Zion ten days after Jesus has been coronated and proclaimed King of the messianic age during the Feast of Trumpets.

On this holy day, perhaps Jesus will stand on Mount Zion dressed in pure white garments that symbolize His priesthood, with the golden crown of kingship on His head, as rows and rows of purified saints from Israel and the nations stand before Him.

With the crowds gathered, Jesus then takes a large flask of golden oil and pours it forth over the earth on the site where the future Temple will be built, anointing the most holy place just as Daniel 9:24 prophesied. Then Jesus raises His voice, dedicates this sacred space to God, and proclaims the word of the Lord: "My house will be called a house of prayer for all peoples," so "exalt the LORD our God and worship at His holy hill, for the LORD our God is holy!" to which all those in attendance respond by proclaiming, "Amen! How lovely are Your dwelling places, O LORD of hosts! Our souls long and even yearn for the courts of the LORD" (Isa. 57:6; Ps. 99:9; Ps. 84:1–2).

Maybe at this time the Temple altar will also be consecrated and the first sacrifices of the millennium will be made. Then with the holy space of the sanctuary duly consecrated, Jesus is handed a ram's horn trumpet (shofar) and proceeds to sound forth a long blast proclaiming the year of Jubilee. From this point on, having been cleansed of defilement and death, the land of Israel is made holy and set apart for God's service, the construction of the millennial Temple begins, and the twelve tribes are given their inheritance in the regions promised to Abraham, Isaac, and Jacob, never again to be exiled, never again to be separated from their property, and never again to experience slavery. For the age of atonement and jubilee will have arrived.

THE GOD OF HOLINESS

Of course, this explanation of how Yom Kippur will be fulfilled in the kingdom of God may only give us a shadow of a much greater reality that will be experienced in the messianic age. But still, this focus on a process of cleansing and purification, centered around the people of Israel, the land of Israel, the Messiah's High Priesthood, and the sacred space of the future Temple, brings us much closer to the deeper eschatological layers of this feast than many of the other explanations that are popular in Christian and messianic Jewish circles today.

Above all, the Day of Atonement was concerned with creating a people who could be in contact with the Lord and a sacred space suitable for His glory. After the Messiah is victorious over the forces of evil, He will then systematically work for a period of many months to bring the Day of Atonement to a glorious prophetic fulfillment in the kingdom of God, which will in turn mark the beginning of His reign as the great King-Priest of the millennium and set the stage for the glory of God to return to the earth.

CHAPTER SUMMARY

Below are the main points from this chapter that summarize how the Day of Atonement relates to the Second Coming:

1. It is common to hear that the Day of Atonement will be fulfilled ten days after Jesus returns. This view, however, is rooted in the mistaken idea that only the fall feasts relate to the Messiah's Second Coming, and it also overlooks the elaborate sequence of events that must transpire in the millennium before the purification and final salvation of Israel and the nations can be complete.

2. The Hebrew prophets did use atonement and cleansing language from Leviticus 16 to describe the spiritual purification of Israel and the physical purification of the Promised Land after the Second Coming. However, the prophets are also clear that this holistic purification process will take seven months to complete, which implies that the Day of Atonement will not be fulfilled until many months after Jesus returns. It appears that the purification of Israel will begin after the battle of Armageddon and when the remnant is gathered and the Holy Spirit is poured out to fulfill the Feast of Weeks. Then over the ensuing months Israel and the nations will deepen their relationship with the Lord in preparation for the first Day of Atonement celebration in the kingdom (Ezek. 36:24–25; 39:11–16).

3. Besides its purification aspects, the fulfillment of the Day of Atonement will also be intricately tied to the Messiah's High Priesthood, the consecration of a sacred space for the Temple, and the prophetic realization of the Jubilee. As the great King-Priest of Israel, the Messiah will oversee the construction and operation of the millennial Temple and restore the twelve tribes to their ancestral land (Ezek. 37:26–28; 43:7; Dan. 9:24; Zech. 6:11–15; Ezek. 47:13).

BIBLE STUDY QUESTIONS

1. What messianic and eschatological layers of the Day of Atonement covered in this chapter deepened your understanding of this appointed time the most?

2. Why could the Day of Atonement not reach its prophetic end goal within the first ten days after the Second Coming?

3. How will the fulfillment of the Day of Atonement be tied to the earlier fulfillment of the spring feasts, as well as the fulfillment of the Feast of Trumpets?

4. Why will there be another Temple built after Jesus returns?

10

THE FEAST OF TABERNACLES IN HISTORICAL CONTEXT

JUST AS THE ANNUAL CYCLE of appointed times in Leviticus 23 begins with the seven-day feast of Passover and Unleavened Bread, it also ends with a seven-day feast at the end of the year: The Feast of Tabernacles, which is also called the Feast of Booths, or *Sukkot* based on its Hebrew name.[1] In this chapter, we will study the meaning and observance of the Feast of Tabernacles in its original historical context. Then in the next chapter, we will explore how this capstone celebration on the biblical calendar will be fulfilled after the Messiah's Second Coming.

THE FEAST OF TABERNACLES AND THE AGRICULTURAL HARVEST

The Feast of Tabernacles had important agricultural significance in ancient Israel, as it celebrated the completion of the annual harvest, which concluded in the fall, sometime between September and October

1 Pronounced: *soo-kote.*

in the northern hemisphere. For example, Leviticus 23:39 links Sukkot to the harvest in the seventh month and gives an overview of how this feast was supposed to be celebrated. This verse states:

> On exactly the fifteenth day of the seventh month, when you have gathered in the crops of the land, you shall celebrate the feast of the Lord for seven days, with a rest on the first day and a rest on the eighth day.

Likewise, in Exodus 23:16 the Festival of Tabernacles is called the "Feast of the Ingathering at the end of the year" and this is an important designation. It indicates that one of the core purposes of Sukkot was to celebrate God's provision and the completion of the harvest that had transpired over the previous seven months.

In Deuteronomy 16:13–15, this connection between the harvest and the Feast of Tabernacles is also apparent. But in this context, the Lord highlights how Sukkot was supposed to be a time of great joy and celebration, as the Israelites acknowledged His favor and provision. We read:

> You shall celebrate the Feast of Booths seven days after you have gathered in from your threshing floor and your wine vat; and you shall rejoice in your feast, you and your son and your daughter and your male and female servants and the Levite and the stranger and the orphan and the widow who are in your towns. Seven days you shall celebrate a feast to the Lord your God in the place which the Lord chooses, because the Lord your God will bless you in all your produce and in all the work of your hands, so that you will be altogether joyful. (Deut. 16:13–15)

As noted in earlier chapters, the annual harvest in Israel began in the spring (March/April), on the day of First Fruits, which took place two days after Passover, on the sixteenth of the first biblical month (Aviv/Nisan). During First Fruits the early barley was harvested and then seven weeks later, during the Feast of Weeks, the completion of the wheat harvest was celebrated.

In addition to these spring grain crops, however, other staples of the Israelite diet, including grapes, figs, pomegranates, and olives were not harvested until later in the year. The grape harvest began in June and lasted until September or October. Figs and pomegranates ripened in August and September, and the olive harvest could last from September through November.

The Feast of Tabernacles was observed from the fifteenth through the twenty-first of the seventh biblical month, which would typically fall somewhere between mid-September and the end of October on our modern calendars. As a result, by the time the Feast of Tabernacles was celebrated, all the main staples of the Israelite diet had been harvested or were on the verge of being harvested. The grain stores were full, delicious fruits were enjoyed, and wine and olive oil could be made for the following year.

In light of His provision, God naturally told the Israelites to "rejoice" and be "altogether joyful" at this time of year (Deut. 16:13–15). Whereas the Day of Atonement five days earlier (on the tenth of the seventh month) called for fasting, repentance, and somber reflection, Sukkot was a time to relax and feast. This was the holy week to celebrate the abundance that God provides for His chosen people.

SUKKOT CELEBRATIONS IN THE TIME OF JESUS

During the Second Temple Period (c. 500 BC–AD 70), which included the time when Jesus walked the earth, there were key Jewish traditions incorporated into the observance of Sukkot that highlighted how this was a time of great rejoicing before the Lord, in particular in light of His provision through the agricultural harvest. One of these traditions was called the Water Libation Ceremony, which began on the second morning of Sukkot and took place every morning thereafter until the feast was over.

THE WATER LIBATION CEREMONY

To complete the Water Libation Ceremony, the high priest would lead a joyful procession of Temple worshippers to the Pool of Siloam in

Jerusalem every morning and fill a golden pitcher that held about two pints of water. After this, the high priest would lead the procession back into the walled city through the Water Gate. As the crowds entered the Water Gate with the high priest, a group of Temple musicians would sound forth three loud blasts on their silver trumpets and then a group of priests would proclaim the words of Isaiah 12:3: "With joy you will draw water from the wells of salvation" (NIV).

Once the high priest was back at the Temple the morning sacrifice was offered on the altar, and then immediately after the high priest ascended to the top of the altar and poured the water from the golden pitcher into a silver basin with a small spout at the bottom. At the same time the Water Libation was offered, a drink offering of wine was also poured into another silver basin on top of the alar.

As these offerings were poured into their respective basins, the water and wine would slowly fall from the top of the altar into a drain at the base of the altar, about ten feet below. Simultaneously, the Temple choir would sing Psalms 113–118 "to the accompaniment of flutes," as all the people assembled for the feast joined in the singing and waved palm branches toward the altar.[2] When the Water Libation ceremony was nearly complete, the priests at the Temple would walk in a circle around the altar one time, and then seven times on the last day of the feast.

The main reason the Water Libation Ceremony became a central part of Sukkot was because most of the rain that ensured the next year's harvest fell on the land between Sukkot and Passover. Thus, even as the Israelites celebrated the previous year's harvest during Sukkot, through the Water Libation Ceremony they also entreated God to send the "latter rains" that would guarantee their agricultural harvest in the following year. In essence, the Water Libation Ceremony was an enacted prayer of supplication. It was an appeal to God to send enough rain to sustain the Israelite nation for another twelve months, even as He had done the year prior.

2 Alfred Edersheim, *The Temple: Its Ministry and Services* (Peabody: Hendrickson, 1994), 221.

Rabbinic scholar Joshua Kulp summarizes the purpose of the Water Libation Ceremony:

> The water libation functioned as a supplication to God to bring rain in the upcoming season. [...] [T]he rainy season in Israel is from Sukkot [Tabernacles] to Pesach [Passover]. If enough rain did not fall in this period people's lives would have been in serious danger. In the Temple they would pour water onto the altar to ask God to bring rain from the heavens to fill the cisterns and underground aquifers below.[3]

THE TEMPLE ILLUMINATION CEREMONY

Although the Water Libation Ceremony took place during the day, this observance was also celebrated again in the evening, beginning on the second night of Sukkot. At this time, the people would gather in one of the outer courts of the Temple, known as the Court of the Women. Then late into the night they would celebrate the Temple Illumination Ceremony, which was also known as "the Rejoicing of the House of [Water] Drawing."

The most important feature of the Temple Illumination Ceremony was the four towering lampstands, each about twenty feet tall with four bowls for oil at the top, that were stationed in the Temple court. Once the sun set, young priests would climb up one of four ladders that stood against each lampstand and fill their respective bowls with olive oil. Subsequently, the lamps would be lit, and all the inhabitants of Jerusalem would behold sixteen magnificent flames that illuminated not only the Temple courts but also large portions of the city itself.

From that moment on, the Israelite priests and people would sing various Psalms in the Temple courtyard, even as "elders of the Sanhedrin performed impressive torch dances, while the steady yellow flames of the menorah oil lamps flooded the Temple and the streets of Jerusalem

3 Joshua Kulp, "English Explanation of Mishnah Sukkah," *Sukkah 4.9*, *Sefaria*, online.

with brilliant light."[4] One can only imagine this scene, as the people saw their religious leaders, men whom they normally associated with the somber rites of the Temple, dancing and juggling torches late into the night. This celebration would have resembled something we associate more with the circus than the worship of God! But in any case, according to the Jewish Talmud, the Temple Illumination Ceremony was such an important part of Sukkot, and so spectacular, "that the ancient rabbis said: 'He that hath not beheld the joy of the drawing of water [celebration] hath never seen joy in his life.'"[5] The Temple Illumination Ceremony demonstrated just how seriously the Israelites took God's commandment to be "altogether joyful" during the Feast of Tabernacles (Deut. 16:15).

THE FEAST OF TABERNACLES AND THE EXODUS

In addition to celebrating the fall harvest in the land of Israel, the Feast of Tabernacles, like Passover and the Feast of Trumpets, also commemorated Israel's exodus from Egypt. However, whereas Passover memorialized the deliverance from Egypt, and the Feast of Trumpets memorialized Israel's Sinai encounter, the Feast of Tabernacles memorialized Israel's time of wandering in the wilderness, and perhaps more to the point, the way God sustained the Israelite nation through their harsh years in the barren desert and then brought them into the Promised Land.

After the statement in Leviticus 23:39 that links Sukkot to the fall harvest, the remaining verses in this passage, found in Leviticus 23:40–44, highlight the connection between Sukkot and the exodus:

> Now on the first day you shall take for yourselves the foliage of beautiful trees, palm branches and boughs of leafy trees and willows of the brook, and you shall rejoice before the LORD your God for seven days. You

---

4 Kevin Howard & Marvin Rosenthal, *The Feasts of the Lord: God's Prophetic Calendar from Calvary to the Kingdom* (Orlando: Zion's Hope, 1997), 140.

5 Howard & Rosenthal, *The Feasts of the Lord*, 140; Quote from *Babylonian Talmud, Sukkah* 5:1.

> shall thus celebrate it as a feast to the Lord for seven days in the year. It shall be a perpetual statute throughout your generations; you shall celebrate it in the seventh month. You shall live in booths for seven days; all the native-born in Israel shall live in booths, so that your generations may know that I had the sons of Israel live in booths when I brought them out from the land of Egypt. I am the Lord your God. So Moses declared to the sons of Israel the appointed times of the Lord.

THE FOLIAGE OF BEAUTIFUL TREES

Within Leviticus 23:40–44, there are probably two distinct commandments that were meant to help Israel remember how God preserved them in the wilderness and then brought them into His abundant land. The first is found in verse 40, where God says that on the first day of Sukkot Israel was supposed to gather the "foliage [lit. fruit] of beautiful trees, palm branches, and boughs of leafy trees and willows of the brook."

During the Second Temple Period, a dispute arose between the Pharisees and the Sadducees over the proper interpretation of this verse (Lev. 23:40). The Sadducees argued the booths mentioned in verses 42–43 were supposed to be built using only the natural foliage mentioned in verse 40. The Pharisees, however, argued that the command to gather foliage (v. 40) during the Feast of Tabernacles was distinct from the command to dwell in booths (v. 42–43). As a result, the Pharisees interpreted Leviticus 23:40 to mean that the Israelites were supposed to carry the natural elements mentioned in this verse in their hands as they worshipped at the Temple.

Because of the popularity of the Pharisees' view, when the Feast of Tabernacles was celebrated the Jewish worshippers in the Temple courts would carry in their hands a citron fruit and a small bundle of branches from three other trees: the date palm, the myrtle, and the willow. These were the four natural elements mentioned in Leviticus 23:40, and in modern Judaism they are called the Four Species.[6]

6 One may also hear these elements called the *lulav* and *etrog*, though the *lulav* technically refers only to the date palm and the *etrog* refers to the citron fruit.

Biblical scholar Alfred Edersheim notes that God probably commanded Israel to gather the Four Species during Sukkot because they corresponded to "different stages of their wilderness journey." The date palms were found in the valleys and plains in the wilderness, the boughs of thick trees referred to bushes on "the mountain heights," the willows of the brook were shorter trees that grew along banks and streams, and the citron fruit reminded Israel of the "good land which the Lord had given them."[7]

In a certain sense then, Israel's entire national history was contained in the Four Species. When the Jewish people carried these holy elements to the Temple during the Feast of Tabernacles, they honored the God who had sustained them in the wilderness, brought them into His good land, and taken up residence among them as their King. Thus, as the various ceremonies took place in the Temple toward the end of the seventh month, the Israelites would wave their Four Species before the Lord and celebrate the completeness of their redemption, as well as God's provision at every stage of their long journey as His chosen people.

LIVING IN THE SUKKAH

Along with the Four Species, the most well-known feature of the Feast of Tabernacles is the temporary shelters that are associated with this appointed time in Leviticus 23:42–43. These shelters are called sukkot in these verses, which is the plural form of the Hebrew word *sukkah,* which simply means a dwelling place or small hut. In Leviticus 23:34, the Feast of Tabernacles is literally called Hag Sukkot (i.e., festival of temporary shelters).

During Sukkot, each Israelite family was commanded to live in a sukkah for the seven days of the feast, as a reminder that their ancestors lived in temporary shelters in the wilderness after they departed from Egypt. According to Leviticus God said:

---

7 Edersheim, *The Temple*, 218.

> You shall live in booths [sukkot] for seven days; all the native-born in Israel shall live in booths [sukkot], so that your generations may know that I had the sons of Israel live in booths [sukkot] when I brought them out from the land of Egypt. I am the LORD your God. (Lev. 23:42–43)

Like the Four Species mentioned in Leviticus 23:40, the sukkot that set the Feast of Tabernacles apart from Israel's other moedim helped the people commemorate the exodus and the years of wilderness wandering. Notice how Leviticus 23:43 also says the temporary booths of Sukkot were meant to educate later "generations" of Israelites about their national history, just like the Passover meal and the Feast of Unleavened Bread (Exod. 13:8).

By the time the Second Temple was built, complex regulations governed how large or small a sukkah could be, as well as what it should be made of. We do not need to get into the details here, but we should note that in general a sukkah was a relatively small hut, usually no bigger than ten or fifteen feet in all directions and built from the boughs of trees and natural branches that grew out of the earth. Moreover, due to the compromise between the Pharisees and Sadducees over the interpretation of Leviticus 23:40, a sukkah was often built with many of the same materials that were included in the Four Species, and from ancient to modern times it has been customary to hang different types of fruit from the leafy branches that cover the top of one's sukkah.

For more than two thousand years, the observance of Sukkot in Jerusalem has offered a remarkable site. Even today, during the Feast of Tabernacles, one will find every street in the city lined with the temporary dwellings of the feast in a way that directly parallels what would have been the case in ancient Israel.

Although the Torah originally called for the Israelites to live in these huts for the entirety of the festival, in modern times the Jewish custom is to simply eat a number of meals and enjoy fellowship with friends and family in one's sukkah, in order to fulfill the commandment. When the seven days of Sukkot come to an end, the Jewish people will then gradually deconstruct their shelters until the next year and observe a Sabbath rest on the eighth day to complete the annual cycle of appointed times (Lev. 23:39).

THE SPIRITUAL APPLICATION OF SUKKOT

The core spiritual message of Sukkot is that God protects and preserves His people in the wilderness and then ultimately blesses them with His abundant provision. The sukkah and the Four Species of this festival symbolize how God's people will often be called to endure barren seasons that make us feel as though we are in a spiritual desert. However, they also symbolize how God nevertheless takes care of us at every stage of our spiritual journey, just as He did for Israel in the wilderness, and eventually brings us into seasons of joy, which are symbolized by the harvest aspects of Sukkot.

As we experience life on this earth, we are often caught off guard and disoriented by the difficult circumstances God calls us to endure. In these times, God can seem absent or distant, His provision can seem insufficient, and it often feels as though our prayers go unanswered. Yet, Sukkot reminds us that even these seasons in the wilderness are part of God's plan for our lives because they teach us to rely on Him in a way that only the wilderness can.

Simultaneously, Sukkot also reminds us that God does not bring His people into the wilderness to destroy us, to confuse us, or to abandon us. His goals are always redemptive and mapped out with our best interest in mind. Ultimately, the Feast of Tabernacles teaches us that God will turn our mourning into dancing and our desert into the garden of Eden.

Metaphorically speaking, we will indeed be called to live in the sukkah in this life. We will be called to face the challenges of instability and fragility in the wilderness of this world. But as we do, we can be confident that God will adorn our time in the wilderness with fruitfulness and eventually bring us into the Promised Land, where like the ancient Israelites, we will reap a bountiful harvest and joyfully draw water from the springs of salvation.

At the end of our lives, we will look back and realize that these words of Moses describe both Israel's experience and ours as well:

> The LORD led you through the great and terrible wilderness, with its fiery serpents and scorpions and thirsty ground where there was no water; He brought water for you out of the rock of flint. In the wilderness He fed you manna which your fathers did not know, that He might humble you and that He might test you, to do good for you in the end. (Deut. 8:15–16)

To continue to trust God in the wilderness, anticipating His abundant grace, is to touch the spiritual essence of Sukkot. The Feast of Tabernacles teaches us that God's end goal is always our joy, and in particular, a joy that we can offer back to Him because we have tangibly experienced His salvation and provision at every stage of our spiritual journey.

THE MINISTRY OF JESUS AND SUKKOT

Because every biblical feast has a deeper spiritual and messianic meaning, it should not surprise us that Jesus also said He came to offer people the true spiritual vitality and abundance that the outward observances and ceremonies of Sukkot always symbolized. For example, in John 7:37–39 we find Jesus in Jerusalem on the last day of the Feast of Tabernacles. With the crowds surrounding Him at the Temple, most likely right around the time the Water Libation Ceremony took place, Jesus stood up and cried out, saying:

> If anyone is thirsty, let him come to Me and drink. He who believes in Me, as the Scripture said, "From his innermost being will flow rivers of living water."

Then John adds:

> But this He spoke of the Spirit, whom those who believed in Him were to receive; for the Spirit was not yet given, because Jesus was not yet glorified. (John 7:37–39)

To understand how Jesus' statement in John 7 would have been interpreted by His contemporaries, recall that in the first century, as the water from the Pool of Siloam was carried into Jerusalem through the Water Gate, a group of priests would proclaim the words of Isaiah 12:3: "With joy you will draw water from the wells of salvation" (NIV). Then, the Water Libation Ceremony would be completed at the Temple altar.

The proclamation of Isaiah 12:3 during the Water Libation Ceremony was important, because it confirms that at this time the Jewish people focused on the coming of the Messiah, the very one whom they believed would lead them to the true wells of spiritual salvation and into the physical abundance of the messianic age. In the time of Jesus, the celebration of Sukkot was infused with messianic significance, and this messianic component was clearly on display when Isaiah 12:3 was read to the people every morning before the festival offerings were made.

With this background in mind, consider the profound boldness of Jesus' statement in John 7:37–39. When Jesus described Himself as the one who can create "rivers of living water" in the "innermost being" of His people, He was declaring Himself to be the mediator of the messianic redemption that every element of Sukkot, and in particular the Water Libation Ceremony, prophetically foreshadowed. He was saying, "I'm the only one who can lead you to the wells of salvation and spiritual abundance that you express so much longing for at this time of year."

It is also noteworthy that Jesus' Hebrew name is Yeshua, which means "salvation." This is the exact Hebrew word from Isaiah 12:3 that announced the Water Libation Ceremony with a reference to the "wells of salvation," or literally, "the wells of yeshua."

When this Hebrew nuance is understood, we can understand why some would have experienced joy and others consternation when they heard Jesus' teaching in the Temple during Sukkot. In John 7 we see the man Yeshua proclaiming Himself to be the path to the wells of salvation (yeshua) that the entire Jewish population expressed joyous longing for at the end of every year.

These were bold claims to be sure, but they also reveal a vital lesson for all God's people across the ages. As we find ourselves walking through the wilderness of this world, we can trust that the man from Nazareth will preserve us until the messianic age. The Spirit He gives to those who believe in Him provides the only living water than can sustain us in this world and prepare us for the next. We often find ourselves spiritually dry because we seek to hydrate our souls with everything but the Messiah. However, to be refreshed at the wells of salvation (yeshua), we only need to turn to the source of our life, Yeshua Himself, the very one whose mission it is to bring us into the joy and abundance of Sukkot. As Jesus made clear when He celebrated the Feast of Tabernacles with His Jewish kin, He is the water that our souls are thirsty for.

THE FEAST OF TABERNACLES IN HISTORICAL CONTEXT

In the next chapter we will cover how Jesus will bring us into the deepest levels of Sukkot joy and abundance in the messianic age. But to conclude this chapter, let us review the main points that clarify the meaning of the Feast of Tabernacles in its original historical context.

As the seventh annual feast on the biblical calendar, the Feast of Tabernacles was the climax of the Israelite year in the same way the seventh-day Sabbath was the climax of the Israelite week. Earlier in the year, Israel celebrated their miraculous deliverance from Egypt during Passover and Unleavened Bread, their early barley harvest during First Fruits, their wheat harvest during the Feast of Weeks, their encounter with God at Mount Sinai during the Feast of Trumpets, and His holy presence abiding in their midst on the Day of Atonement. With these appointed times observed as a foundation, Sukkot, the seventh annual festival, observed in the seventh month, for seven days,[8] then became the consummate time of joy in God's presence that looked back on and celebrated everything He had done for His people in Egypt, in the wilderness, and in the Promised Land. God saved Israel, established His throne in their midst, and provided for their every need. In light of this, Sukkot was the time to say thank you, to feast, and to rejoice in the Lord.

CHAPTER SUMMARY

The following points summarize the original historical meaning of the Feast of Tabernacles:

1. First and foremost, Sukkot was instituted to honor God for the prior year's harvest. After the barley and wheat were harvested in the spring, the Israelites harvested other vital staples, such as grapes, figs, pomegranates, and olives in the fall, and for this reason Sukkot was recognized as the climactic harvest festival on the biblical calendar. During Sukkot, Israel rejoiced in God's provision for seven days and then observed a closing Sabbath rest on the eighth day, which officially brought the annual cycle of appointed times to an end (Lev. 23:33–43; Deut. 16:13–16).

2. Sukkot was also a time to remember how God sustained Israel through their difficult years of wandering in the wilderness. The Four Species carried to the Temple by Jewish worshippers during Sukkot, as well as the temporary shelters Israel lived in for the seven days of this feast, were the tangible elements of this festival that commemorated Israel's desert years after their exodus from Egypt.

---

8 Notice the 777 designating perfect completion.

3. In the time of Jesus, the Feast of Tabernacles was saturated with messianic and eschatological overtones. The Water Libation Ceremony and the Temple Illumination Ceremony were a time to entreat God for the latter rains and rejoice in His provision. However, these ceremonies also marked a time when the Jewish people looked forward to the coming of the Messiah and the abundance of the messianic age (Isa. 12:3; Jn. 7:37–39).

BIBLE STUDY QUESTIONS

1. In what ways is the Feast of Tabernacles tied to the theme of completion?

2. How dd the Feast of Tabernacles relate to both Israel's harvest cycle and their national history?

3. What aspects of Sukkot covered in this chapter did you find the most interesting or beneficial to ponder?

4. How would you summarize the spiritual lessons of the Feast of Tabernacles?

11

THE FEAST OF TABERNACLES & THE RETURN OF JESUS

IN MANY WAYS, the Feast of Tabernacles is the natural extension of the Feast of Trumpets and the Day of Atonement. At the beginning of the seventh month God is enthroned with trumpet blasts and shouts of praise (teruah). Then on the tenth of the month the physical place of His throne is purified, and subsequently, during the Feast of Tabernacles, the benefits of living under God's reign, which include material provision and spiritual blessings, are celebrated with one final seven-day feast.

Stated somewhat differently, though every fall feast centers around God's kingship in some way, the first two fall feasts officially establish His kingship whereas the Feast of Tabernacles is the time to rejoice in His presence and to acknowledge that He is now living among and ruling His people. The Feast of Tabernacles is the climax on the biblical calendar because it signifies the end goal of God's entire redemptive plan. The Lord redeems His people and defeats their enemies (Passover and Unleavened Bread), provides for them (First Fruits and Weeks), establishes His throne and sanctuary in their midst (Trumpets and Atonement), and thus, during the Feast of Tabernacles, the people can relax and rejoice in the King of kings who rules over them, provides for them, and continues to protect them.

Given this relationship between the Feast of Tabernacles and the reign of God, it should not surprise us that the Hebrew prophets frequently spoke of events in the millennial kingdom using the language and themes associated with this feast in the Torah. In this chapter, we will study the future fulfillment of the Sukkot in the kingdom of God and see how it points forward to the time when God will bless the earth with unprecedented levels of agricultural abundance, dwell among His people, and bring all the nations into the experience of His kingship.

THE FEAST OF TABERNACLES IN ZECHARIAH 14

There is one prophecy in Zechariah that mentions the Feast of Tabernacles and notes that this appointed time will be celebrated every year after the Messiah's Second Coming. In Zechariah 14:16–19 we read:

> Then the survivors from all the nations that have attacked Jerusalem will go up year after year to worship the King, the LORD Almighty, and to celebrate the Festival of Tabernacles. If any of the peoples of the earth do not go up to Jerusalem to worship the King, the LORD Almighty, they will have no rain. If the Egyptian people do not go up and take part, they will have no rain. [...] This will be the punishment of Egypt and the punishment of all the nations that do not go up to celebrate the Festival of Tabernacles (NIV).

It is no coincidence that in Zechariah 14:16–19, the Feast of Tabernacles is linked to God's kingship. The main idea articulated in this passage is that after the Messiah's coronation ceremony in the seventh month, which will then lead to the building of the millennial Temple, all the inhabitants of the earth will "go up to Jerusalem" in the days of the millennium to "worship the King, the LORD Almighty" during Sukkot.

At this time, people from the nations will acknowledge God's rule and honor Him for blessing them in the prior year, which will consequently ensure their harvest in the following year. However, Zechariah 14 also says that if any nations in the millennium do not honor God as the King who sustains their lives, "they will have no rain" in the following year and will experience drought until they formally submit to God's rule during the Feast of Tabernacles.

As we saw in the last chapter, Sukkot was a time to celebrate the prior year's harvest and a time to entreat God to send the latter rains that guaranteed the agricultural harvest in the next year. Moreover, in the time of Jesus, it was through the Water Libation Ceremony in the Temple that Israel formalized their expressions of dependence upon God for the following year's harvest. Thus, it makes perfect sense that in the millennium, the observance of Sukkot will once again be tied to the latter rains and the provision of the King, just as it was in ancient Israel.

THE ABUNDANCE OF THE MESSIANIC AGE IN JOEL 2

Besides Zechariah 14, there are a number of other prophecies in the Hebrew Bible that speak of the agricultural abundance we will experience in the messianic age. Although these prophecies do not mention Sukkot directly, they are related to the future fulfillment of Sukkot because they highlight God's provision through the earth, which we know from Zechariah 14 will be celebrated every year of the Messiah's millennial reign during the Feast of Tabernacles.

For example, Joel mentions how God will bless the earth after the Messiah returns. He writes:

> Do not fear, O land, rejoice and be glad, for the LORD has done great things. Do not fear, beasts of the field, for the pastures of the wilderness have turned green, for the tree has borne its fruit, the fig tree and the vine have yielded in full.

> So rejoice, O sons of Zion, and be glad in the Lord your God; for He has given you the early rain for your vindication. And He has poured down for you the rain, the early and latter rain as before. The threshing floors will be full of grain, and the vats will overflow with the new wine and oil.
>
> You will have plenty to eat and be satisfied, and praise the name of the Lord your God, Who has dealt wondrously with you; Then My people will never be put to shame. (Joel 2:21–26)

In this passage we see many of the same elements that are also present in the portions of the Torah that speak of Sukkot. First, God tells the "sons of Zion" to "rejoice" and "be glad." Second, God mentions the "early and latter" rains that will cause the threshing floors to be full of grain and the storage vats to be full of new wine and oil. Finally, God speaks of the fig trees and the grape vines yielding a full harvest.

The reappearance of these Sukkot element from the Torah in Joel 2 (i.e., rejoicing, harvest, and latter rain) indicate that this prophecy gives us a picture of the prophetic fulfillment of Sukkot in the messianic age. It reveals that after the Messiah's Second Coming, the land of Israel, and even the entire earth, will be blessed with a level of agricultural abundance never experienced before in the history of mankind. As a result, every year during the Feast of Tabernacles the nations will stream to Jerusalem to rejoice in the Lord and celebrate His generosity. The earth will be healed, and the war-torn landscapes of the Tribulation will blossom into orchards of fruit trees and rolling fields of ripe grain.

Right now, we live in a world of pollution and depleted soil to the extent that even the best produce we can find is inferior by God's standards. But in the millennium, the earth will be purified as in the days of the garden of Eden. Consequently, the bounty from the natural world will be extravagantly rich, and people will enjoy a wealth of amazing fruits that will far surpass what our minds can now fathom in terms of both quantity and quality.

Often when I eat a plump jammy fig, or a mango dripping with sweet nectar, or a crisp juicy grape, or a bright red watermelon, I think about what it will be like to celebrate the Feast of Tabernacles in the kingdom of God after the fruits of the earth have been harvested and taken to Jerusalem to be enjoyed with the Messiah. Though this aspect of God's prophetic plan is rarely discussed, one of the central features of our experience in the millennium will be the consumption of ridiculously good food, and fruit in particular.

FEASTING IN THE KINGDOM

Interestingly, though we call the appointed times of Leviticus 23 "feasts" in English, none of them besides the Feast of Tabernacles centered around proper feasting in their original historical context. The Passover meal originally included only lamb, unleavened bread, and bitter herbs. The Feast of Weeks was associated with the wheat harvest, but no feast was eaten by the entire population when it was observed, and the same can also be said of the Feast of Trumpets and the Day of Atonement (which was a fast day).

This does not mean there will not be feasting when these appointed times are celebrated in the kingdom in the future. I suspect that there will be, and as noted in chapter 3, Jesus referenced a Passover feast that will be celebrated when this holy day is "fulfilled in the kingdom of God" (Lk. 22:15–16).

Yet still, I also suspect that the feasting and celebrations that will take place during the Feast of Tabernacles in the millennial kingdom will be unparalleled. In contrast to the other appointed times, Sukkot was instituted simply to give God's people a chance to feast, and to enjoy the bountiful harvest that had been reaped earlier in the year.

As a result, the Feast of Tabernacles no doubt points forward to the time when words such as those found in Isaiah 25:6 will be realized. In this passage, Isaiah wrote:

> On this mountain the Lord Almighty will prepare a feast of rich food for all peoples, a banquet of aged wine, the best of meats, and the finest of wines.

Admittedly, Isaiah does not say exactly when this meal will be enjoyed. However, this prophecy still outlines in a general way what God's people will experience every year during the Feast of Tabernacles. This will be the time when we will feast in lavish banquet style with the Messiah, the King, for seven days, and every Feast of Tabernacles and every holiday feast we celebrate until then offers only a small foretaste of what our experience in the kingdom will be. Some have also connected the Feast of Tabernacles to the marriage supper of the Lamb, which is referenced in Revelation 19, and it is certainly possible that the Messiah's marriage covenant with Israel and the nations could be celebrated in the millennium at this time.

THE TEMPLE, THE GLORY OF GOD, AND THE SEVENTH MONTH

Besides the way in which Sukkot will commemorate the annual harvest in the kingdom, and involve banquet feasting, there are also clues in the Hebrew Bible that this festival points forward to how the glory of God will again dwell on the earth in the messianic age, particularly in the millennial Temple. For example, the book of 1 Kings records that Solomon brought the ark of the covenant into Jerusalem "in the seventh month" (1 Kings 8:2) and dedicated the first Temple during the Feast of Tabernacles. This passage also notes that the glory of God entered the Temple at this time as well (1 Kings 8:65-66).

The following passage from 1 Kings 8:1–11 describes what took place when Sukkot was celebrated in the time of Solomon:

> Then Solomon assembled the elders of Israel and all the heads of the tribes, the leaders of the fathers' households of the sons of Israel, to King Solomon in Jerusalem, to bring up the ark of the covenant of the Lord from the city of David, which is Zion. All the men of Israel

> assembled themselves to King Solomon at the feast, in the month Ethanim, which is the seventh month. Then all the elders of Israel came, and the priests took up the ark. They brought up the ark of the LORD and the tent of meeting and all the holy utensils, which were in the tent, and the priests and the Levites brought them up. [...]
>
> Then the priests brought the ark of the covenant of the LORD to its place, into the inner sanctuary of the house, to the most holy place, under the wings of the cherubim. [...]
>
> It happened that when the priests came from the holy place, the cloud filled the house of the LORD, so that the priests could not stand to minister because of the cloud, for the glory of the LORD filled the house of the LORD. [...]

This text in 1 Kings 8 highlights that the Feast of Tabernacles was always about much more than just the agricultural harvest. At the deepest level, Sukkot celebrates that God dwells among His people and reigns as their King, and this is why the glory of the Lord filled His house during Sukkot in the days of Solomon. The tangible presence of God in the Temple signified that His heavenly reign would be mediated through His earthly king in Jerusalem.

Moreover, we may not be able to deduce from this passage exactly when God's glory will return to the earth during the millennium. However, 1 Kings 8 does indicate, even if only in a general way, that the Feast of Tabernacles points forward to the time when God's manifest glory will again dwell on the earth. And who knows, because the seventh month is so closely tied to key Temple events in 1 Kings 8, it is possible that after the Messiah is enthroned on Mount Zion and construction of the millennial Temple begins, God's glory will return to the earth during Sukkot, just as it did in the days of Solomon.

THE GLORY OF GOD RETURNS TO THE EARTH

Regardless of which scenario is correct, however, the most important point to note here is that the Feast of Tabernacles does foreshadow how the inhabitants of the earth will have supernatural encounters with the manifest glory of God the Father in the millennium. Thus, Ezekiel described the time when God's glory will return to the earth after the Second Coming and dwell in the millennial Temple:

> Then the man brought me to the gate facing east, and I saw the glory of the God of Israel coming from the east. His voice was like the roar of rushing waters, and the land was radiant with His glory. The vision I saw was like the vision I had seen when He came to destroy the city and like the visions I had seen by the Kebar River, and I fell facedown.
>
> The glory of the Lord entered the temple through the gate facing east. Then the Spirit lifted me up and brought me into the inner court, and the glory of the Lord filled the temple. While the man was standing beside me, I heard someone speaking to me from inside the temple. He said: "Son of man, this is the place of my throne and the place for the soles of my feet. This is where I will live among the Israelites forever." (Ezek. 43:1–7, NIV)

Earlier in Ezekiel, at the start of his ministry, Ezekiel also articulated what the glory of God will look like when He again resides in His Jerusalem Temple during the messianic age. Ezekiel wrote:

> [There was] a throne of lapis lazuli, and high above on the throne was a figure like that of a man. I saw that from what appeared to be His waist up he looked like glowing metal, as if full of fire, and that from there down He looked like fire; and brilliant light surrounded Him. Like the appearance of a rainbow in the clouds on a rainy day, so was the radiance around Him. This was the appearance of the likeness of the glory of the Lord. When I saw it, I fell facedown, and I heard the voice of one speaking. (Ezek. 1:16–28; cf. Rev. 4)

Usually when people think about the return of Jesus, they only look forward to interacting with Jesus Himself in the messianic age. Also, because most people do not realize that God the Father can appear in a physical form, they are not able to fully appreciate what our fellowship with the Triune God in the millennium will entail.

No doubt it will be glorious to interact with Jesus and to experience the power of the Holy Spirit in the kingdom God. However, Scripture is also clear that in the messianic age God the Father will tangibly and visibly dwell in His Temple.

The experience of God's glory does not belong only to the prophets of old or to some bygone era. Rather, the full vision of God's glory belongs to all the children of God, and physical encounters with the manifest presence of the Father will be a central feature of our relationship with Him in the messianic age.

In Ezekiel 1, Ezekiel saw God the Father sitting on a crystal blue throne, bathed in fire, with radiant light and the brilliance of rainbow hues surrounding Him. And then, Ezekiel says in Ezekiel 43 that this is exactly what we will see when the glory of God returns to the earth after the Second Coming.[1]

During the millennium, our experience with God will be thoroughly Trinitarian. We will enter the unfathomable depths of joy through a dynamic relationship with the Father, the Son, and the Holy Spirit. As

---

1 Because John 1:18 says, "no one has seen God at any time," many Christians are under the mistaken impression that God the Father is completely invisible or incorporeal, meaning, they believe He doesn't exist in a visible/physical form. In reality, however, there are numerous places in the Bible where God is seen, and not every visible appearance of God is simply a manifestion of Jesus. For exampe, in Daniel 7:9 Daniel sees "the Ancient of Days" (i.e., God the Father) with the Son of Man (i.e., Jesus), and in Revelation 4–5 John sees God (the Father) and Jesus (the Lamb) in heaven. Therefore, when John 1:18 says, "no one has seen God," the context makes clear that this means no one can fully know God apart from Jesus, and indeed, the Greek term used for "see" here can carry the connation of mental understanding more than visible sight. All that to say, the notion that God the Father is an invisible and ethereal being only became popular in Christianity after the first century, when the Greek philosophy of Plato, which tends to value the spiritual over the physical, corrupted Christian theology. The Bible is clear that God the Father often manifests His glory in a visible way (e.g., Ezekiel 1), and it is also clear that He will dwell on the earth during the millennium.

Jesus sits on His throne in the millennial Temple, the glory of God the Father will abide there as well, and the Holy Spirit will work on their behalf to renew the entire world.

THE FULFILLMENT OF SUKKOT IN REVELATION 21

One of the primary prophetic purposes of the Feast of Tabernacles is to inspire hope in this time when God's manifest glory will again dwell on the earth. This important festival points forward to the abundance we will experience after we leave the wilderness of this world behind and enter into the fullness of joy in the presence of God.

Not surprisingly therefore, in Revelation 21:3, the Apostle John elaborated on how the Feast of Tabernacles will be ultimately fulfilled not only when God's people dwell in the sukkah, but also when God builds His sukkah among us. Elaborating on this point, John wrote that after the Messiah returns it will again be said on the earth:

> Behold, the tabernacle [*skene*] of God is among men, and He will dwell among them, and they shall be His people, and God Himself will be among them. (Rev. 21:3)

There are debates over when the events in Revelation 21:3 will take place, but we do not need to delve into the minutiae here. What we can be sure of is that this verse must speak in some way of the millennium because we know from Ezekiel 43 that God's glory will dwell on the earth at this time.

Interestingly, when speaking in Revelation 21:3 of how God will tabernacle among His people in the millennium, John uses the Greek equivalent (skene) of the Hebrew word sukkah (tabernacle). This word usage confirms that John saw the glory of God coming to the earth in the millennium as a fulfillment of the Feast of Tabernacles. Also notice that John does not simply say, "the tabernacle of the Messiah will be among men." Rather, John says, "the tabernacle of God is among men." John understood that during the millennium the manifest glory of God the Father, which Moses saw while on Mount Sinai and Ezekiel saw while in exile, will again dwell on the earth.

THE FEAST OF TABERNACLES IN THE KINGDOM OF GOD

At its core, Sukkot provides a prophetic foretaste of the natural abundance and magnificent joy in God's presence that we will experience in the millennium. In a remarkable way, just as the first six days of creation led up to the blessings of the garden of Eden on the seventh day, the first six feasts on the calendar will lead up to the complete blessings of the messianic age during Sukkot (the seventh feast), which will in many ways mirror those first experienced by Adam and Eve in Genesis.

After His victory over the powers of darkness (Passover and Unleavened Bread), His saving work among Israel and the nations (First Fruits and Weeks), and His enthronement as the King-Priest of the millennium (Trumpets and Atonement), the Messiah will invite all the peoples of the earth to rejoice and feast in God's presence on Mount Zion for seven days during the Feast of Tabernacles. At this time, we will not only enjoy the natural abundance of the earth and rejoice in the Messiah, but we will also celebrate how God carried us through the difficult wilderness seasons of life and brought us safely into His good land. We will look back on our entire spiritual journey and realize that enduring the temporary trials of this life was not so bad after all, because by that point, we will fully understand where God was leading us the entire time.

When the first great Sukkot celebration takes place in the kingdom, perhaps Jesus will hold up a large basket of magnificent fruits from the earth, including grapes, figs, pomegranates, dates, and olives, and then recite the traditional Jewish blessing that praises God for creating the fruits of the earth. Then the party will begin, and we will all experience the most amazing times of joy and fellowship with believers and saints from across the ages. At that point, construction of the millennial Temple will be well underway, and soon God's glory will return to the earth to tabernacle among His people. Finally, at long last, all the biblical feasts will be officially fulfilled in the kingdom of God, and we will repeat the entire cycle again month after month, year after year, as we celebrate the complete redemptive work of God and move deeper and deeper into the glorious days of the millennium.

CHAPTER SUMMARY

Below are the main points from this chapter that summarize how the Feast of Tabernacles will be fulfilled in the kingdom of God:

1. Zechariah says the Feast of Tabernacles will be celebrated by all nations after the Messiah returns, and he connects the observance of this festival to rain and agricultural abundance in the messianic age (Zech. 14:16–19).

2. Other passages also use Sukkot language when speaking of how the land will be blessed by God, and how all the peoples of the earth will feast in God's presence, during the millennium (Joel 2:21–26; Isa. 25:6).

3. Besides the way the Feast of Tabernacles points forward to agricultural abundance and feasting in the messianic age, this holy festival will also have a fulfillment when the glory of God the Father returns to the earth and once again tabernacles among His people (1 Kings 8:1–11; Ezek. 43:1–7; Rev. 21:3).

4. Because Sukkot is the seventh feast on the biblical calendar, which occurs in the seventh month for seven days, this appointed time is closely tied to the idea of, and the numerical symbol for, completion (777). Thus, when Sukkot is fulfilled in the kingdom, this will mark the time when God's redemptive plan will in many ways be complete, and we will enter a new phase in redemptive history. For one thousand years the inhabitants of the world will live in harmonious union with God, enjoy His provision from the earth, and see His glory. Subsequently, from that point on, we will move from glory to glory in the millennium and then finally experience the full reality of the new heavens and the new earth for all eternity.

BIBLE STUDY QUESTIONS

1. What events in the millennium does the Feast of Tabernacles foreshadow?

2. How will the fulfillment of the Feast of Tabernacles be tied to its original historical meaning in ancient Israel?

3. What aspect of Sukkot covered in this chapter was the most surprising or encouraging to you?

4. Why do you think it is important to emphasize that our fellowship with God during the millennium will be Trinitarian in nature?

THANK YOU FOR READING THIS BOOK!

Would you also consider helping me share the *The Biblical Feasts and the Return of Jesus* with more people? If so, here are a few practical steps you can take:

1. Please leave a short review of *The Biblical Feasts and the Return of Jesus* on Amazon. Other potential readers will enjoy hearing your perspective, and this helps to spread the message to a wider audience as well. Please also consider recommending this book through your social media accounts.

2. Follow Travis M. Snow on Twitter, subscribe to Travis M. Snow on YouTube, and sign-up for our ministry email list at shilohmedia.org. This will ensure that you stay up to date with forthcoming book releases, ministry projects, and prayer requests. We also produce regular devotional and Bible teaching content on our social media platforms as well.

3. Consider making a tax-deductible donation to Shiloh Media. We depend on the Lord's provision through His saints to do the work of the ministry and to fulfill the Great Commission before the return of Jesus. We are so grateful for any gifts or prayers that the Lord lays on your heart.

Many blessings to you friend. I look forward to meeting you in the kingdom of God!

—TRAVIS SNOW

SCRIPTURE INDEX

GENESIS

1:2, 45–46, 79, 99

8:13, 98

8:20–22, 46

EXODUS

1:13–14, 25

3:7–20, 28

7:10–21, 31

8:1–24, 29

9:1–26, 29, 38

10:1–23, 29

11:1–7, 30

12:2–39, 6, 41–42, 51–52

14:1–31, 42–44, 46–47

15:1-18; 43–45, 175

19:1, 115–117

19:16–20, 149–151

23:16, 4–6, 115

24:7, 151

25:8, 185

25:22, 2

31:3, 137

34:22, 4–6

LEVITICUS

4:1–35, 189, 191

12–19, 188

16:7–27, 193–196

16:29–30, 184

23:1–2, 2

23:9–14, 54–55

23:15–16, 111–112

23:16–21, 112–115, 128

23:23–25, 143, 147–151, 165–166

23:26–27, 183

23:39, 220

23:40–44, 224–227

25:8–10, 214

NUMBERS

10:9, 148

10:10, 163

24:5–9, 73–76

DEUTERONOMY

4:25–30, 66

8:15–16, 229

16:13–15, 220

28:68, 67

JOSHUA
4:19, 99
6:16, 148

1 SAMUEL
10:24, 153

1 KINGS
1:34, 153
8:1–11, 239–240

PSALMS
2:2, 173
24:7–8, 154
37:10, 138
47:5–9, 178–179
98:4–6, 153, 180
132:13–14, 173

ISAIAH
2:2–4, 176–177
10:16–17, 76
11:1–5, 137
11:11, 67
11:15–16, 77
12:3, 222
13:12–13, 123
18:3–7, 177–178
25:6, 238–239
27:12–13, 67, 71–72, 177–178
19:1, 69–71
49:22–23, 126
61:1, 136
61:4–7, 138
63:1–6, 83–84
66:18–21, 125, 128, 204

JEREMIAH
30:5–7, 63

EZEKIEL
1:16–28, 241–242
36:24–25, 203–204
36:27, 133
37:25, 215
37:26–28, 212
38:8–23, 85–90
39:28–29, 132
39:11–16, 206–209
43:7, 211
43:1–7, 241
47:13, 215

DANIEL
9:24, 212
9:27, 63
12:7, 63

JOEL
2:21–26, 236–237
2:28–29, 129–131, 134–136

HABAKKUK
3:3–15, 80–83

ZECHARIAH
2:10–12, 174
6:11–15, 213
8:3, 173
8:6–8, 126
9:13–17, 84
10:10–11, 78
12:10, 131
14:2, 64
14:3–4, 68
14:10–11, 175–176
14:12–15, 91
14:16, 123
14:16–19, 235–236

MATTHEW
16:11–12, 53
24:31, 162

LUKE
21:20–24, 64–65
22:15–16, 58–62, 96–98, 119

JOHN
3:5, 129
6:51, 53
7:37–39, 229–231

ACTS
2:1–4, 121–122

ROMANS
8:23, 139

1 CORINTHIANS
5:6–8, 52-54
15:20–23, 56, 100
15:52, 133, 162

EPHESIANS
5:5, 134
5:18–19, 137

COLOSSIANS
2:16–17, 12–13

1 THESSALONIANS
4:16–17, 124, 161

HEBREWS
9:11–12, 199
10:1–3, 199
10:20–22, 200–201
12:18–25, 155–156
13:12, 201

REVELATION
2:27, 137
16:1–21, 91–94
20:1–3, 134
20:4–15, 124
21:3, 243

Printed in Poland
by Amazon Fulfillment
Poland Sp. z o.o., Wrocław

23504588R00150